FREEDOM OF THE PRESS

FREEDOM OF THE PRESS

Rights and Liberties under the Law

NANCY C. CORNWELL

A B C • C L I O

Santa Barbara, California • Denver, Colorado • Oxford, England

Library of Congress Cataloging-in-Publication Data
Cornwell, Nancy, 1959-
  Freedom of the press : rights and liberties under the law / Nancy C. Cornwell.
     p. cm.—(America's freedoms)
  Includes bibliographical references and index.
  ISBN 1-85109-471-7 (alk. paper)—ISBN 1-85109-476-8 (e-book)   1.
Freedom of the press—United States.   I. Title. II. Series.
PN4738.C67 2004
323.44'5'0973—dc22

                                                                2004021071

07 06 05 04 10 9 8 7 6 5 4 3 2 1

This book is also available on the World Wide Web as an e-book. Visit abc-clio.com for details.

ABC-CLIO, Inc.
130 Cremona Drive, P.O. Box 1911
Santa Barbara, California 93116-1911

This book is printed on acid-free paper.
Manufactured in the United States of America

CONTENTS

v

SERIES FOREWORD

America's Freedoms promises a series of books that address the origin, development, meaning, and future of the nation's fundamental liberties, as well as the individuals, circumstances, and events that have shaped them. These freedoms are chiefly enshrined explicitly or implicitly in the Bill of Rights and other amendments to the Constitution of the United States and have much to do with the quality of life Americans enjoy. Without them, America would be a far different place in which to live. Oddly enough, however, the Constitution was drafted and signed in Philadelphia in 1787 without a bill of rights. That was an afterthought, emerging only after a debate among the foremost political minds of the day.

At the time, Thomas Jefferson was in France on a diplomatic mission. Upon receiving a copy of the proposed Constitution from his friend James Madison, who had helped write the document, Jefferson let him know as fast as the slow sailing-ship mails of the day allowed that the new plan of government suffered one major defect—it lacked a bill of rights. This, Jefferson argued, "is what the people are entitled to against every government on earth." Madison should not have been surprised at Jefferson's reaction. The Declaration of Independence of 1776 had largely been Jefferson's handiwork, including its core statement of principle:

> We hold these truths to be self-evident, that all men are created equal,
> that they are endowed by their Creator with certain unalienable
> Rights, that among these are Life, Liberty, and the pursuit of Happi-
> ness. That to secure these rights, Governments are instituted among
> Men, deriving their just powers from the consent of the governed.

Jefferson rejected the conclusion of many of the framers that
the Constitution's design—a system of both separation of powers
among the legislative, executive, and judicial branches, and a
federal division of powers between national and state
governments—would safeguard liberty. Even when combined
with elections, he believed strongly that such structural checks
would fall short.

Jefferson and other critics of the proposed Constitution
ultimately had their way. In one of the first items of business in
the First Congress in 1789, Madison, as a member of the House of
Representatives from Virginia, introduced amendments to protect
liberty. Ten were ratified by 1791 and have become known as the
Bill of Rights.

America's Bill of Rights reflects the founding generation's
understanding of the necessary link between personal freedom
and representative government, as well as their experience with
threats to liberty. The First Amendment protects expression—in
speech, press, assembly, petition, and religion—and guards against
a union of church and state. The Second Amendment secures
liberty against national tyranny by affirming the self-defense of
the states. Members of state-authorized local militia—citizens
primarily, soldiers occasionally—retained a right to bear arms.
The ban in the Third Amendment on forcibly quartering troops in
houses reflects the emphasis the framers placed on the integrity
and sanctity of the home.

Other provisions in the Fourth, Fifth, Sixth, Seventh, and
Eighth amendments safeguard freedom by setting forth standards
that government must follow in administering the law, especially

regarding persons accused of crimes. The framers knew firsthand the dangers that government-as-prosecutor could pose to liberty. Even today, authoritarian regimes in other lands routinely use the tools of law enforcement—arrests, searches, detentions, as well as trials—to squelch peaceful political opposition. Limits in the Bill of Rights on crime-fighting powers thus help maintain democracy by demanding a high level of legal scrutiny of the government's practices.

In addition, one clause in the Fifth Amendment forbids the taking of private property for public use without paying the owner just compensation and thereby limits the power of eminent domain, the authority to seize a person's property. Along with taxation and conscription, eminent domain is one of the most awesome powers any government can possess.

The Ninth Amendment makes sure that the listing of some rights does not imply that others necessarily have been abandoned. If the Ninth Amendment offered reassurances to the people, the Tenth Amendment was designed to reassure the states that they or the people retained those powers not delegated to the national government. Today, the Tenth Amendment is a reminder of the integral role states play in the federal plan of union that the Constitution ordained.

Despite this legacy of freedom, however, we Americans today sometimes wonder about the origin, development, meaning, and future of our liberties. This concern is entirely understandable, because liberty is central to the idea of what it means *to be American*. In this way, the United States stands apart from virtually every other nation on earth. Other countries typically define their national identities through a common ethnicity, origin, ancestral bond, religion, or history. But none of these accounts for the American identity. In terms of ethnicity, ancestry, and religion, the United States is the most diverse place on earth. From the beginning, America has been a land of immigrants. Neither is there a single historical experience to which all current citizens can directly relate: someone who arrived a decade ago from, say, Southeast Asia and was naturalized as a citizen only last year is just as much an American as someone whose forebears served in General George Washington's army at Valley Forge during the American War of Independence (1776–1783). In religious as in political affairs, the United States has been a beacon to those suffering oppression abroad: "the last, best hope of earth," Abraham Lincoln said. So, the American identity is ideological. It consists of faith in the value and importance of liberty for each individual.

Nonetheless, a longstanding consensus among Americans on the *principle* that individual liberty is essential, highly prized, and widely shared hardly assures agreement about liberty *in practice*. This is because the concept of liberty, as it has developed in the United States, has several dimensions.

First, there is an unavoidable tension between liberty and restraint. Liberty means freedom: we say that a person has a "right" to do this or that. But that *right* is meaningless unless there is a corresponding *duty* on the part of others (such as police officers and elected officials) not to interfere. Thus, protection of the liberty of one person necessarily involves restraints imposed on someone else. This is why we speak of a *civil* right or a *civil* liberty: it is a claim on the behavior of another that is enforceable through the legal process. Moreover, some degree of order (restrictions on the behavior of all) is necessary if everyone's liberties are to be protected. Just as too much order crushes freedom, too little invites social chaos that also threatens freedom. Determining the proper balance between freedom and order, however, is more easily sought than found. "To make a government requires no great prudence," declared English statesman and political philosopher Edmund Burke in 1790. "Settle the seat of power; teach obedience; and the work is done. To give freedom is still more easy. It is not necessary to guide; it only requires to let go the rein. But to form a *free government;* that is, to temper together these opposite elements of liberty and restraint in one consistent work, requires much thought; deep reflection; a sagacious, powerful, and combining mind."

Second, the Constitution does not define the freedoms that it protects. Chief Justice John Marshall once acknowledged that the Constitution was a document "of enumeration, and not of definition." There are, for example, lists of the powers of Congress in Article I, or the rights of individuals in the Bill of Rights, but those powers and limitations are not explained. What is the "freedom of speech" that the First Amendment guarantees? What are "unreasonable searches and seizures" that are proscribed by the Fourth Amendment? What is the "due process of law" secured by both the Fifth and Fourteenth Amendments? Reasonable people, all of whom favor individual liberty, can arrive at very different answers to these questions.

A third dimension—breadth—is closely related to the second. How widely shared is a particular freedom? Consider voting, for example. One could write a political history of the United States by cataloging the efforts to extend the vote or franchise to groups such as women and nonwhites that had been previously excluded. Or consider the First Amendment's freedom of speech. Does it include the expression of *all* points of view or merely *some?* Does the same amendment's protection of the "free exercise of religion" include all faiths, even obscure ones that may seem weird or even irritating? At different times questions like these have yielded different answers.

Similarly, the historical record contains notorious lapses. Despite all the safeguards that are supposed to shore up freedom's foundations, constitutional protections have sometimes been worth the least when they have been desperately needed. In our history the most frequent and often the most serious threats to freedom have come not from people intent on throwing the Bill of Rights away outright but from well-meaning people who find the

Bill of Rights a temporary bother, standing in the way of some objective they want to reach.

There is also a question that dates to the very beginning of American government under the Constitution. Does the Constitution protect rights not spelled out in, or fairly implied by, the words of the document? The answer to that question largely depends on what a person concludes about the source of rights. One tradition, reflected in the Declaration of Independence, asserts that rights predate government and that government's chief duty is to protect the rights that everyone naturally possesses. Thus, if the Constitution is read as a document designed, among other things, to protect liberty, then protected liberties are not limited to those in the text of the Constitution but may also be derived from experience, for example, or from one's assessment of the requirements of a free society. This tradition places a lot of discretion in the hands of judges, because in the American political system, it is largely the judiciary that decides what the Constitution means. Partly due to this dynamic, a competing tradition looks to the text of the Constitution, as well as to statutes passed consistent with the Constitution, as a *complete* code of law containing *all* the liberties that Americans possess. Judges, therefore, are not free to go outside the text to "discover" rights that the people, through the process of lawmaking and constitutional amendment, have not declared. Doing so is undemocratic because it bypasses "rule by the people." The tension between these two ways of thinking explains the ongoing debate about a right to privacy, itself nowhere mentioned in the words of the Constitution. "I like my privacy as well as the next one," once admitted Justice Hugo Black, "but I am nevertheless compelled to admit that government has a right to invade it unless prohibited by some specific constitutional provision." Otherwise, he said, judges are forced "to determine what is or is not constitutional on the basis of their own appraisal of what laws are unwise or unnecessary." Black thought that was the job of elected legislators who would answer to the people.

Fifth, it is often forgotten that at the outset, and for many years afterward, the Bill of Rights applied only to the national government, not to the states. Except for a very few restrictions, such as those in section 10 of Article I in the main body of the Constitution, which expressly limited state power, states were restrained only by their individual constitutions and state laws, not by the U.S. Bill of Rights. So, Pennsylvania or any other state, for example, could shut down a newspaper or barricade the doors of a church without violating the First Amendment. For many in the founding generation, the new central government loomed as a colossus that might threaten liberty. Few at that time thought that individual freedom needed *national* protection against *state* invasions of the rights of the people.

The first step in removing this double standard came with ratification of the Fourteenth Amendment after the Civil War in 1868. Section 1 contained majestic, but undefined, checks on states: "*No State* shall make or enforce any law which shall abridge the privileges or immunities of citizens of the United States; nor shall any *State* deprive any person of life, liberty, or property, without due process of law; nor deny to any person with in its jurisdiction the equal protections of the laws" (emphasis added). Such vague language begged for interpretation. In a series of cases mainly between 1920 and 1968, the Supreme Court construed the Fourteenth Amendment to include within its meaning almost every provision of the Bill of Rights. This process of "incorporation" (applying the Bill of Rights to the states by way of the Fourteenth Amendment) was the second step in eliminating the double standard of 1791. State and local governments became bound by the same restrictions that had applied all along to the national government. The consequences of this development scarcely can be exaggerated because most governmental action in the United States is the work of state and local governments. For instance, ordinary citizens are far more likely to encounter a local police officer than an agent of the Federal Bureau of Investigation or the Secret Service.

A sixth dimension reflects an irony. A society premised on individual freedom assumes not only the worth of each person but citizens capable of rational thought, considered judgment, and measured actions. Otherwise democratic government would be futile. Yet, we lodge the most important freedoms in the Constitution precisely because we want to give those freedoms extra protection. "The very purpose of a Bill of Rights was to . . . place [certain subjects] beyond the reach of majorities and officials and to establish them as legal principles to be applied by the courts," explained Justice Robert H. Jackson. "One's right to life, liberty, and property, to free speech, a free press, freedom of worship and assembly, and other fundamental rights may not be submitted to vote; they depend on the outcome of no elections." Jackson referred to a hard lesson learned from experience: basic rights require extra protection because they are fragile. On occasion, people have been willing to violate the freedoms of others. That reality demanded a written constitution.

This irony reflects the changing nature of a bill of rights in history. Americans did not invent the idea of a bill of rights in 1791. Instead it drew from and was inspired by colonial documents such as the Pennsylvania colony's Charter of Liberties (1701) and the English Bill of Rights (1689), Petition of Right (1628), and Magna Carta (1215). However, these early and often unsuccessful attempts to limit government power were devices to protect the many (the people) from the few (the English Crown). With the emergence of democratic political systems in the eighteenth century, however, political power shifted from the few to the many. The right to rule belonged to the person who received the most votes in an election, not necessarily to the firstborn, the wealthiest, or the most physically powerful. So the focus of a bill of rights had to shift too. No longer was it designed to shelter the majority from the minority, but to shelter the minority from the majority. "Wherever the real power in a Government lies, there is the danger of oppression," commented Madison in his exchange of letters with Jefferson in 1788. "In our Government, the real power lies in the majority of the Community, and the invasion of private rights is *chiefly* to be apprehended, not from acts of government contrary to the sense of its constituents, but from acts in which the Government is the mere instrument of the major number of the Constituents."

Americans, however, do deserve credit for having discovered a way to enforce a bill of rights. Without an enforcement mechanism, a bill of rights is no more than a list of aspirations: standards to aim for, but with no redress other than violent protest or revolution. Indeed this had been the experience in England with which the framers were thoroughly familiar. Thanks to judicial review—the authority courts in the United States possess to invalidate actions taken by the other branches of government that, in the judges' view, conflict with the Constitution—the provisions in the Bill of Rights and other constitutionally protected liberties became judicially enforceable.

Judicial review was a tradition that was beginning to emerge in the states on a small scale in the 1780s and 1790s and that would blossom in the U.S. Supreme Court in the nineteenth and twentieth centuries. "In the arguments in favor of a declaration of rights," Jefferson presciently told Madison in the late winter of 1789 after the Constitution had been ratified, "you omit one which has great weight with me, the legal check which it puts into the hands of the judiciary." This is the reason why each of the volumes in this series focuses extensively on judicial decisions. Liberties have largely been defined by judges in the context of deciding cases in situations where individuals thought the power of government extended too far.

Designed to help democracy protect itself, the Constitution ultimately needs the support of those—the majority—who endure its restraints. Without sufficient support among the people, its freedoms rest on a weak foundation. The earnest hope of *America's Freedoms* is that this series will offer Americans a renewed appreciation and understanding of their heritage of liberty.

Yet there would be no series on America's freedoms without the interest and support of Alicia Merritt at ABC-CLIO. The series was her idea. She approached me originally about the series and was very adept at overcoming my initial hesitations as series editor. She not only helped me shape the particular topics that the series would include but also guided me toward prospective authors. As a result, the topic of each book has been matched with the most appropriate person as author. The goal in each instance as been to pair topics with authors who are recognized teachers and scholars in their field. The results have been gratifying. A series editor could hardly wish for authors who have been more cooperative, helpful, and accommodating.

Donald Grier Stephenson, Jr.

PREFACE AND
ACKNOWLEDGMENTS

Were it left to me to decide whether we should have a government without newspapers, or newspapers without a government, I should not hesitate a moment to prefer the latter.

—Thomas Jefferson (1787)

This book examines the tradition of a free press in American society. The right to a free press is explicitly guaranteed by the First Amendment to the U.S. Constitution. It is a right that affects Americans directly, on a daily basis, usually without our thinking about it. Although the press is accused, at various times, of being influenced by government, business interests, corporate ownership, demands to increase profits and reduce expenses, sensationalism, pressure to scoop the competition, its own liberal leanings, and its own conservative leanings, Americans generally assume that the press is free from censorship and that it offers its audience a version of reality that approximates the truth.

If we have a constitutional guarantee of a free press, why is there any concern about undue influence on the press? Why *is* the press restricted during military conflicts? Why are there a multitude of Supreme Court decisions clarifying a seemingly simple guarantee? Why is the growing number of libel and invasion of privacy lawsuits raising concerns about press freedoms? Has the meaning of a free press changed over time?

These kinds of questions form the basis of this book. The right of a free press is complex, and it has transformed over time. The authors of the Bill of Rights never anticipated radio, television, cable, and the Internet. They never imagined distribution systems like the telegraph, satellite, and videophone. During an age of extensive pamphleteering, when cities were brimming with newspapers of diverse perspectives, the drafters of the First Amendment could not have expected the kinds of media ownership patterns seen in the United States today.

So what does a guarantee of a free press mean? A literal and narrow reading of the First Amendment's press clause leaves room for dramatic press restrictions. With a literal reading, only Congress is expressly restricted from passing laws limiting the freedom of the press. The amendment says nothing about the ability of states to restrict the press or of the government's ability to punish the press after it exercises its constitutional freedom. A more expansive yet still literal reading of the press clause in which the word "Congress" is interpreted to mean "government" does little to account for the larger democratic role of the news media. It suggests little about the social responsibility the press might have toward its audience. It says nothing about the potential of media ownership concentration to limit the range of ideas that might reach the public. Certainly an interpretivist reading of the press clause might suggest that the press has a formal, codifiable responsibility to its audiences, and broadcast regulations have suggested as much. But the regulatory climate since the 1980s has been hostile to any notion of enforcing an obligation on the press in a way that might impinge on content (e.g., requiring genuinely educational programming), create ownership limits (e.g., limiting concentration of ownership or cross-ownership of media in the same market), establish requirements of balanced coverage (e.g., the Fairness Doctrine or political editorial rules), or have any

other effect that might mean an increasingly expansive interpretation of "freedom of the press."

Thus a succession of court decisions have attempted to navigate
these murky waters with consideration of both the original intent
of the authors of the Bill of Rights and the historical context in
which the press clause was written. For example, the courts have
tried to make sense of the role that new technologies, such as the
Internet, satellite distribution, and videophones, have in
redefining the extent of press freedoms during times of military
conflict.

As a result of many unanswered questions about the functional
meaning of freedom of the press, the twentieth-century Supreme
Court actively engaged questions of national security, libel,
invasion of privacy, and pretrial publicity, among others. The
resulting decisions show a court struggling to balance freedom of
the press with a host of competing rights. The accelerated pattern
of technological innovation since the latter half of the twentieth
century only confounded the problem. The Court and Congress
struggle to keep up with the pace of technological innovation and
face growing concerns about privacy, media ownership
convergence, and the explosive growth of pornography on the
Internet. Efforts to legislate restrictions on pornography have not
survived judicial challenges under the First Amendment.
Legislative efforts to control "spam" on the Internet are likely to
face a similar First Amendment challenge.

Any attempt to understand the future of press freedoms
requires an understanding of the key judicial decisions that have
shaped the contemporary meaning of a free press and of the
historical and political context of such decisions—these are the
topics of Chapters 2 and 3. With this groundwork laid, the future
impact of media ownership, technological innovation, and
nonjudicial influences on freedom of the press, part of the focus in
Chapter 4, will be contextualized and make more sense. Today,
with much of the media's attention focused on the military

occupation of Iraq, corporate misconduct (including some corporate media), relaxation of media ownership rules, and presidential election campaigns, it seems timely to look back at how early principles of press freedom have led us to this moment in history.

My interest in free expression issues generally and freedom of the press in particular started with my work as a media professional. I worked as a journalist, news director, and producer for the Southern Command Television Network in the Republic of Panama. There I gained firsthand knowledge of military censorship of the press as I faced sometimes legitimate and sometimes quirky decisions to excise news stories in a way reminiscent of those facing the irreverent deejay Adrian Cronauer in the movie *Good Morning Vietnam.* My work for a large cable television company taught me about how First Amendment rights might bump up against community sensitivities as I talked with city council members about the presence of the Playboy Channel on the local cable television system. But it was probably my own academic research and involvement with the American Civil Liberties Union that solidified my interest in First Amendment issues. In a time of growing media concentration and technological innovation, never have the questions raised about freedom of the press been more intriguing or had more significant implications for democratic participation.

For the opportunity to indulge my fascination with press freedoms, I extend my gratitude to ABC-CLIO. I also want to thank Donald Grier Stephenson, series editor for America's Freedoms, and Alicia Merritt, ABC-CLIO's acquisitions editor, for their support and patience as I attempted to begin work on this book during a cross-country move and in the throes of a new job. Jenny Wolstenholm provided excellent research assistance, transcribed documents, and helped annotate key cases and concepts. ABC-CLIO senior production editor Melanie Stafford kept the manuscript moving toward a timely publication, and

John Guardiano, "expert" copy editor, quite simply, made the book better. Marv Henberg, Linfield College's Dean of Faculty, and Dave Gilbert, chair of the Mass Communication Department when I began the book and now professor emeritus, provided me with support, encouragement, and release time to complete the book in a timely manner. The Linfield College Faculty Development Committee provided much-needed funding to support a summer research assistant. I want to thank the Linfield community itself, made up of some of the most interesting, friendly, and collegial students, faculty, staff, and administrators I have had the pleasure to meet. It was a unique combination of openness, patience, curiosity, and serendipity that brought me here, and I have come to understand those very qualities that permeate this fine institution. Thank you for making my transition to Linfield simply delightful.

A heartfelt appreciation goes to the "Julies" in my life, one my sister and one a friend. Both are generous of heart and time, always willing to listen, and unconditionally supportive. I look forward to more face time now that the writing is done.

I dedicate this book to Emily and Graham, who fill my days with music, laughter, great conversations about everything, including the ideas in this book, and, of course, general silliness. Full of exuberant energy and ready for any adventure, they are a constant reminder of how fun life really is.

Nancy C. Cornwell

1

INTRODUCTION

In the early morning hours of March 20, 2003, explosions rocked the city of Baghdad, Iraq. U.S. missiles struck government buildings and the palace of Iraqi president Saddam Hussein, among other strategic targets. That morning marked the beginning of the U.S. "shock and awe" campaign and the culmination of three weeks of U.S. and coalition troop movement from southern Iraq toward the capital. The events that unfolded on each of the preceding twenty-one days, as well as during the months of occupation that followed, were reported in excruciating detail by more than 500 journalists "embedded" among U.S. and coalition military units. Many more journalists reported from Kuwait, Bahrain, and other locales on the periphery of the war zone. American television, radio, newspapers, magazines, and Internet news sources were flooded with continuous coverage. When live images were not available, the analysts took over. Media and political analysts compared U.S. press coverage—in principle protected by the U.S. Constitution and free from government influence—and other media, such as the Qatar-based Al Jazeera satellite network, whose information was analyzed skeptically because it was considered tainted by an Arab political agenda and sympathetic to the Iraqi perspective (Sharkey 2003). American media sources were saturated with war coverage. Information overload seemed more a problem than concerns about censorship or disinformation.

In the aftermath of the war, with more time for reflection as the media covered the continuing military occupation, questions emerged about the press's objectivity and freedom in its war coverage. Did the practice of embedding journalists in the war zone serve the principles of a free press? Were the American people, or the world for that matter, watching freedom of the press functioning at its best, or were they witnessing a press subjected to government restrictions in a way that distorted the reality of war? Of even greater concern: Did the process of embedding journalists create the *illusion* of a free press when, in fact, information and images were restricted and manipulated by the government to shape public opinion about the war? How does this scenario fit into a worldview in which the American press is "free"? To answer this question it is necessary to understand what freedom of the press actually means. There is no simple answer.

The First Amendment to the U.S. Constitution reads as follows: "Congress shall make no law respecting an establishment of religion, or prohibiting the free exercise thereof; or abridging the freedom of speech, or of the press; or the right of the people peaceably to assemble, and to petition the government for a redress of grievances." These forty-five words specify six specific freedoms and guarantee them under the Constitution. So important are these guarantees, so central to our tradition of individual freedom and democratic participation, that this entire book is devoted to just one of them: freedom of the press. The United States is the only nation that provides constitutional protection to the press, and the U.S. press is the only private business whose activities receive direct protection under the U.S. Constitution. The American tradition of protecting the press from governmental influence and pressure is unmatched anywhere in the world.

Freedom of the press is not an absolute freedom, even though the language of the First Amendment might imply otherwise. The statement "Congress shall make no law . . . abridging the freedom of . . . the press" sounds comprehensive and clear. In 1960, U.S. Supreme Court Justice Hugo Black stated, "It is my belief that there *are* 'absolutes' in our Bill of Rights and that they were put there on purpose by men who knew what words meant and meant their prohibitions to be 'absolutes'" (Black 1960, 867). His words suggest that all speech is protected and that the First Amendment protects the news media from any censorship or punishment after publication. That, of course, means no libel or invasion of privacy lawsuits and no restrictions in the name of copyright or national security.

Justice Black held the view that any speech involving public matters would be enfolded within the protection of the First Amendment. It has been noted that for Justice Black, this meant that obscenity, libel, and slander are protected expression. Even today's Supreme Court does not go this far. The constraints placed on the press during the war in Iraq, as in many other military conflicts, make it clear that freedom of the press is tempered, in part, by other competing needs and rights, national security being just one example. Thus, in some ways, freedom of the press is not so clear. It can be more fluid and subject to external pressures and competing interests and rights. What constitutes freedom of the press, and what it meant when the authors of the Bill of Rights wrote the words "Congress shall make no law abridging . . . freedom of . . . the press," remains a remarkably complex issue.

JUSTIFICATIONS FOR PROTECTING EXPRESSION

It may seem self-evident, but it is worthwhile discussing why a society would seek to protect expression. There are plenty of cultures and nation-states that restrict expression for all sort of reasons, ranging from the political to the cultural to the religious. Yet we have chosen to broadly and fundamentally protect expressive freedoms. That choice is based on a belief that freedom of expression has some value. The question is, then, What values justify protecting expression? And do these values hold any connection to why we protect the press?

First Amendment scholar Thomas Emerson reviewed the body of First Amendment jurisprudence up to the mid-1960s and culled four values supporting the principle of free and unfettered expression (Emerson 1966). The first value echoed the words and ideas of the classical liberal theorists (discussed in Chapter 2). Emerson suggested that a central value of free and open debate is the discovery of truth and knowledge through the free trade of ideas. In language that is reminiscent of John Milton's *Areopagitica* and John Stuart Mill's *On Liberty*, Emerson stated,

> an individual who seeks knowledge and truth must hear all sides of the question, consider all alternatives, test his judgment by exposing it to opposition, and make full use of different minds. Discussion must be kept open no matter how certainly true an accepted opinion may be; many of the most widely acknowledged truths have turned out to be erroneous. (Emerson 1970, 6–7)

The idea that free expression is central to discovering truth is not just discussed in philosophical tomes of the seventeenth and eighteenth centuries. It appears in Supreme Court Justice Oliver Wendell Holmes's 1919 dissent in *Abrams*, in which he passionately stated, "[T]he ultimate good desired is better reached by free trade in ideas—that the best test of truth is the power of the thought to get itself accepted in the competition of the marketplace" (*Abrams v. United States* [1919] 630). It also appears in Justice Louis D. Brandeis's 1927 concurring opinion in *Whitney*, in which he referred to the Founding Fathers and how "they believed that freedom to think as you will and to speak as you think are means indispensable to the discovery and spread of political truth" (*Whitney v. California* [1927] 375). Brandeis added, "If there be time to expose through discussion the falsehood and fallacies, to avert the evil by the processes of education, the remedy to be applied is more speech, not enforced silence" (*Whitney v. California* [1927] 377). The idea of protecting the press nests quite nicely with the effort to discover truth or knowledge. In spite of the growth of tabloid journalism and cynicism about the press, there is a general belief that part of the function of the press in a democratic society is to inform citizens about events that interest or affect them (Sanford 1999).

Emerson suggested that there is a fundamental need in human nature to express oneself as part of the process of self-actualization. To restrict freedom of expression is "a negation of man's essential nature" (Emerson 1970, 6). Emerson believed that part of the need for self-fulfillment is realized in one's right to participate in decisions that affect one's life (Emerson 1970). Given the role the press plays in providing information that may form the basis of such decision-making, the importance of protecting the press as part of the value of individual self-fulfillment is evident. These first two values—discovery of truth and individual self-fulfillment—connect most closely with the individual value of protecting expression. But protecting freedom of the press facilitates those individualistic values.

Emerson's next two values extend beyond the individual value of protecting expression and consider the larger social values associated with a system of free expression. He suggested that protecting expression provides an important safety valve for a society as it changes over time. Society demands, at some level, a certain amount of cohesion, yet it must also adapt and change with new ideas. The free exchange of ideas plays an essential role in revealing and diffusing the tensions built up while oscillating between what Emerson called a "healthy cleavage and necessary consensus" (Emerson 1970, 7). This delicate balance is facilitated by open discussion of the issues and concerns that face the citizenry. As Emerson stated, "[P]eople are more ready to accept decisions that go against them if they have a part in the decision-making process" (Emerson 1970, 7). When most public information is disseminated through the mass media, access to those forms of communication is increasingly essential. It was suggested, for example, in the aftermath of the 2000 national election campaign that fringe candidates such as Ralph Nader would have performed better in the polls if they had as much access to the mass media and the televised presidential debates as the mainstream candidates.

Emerson's fourth value for protecting expression was presented with an eye toward the ideal of participatory democracy. The ability to contribute to the democratic process is a value of free expression that extends from the right to share in common decisions. Even if scholars differ on the extent of protection the authors of the Bill of Rights intended with First Amendment protections of expression, they agree that the intent was to protect political expression from government censorship. For Emerson, this right of participation moves far beyond political expression and "embraces the right to participate in the building of the whole culture, and includes freedom of expression in religion, literature, art, science, and all areas of human learning and knowledge" (Emerson 1970, 7).

These values offer a broad justification for protecting expression in a democratic society. The role of a free press is central to facilitating both the individualistic and the social values presented by Emerson.

THEORIES OF THE PRESS

The press operates differently in different societies. It has different ranges of freedom, it is funded differently, and its relationship with the government ranges from being government owned and operated to operating as a "watchdog" of government. In contemporary society, the press falls into five loosely constructed theoretical frameworks or models. The lines between them are diffuse, and some media systems, including our own, straddle different models.

The authoritarian model (see Chapter 2) describes how the press operated in sixteenth- and seventeenth-century England before the abolition of prior restraint (Siebert, Peterson, and Schramm 1956). It is still the model for the press in some parts of the world. Press operating under this model would be completely controlled by and operate for the benefit of the power controlling it—the government, the monarchy, the dictator, or the like. The government determines who operates the press, including whether the press operates itself. It doesn't necessarily have to be government owned, but control of the press tends to be absolute, so there is little media criticism of the government.

Closely related is the socialist/communist model of the press (Siebert, Peterson, and Schramm 1956). The best example of this model was the press in the Soviet Union before its dissolution. The press operating under this model would clearly be state owned and controlled. Information is controlled and filtered to facilitate and further the goals of the state. There is some overlap between this model and the authoritarian model, but in the socialist model the press would never be privately owned and state control reflects a "public ownership," whereas in the authoritarian model the press may be privately owned, but only at the grace of a dictator, a monarchy, or the like.

As concerns about media in developing nations came to the fore, another model of the press emerged (McQuail, 1987). Drawn from ideas debated in the UN Educational, Scientific and Cultural Organization (UNESCO) in the early 1980s, this new model countered the traditional kinds of press, which did not fit the particular technological, economic, or political conditions or needs of developing nations. Under the "development theory," the press may or may not be owned by the state, and the degree of state control varies. But the press is seen less as a watchdog of government and more as an advocate of the government's efforts to develop the country. That advocacy can bump up against freedom of the press when the publication of material might be harmful to the government's development efforts.

The next two models help describe the American press. The libertarian model explains the press as it functioned after the press licensing system was abolished in England (Siebert, Peterson, and Schramm 1956). It is the model that best describes the traditions we inherited in the United States. In this model the press is privately owned by anyone who has the money to start a newspaper or other media outlet. Its objective is not to further the agenda of the state or those in power but instead to inform, to entertain, and to sell. There is little control of the press, aside from the controls imposed by certain court decisions (e.g., those related to libel, obscenity, invasion of privacy, and national security) and the free market. Internal guidelines, ethics, and professional standards of behavior, more than any kind of formal requirements, drive the press to serve larger social goals.

The social responsibility model of the press emerged in the United States in the twentieth century (Siebert, Peterson, and Schramm 1956). It rose as a result of concerns about whether the press was acting in a socially responsible manner. The press under this model has detailed codes of conduct and some mechanism to encourage discussion, feedback, or responses within its forum. The potential exists for the government to step in and correct those in media who fail to meet their responsibility to society. Such intervention could range from regulatory requirements to the taking over of the media company.

In the United States the press operates with a blending of the libertarian and social responsibility models. Where the press falls along the continuum between the two models depends on the nature of the media (television versus print; tabloid versus *New York Times*). The American press enjoys tremendous protection in a manner consistent with the libertarian model. For example, it is almost inconceivable to imagine extensive content regulation of the American press by the state. Additionally, the American press embraces a sense of mission to serve as the watchdog of government and to inform the public on important issues of the day. Although the media's success in meeting this mission varies, for a multitude of reasons, it remains a guiding ethic for much of the press and provides a strong connection to the social responsibility model.

ORGANIZATION OF THE BOOK

It is with this general understanding of the justification for free expression and this theoretical framework for understanding the role of the press in the United States that this book investigates the development and meaning of press liberties in the United States.

Because of the unique role of historical circumstances, technological innovations, court decisions, and precedence in shaping the contemporary meaning of a free press, the text is organized chronologically. This format also provides a context for the historical, political, and social realities of decisive moments in the history of press freedoms. Generally, the development and clarification of press freedoms were not smooth, nor consistent, but the development of contemporary press freedoms is a remarkable story, and it is unique to the United States.

The story does not begin in the United States, however. The roots of contemporary press freedoms stretch back to the writings of Milton, Locke, and Hobbes—English Libertarians who wrote passionately about the importance of individual rights and the problems associated with licensing the press in seventeenth-century England (Altschull 1990). Related French Enlightenment thinkers such as Montesquieu, Voltaire, and Rousseau looked at ideas of democratic principles and social responsibility—values that manifest themselves in the American press's role as a watchdog of government (Altschull 1990). The contribution of these varied philosophical principles to journalism is evident in their repeated appearance in American judicial decisions attempting to clarify the scope and meaning of a free press.

A discussion of these intellectual roots of American press freedoms forms the beginning of Chapter 2. These principles, emerging as part of the larger Enlightenment movement, played a role in the political debates and struggles in seventeenth- and eighteenth-century England. For example, challenges to the English licensing system and the Crown's practice of controlling publishing through the Stationers' Company (chartered in 1557) were wrapped up in a larger struggle over the monarchy's authority to rule Britain. After the authority of the parliamentary system was established in the late seventeenth century, ubiquitous control of printing in England became administratively unmanageable. As a result, more than a century of licensing printers ended in 1694 as the last licensing law expired, and English common law subsequently recognized that there could be no prior restraint imposed on the press. In other words, the government could not prevent the press from publishing. There continued to be mechanisms for punishing the press after it published something "improper, mischievous, or illegal" (Blackstone 1818, 151). Likewise, varied forms of common law prosecution for libel were fundamentally altered in the colonies after the trial of John Peter Zenger for seditious libel in 1744. Before the Zenger trial, truth was no defense against a charge of libel. In fact, in the case of seditious libel, it was thought that truthful criticism of British authority was worse, as it might stir up dissent among the Crown's subjects. The decision in the Zenger trial, initially informally and ultimately formally, established truth as a defense against any libel charge.

The philosophical influences on the Founding Fathers, English common law protections for press, and growing resistance to the British decision to tax newsprint under the Stamp Act of 1765 all helped shape the development of the Bill of Rights in 1791. The common law protection against prior restraint and the early developments in libel law were already part of the framework in which the authors of the Bill of Rights worked. But, as Chapter 2 demonstrates, the road to the freedom of press clause in the Bill of Rights was not simple or smooth. There was resistance generally to a Bill of Rights among the Federalists, and even while the Bill of Rights was being penned, the freedom of press clause was not unanimously supported by the thirteen states.

It is generally agreed that one of the intentions of the authors of the Bill of Rights was to prevent government from intruding on the right of the press to publish by preventing publication, licensing publishers, levying taxes, or controlling the sources of newsprint. Even after the Bill of Rights was ratified in 1791, the meaning of a free press remained unclear. The remainder of Chapter 2 discusses attempts to undermine, limit, challenge, interpret, and reinterpret the meaning of a free press during the eighteenth and nineteenth centuries.

The 1800s are noted for the judicial activity undertaken to regulate speech and the press at the state level (Dickerson 1990). During that century, it was thought that the Bill of Rights prevented only Congress, the federal legislature, from passing laws abridging the freedom of the press. Few cases addressing press freedoms came before the U.S. Supreme Court during the nineteenth century.

The twentieth century was the most judicially active century for the press. Two world wars, perceived threats of fascism and communism, national security concerns arising out of those fears, and the rise of electronic media all formed the impetus for judicial attempts to clarify the meaning of a free press. Journalists developed substantial protection against libel lawsuits, especially concerning public figures. As surveillance technology developed, concerns about invasion of privacy increased. While the press became vulnerable to potential invasion of privacy suits, protections developed that recognized the value of news.

The numerous military conflicts involving the United States during the twentieth century and beyond—the two world wars, the Korean War, the Vietnam War, the invasions of Grenada and Panama in the 1980s, and the Gulf War in 1990, and then the invasion of Afghanistan in 2001 and the invasion of Iraq in 2003—all invite an effort to understand the role and limitation of the press during times of war. Furthermore, general national security concerns, including the publication of classified documents by the press, were hot spots of judicial activity during the 1900s. Throughout most of the 1900s, the courts reflected back on the early philosophical principles embraced as part of the rationale for protecting the press. The courts attempted to remain true to those principles within a contemporary context complicated by the development of electronic media, shifts in media ownership patterns, and accelerating technological innovation.

Chapter 4 extends discussions of major press themes to the twenty-first century. This century looks to be one of the most fascinating with regard to press freedoms. The past century provided us with a relatively clear understanding of governmental limits on censoring the press and the conditions under which the press is protected from libel and privacy lawsuits. But the twenty-first century has already introduced new challenges to press freedoms. It is here that we will see the enormous role technological innovation has played in reshaping the practice of the press in the United States. Satellite and videophone technologies have confounded government efforts to control the press in the name of national security. Enhanced surveillance technology increases the complexity of balancing privacy with freedom of the press. More and more invasion of privacy lawsuits are targeting paparazzi and other celebrity journalists who aggressively photograph, videotape, and document every possible movement of movie stars and television personalities. New distribution technologies, in combination with the relaxation of media ownership rules, have facilitated the streamlining of news operations, ultimately reducing the number of journalists.

As we look forward into the century ahead, an interesting conundrum emerges. There is, at times, a divergence between a free press in principle and a free press in practice. There are wide-ranging protections for journalistic endeavors, yet there are increasing criticisms of the quality of journalism, the range of views journalists present, and the narrowing of news sources at the very time in history that the variety of news outlets has burgeoned to unprecedented numbers. In an age when Americans may get news and information from radio, television, magazines, newspapers, and the Internet, limits on media ownership—justified on the principle of spectrum scarcity for the broadcast media and of media outlet scarcity within a market—are ringing hollow in the halls of the Federal Communications Commission. Over the past twenty-five years, the number of broadcast radio and television stations a corporation can own has increased. Restrictions on the number and kinds of media a corporation can own within a single market are disappearing or are under increasing scrutiny on First Amendment grounds. Critics of the relaxed ownership rules argue, however, that media concentration does not serve the larger ideals that justify freedom of speech or freedom of the press. They argue that in order to preserve the democratic principles justifying those freedoms, the government must in fact set limits on ownership across markets and on cross-ownership within markets.

At issue are competing interpretations of the freedom of press clause. Does the clause articulate a negative liberty, meaning that it prohibits any regulatory or legislative agenda? Or can it be read more broadly, as a positive liberty? Can the government take an activist role and encourage the widest range and dissemination of information and ideas to the public? Regulations and legislation that limit the range of ideas are expressly prohibited, but policies that enhance freedom of expression serve the larger principles behind the First Amendment's freedom of speech and press clauses (Fiss 1996).

Judicial precedent leans in the favor of the freedom of press clause reflecting a negative liberty. In other words, the government is restricted from infringing on the liberty of the press without showing that the restriction serves a more important interest. Still, there are examples in the history of electronic media regulation: the public interest requirement of broadcasters, the old Fairness Doctrine, and the now-diluted Federal Communications Commission restrictions on ownership. The rationale behind all of these electronic media policies is the belief that balanced presentations of wide-ranging ideas serve the public and the democratic process. In the end, any analysis of what freedom of the press means in this country will recognize that much of the development and refinement of the freedom of press clause is more about fine-tuning the balance between competing rights, needs, and responsibilities than believing that the tension may ever be resolved.

The remaining chapters of the book serve as a source of information and research resources for readers. Chapter 5 lists and defines key concepts, events, people, and terms. Ordered alphabetically, the chapter provides an accessible resource for understanding terms and ideas that appear in the first four chapters. Chapter 6 provides readers with excerpts from key original documents pertaining to freedom of the press. Excerpts are presented from a wide range of writings, including those of the English libertarian philosophers and the Anti-Federalists, Supreme Court opinions, and other sources. Finally, the book includes a table of key court cases that have affected press freedoms, a chronology of key events related to press freedoms, and an annotated bibliography to facilitate additional focused research. I hope this book will provide readers with an accessible overview of freedom of the press along with the resources for readers to explore more in-depth one of this country's most cherished freedoms.

References and Further Reading

Altschull, J. Herbert. 1990. *From Milton to McLuhan: The Ideas Behind American Journalism.* New York: Longman Press.

Black, Hugo L. 1960. "The Bill of Rights." *New York University Law Review* 35:865–881.

Blackstone, Sir William. 1818. *Commentaries on the Laws of England,* Vol. 4. Boston: T.B. Wait and Sons.

Clarke, Victoria. 2002. "Striking a Balance: Government's Needs Versus Those of the Media." *Columbia Journalism Review* (Sept./Oct.): 72–73.

Dennis, Everette E., David Stebenne, John Pavlik, Mark Thalhimer, Craig LaMay, Dirk Smilli, Martha FitzSimon, Shirley Gazsi, and Seth Rachlin. 1991. *The Media at War: The Press and the Persian Gulf.* New York: Gannett Foundation Media Center.

Dickerson, Donna. 1990. *The Course of Tolerance: Freedom of Press in Nineteenth-Century America.* Westport, CT: Greenwood Press.

Emerson, Thomas. 1966. *Toward a General Theory of the First Amendment.* New York: Random House.

Emerson, Thomas. 1970. *The System of Freedom of Expression.* New York: Random House.

Fiss, Owen M. 1996. *Liberalism Divided: Freedom of Speech and the Many Uses of State Power.* Boulder, CO: Westview Press.

Langewiesche, William. 2002. "American Ground: Unbuilding the World Trade Center." *Atlantic Monthly* 290(1):42–76.

McQuail, Denis. 1987. *Mass Communication Theory.* 2nd ed. Beverly Hills, CA: Sage.

Newman, Roger K. 1999. "The Populist Hugo Black." *American Lawyer* 21:40–41.

Sanford, Bruce W. 1999. *Don't Shoot the Messenger: How Our Growing Hatred of the Media Threatens Free Speech for All of Us.* Lanham, MD: Rowman and Littlefield.

Sharkey, Jacqueline. 1991. *Under Fire: U.S. Military Restrictions of the Media from Grenada to the Persian Gulf.* Washington, DC: Center for Public Integrity.

———. 2003. "The Rise of Arab TV." *American Journalism Review* (May):26–27.

Siebert, Frederick Seaton. 1965. *Freedom of the Press in England: 1476–1776.* Urbana: University of Illinois Press.

Siebert, Frederick Seaton, Theodore Peterson, and Wilbur Schramm. 1956. *Four Theories of the Press.* Urbana: University of Illinois Press.

2

ORIGINS AND
EARLY DEVELOPMENTS

As we search back through time, the origins of freedom of speech and freedom of the press are a bit blurry. Key moments that helped in the development of a free press, for example, were sometimes more about free expression generally than about the press. With that in mind, seeking out the origins of our press system has the potential to be a diffuse journey. The ratification of the Bill of Rights in 1791 might be seen as the origin of the freedom of the press in the United States, in a literal sense. But that would leave out the clear influence of the British legal system on colonial development. If the history of our press freedoms is considered more broadly and from a regulatory perspective, the abolition of licensing might be seen as the origin of the freedom of press clause in the Bill of Rights. The colonies certainly benefited from the shift to common law. However, the abolition of licensing was not an arbitrary decision; it had roots both in the inability of authorities to enforce licensing and in the long-standing philosophical arguments for the free flow of ideas.

Harking back to the philosophical writings of John Stuart Mill or John Milton might arguably lead us to the first efforts to explain the

crucial importance of an unlicensed press and thus the philosophical roots of our traditions. It depends on how far back and how
broadly we are willing to reach to include early influences on the
American protection of press freedoms. In this chapter, we will go
back even further and look at some ancient experiments with free
expression. Because we share intellectual and philosophical roots
with these cultures, their early experiments with expression hold
some relevance for the development of our traditions. The actual
struggle for freedom of the press consisted of more than the debate
of ideas. It consisted of risk, sacrifice, and the death of many who
advocated such revolutionary and heretical ideas. Their story is the
real story of the early struggle for a free press.

ANTECEDENTS IN GREECE AND ROME

Experiments with expressive freedoms have been documented as
far back as 800–600 B.C. in Athens, Greece, peaking in the mid-
400s B.C. (Radin 1927; Tedford and Herbeck 2001). As part of
early democratic endeavors, aristocratic rulers tolerated, to some
degree, the expressive freedoms of certain classes of "citizens."

These "citizens," as has often been pointed out, did not include
women, or resident aliens, or juveniles (DiStefano 1991; Jaggar
1988; Okin 1979; Phillips 1991). Thus, while the scope of expressive freedom expanded for those fortunate enough to enjoy those
rights, the vast majority of the population of Athens, not to mention the rest of the ancient world, enjoyed no such privilege during this period of isolated democratic experimentation. Furthermore, even among the "citizen" class, the Greeks prohibited
slander and sedition (Tedford and Herbeck 2001).

A similar degree of openness existed for a brief time in republican Rome, although scholars disagree on the extent of tolerance
for expressive freedoms (Frank 1927; Momigliano 1942; Robinson
1940). Then, with the shift to the Roman Empire and monarchical
rule, the Caesars controlled the dissemination of information.

Julius Caesar used the *Acta Diurna*, a handwritten news sheet, to disseminate governmental decrees as well as the results of gladiator events. He also used it to attack his opponents in the Roman senate. But the Caesars squelched dissent of their own leadership. This precedent—limiting criticism of those in power—formed the basic practice in England until the struggle to abolish licensing succeeded. Until that time, no Western nation guaranteed freedom of expression to its citizens (Tedford and Herbeck 2001).

ENGLAND AND THE
EMERGENCE OF PRINTING

Prior to the English Bill of Rights, Britain had no articulated rights of expression, only various degrees of restrictions on printing. With the signing of the Magna Carta in 1215, England underwent a shift in the realm of personal liberties that signaled both an extension of its Greek and Roman democratic roots, mentioned above, and a new direction through the establishment of a domain of inalienable rights and liberties that broke from the Greek elitist classification of "citizen." For the next 500 years, the struggle for free expression fit into this evolving notion of individual rights as an extended struggle to eliminate censorship and licensing of written or printed material.

England inherited this history as questions of expressive freedom, over time, came under the control of the Church and the Crown. The Crown did not tolerate criticism of its leadership, and from that intolerance emerged the 1274 *De Scandalis Magnatum* and the beginnings of seditious libel law. This edict targeted political dissent and any criticism of the Crown and its authority. As early as 1275, still two centuries before the invention of the printing press, the statute of Westminster I outlawed "tales whereby discord or occasion of discord or slander may grow between the king and his people or the great men of the realm" (Levy 1985, 6).

The earliest printers, working in the 1400s, suffered little "censorship or control from ecclesiastical or secular authority" (Siebert 1952, 24). In fact, after William Caxton first introduced printing to England, King Richard III in 1484 created an act to encourage foreign printers to set up shops or import foreign materials. Initially the development of printing in England was viewed as a valuable economic and trade activity. That enthusiasm was short lived. From the early 1500s, continuing through the Puritan Revolution, until the late seventeenth century, England passed a series of printing restrictions, controlled by the Crown and implemented through the Church. Regulation of printing was asserted as a royal prerogative.

ORIGINS OF THE ENGLISH LICENSING SYSTEM AND THE RISE OF THE STAR CHAMBER

Beginning with Henry VIII, approximately fifty years after printing was first introduced in England, a variety of royal measures, from warnings about heretical materials to efforts to limit foreign printers, were used to effectively control the press during the king's thirty-eight-year rule. One focused effort attempted to restrict the widespread distribution of William Tyndale's English translation of the New Testament (along with numerous future publications based in part on his translation). After an effort by the king to recall the book and his bishops' efforts to burn as many copies as they could, the Tyndale Bible continued to be distributed and copies were reprinted abroad. The king's effort to control printing culminated in the royal licensing system, established with the Proclamation of 1538 (Siebert 1952). Toward the end of Henry VIII's reign, he added additional antipress legislation to address the continuing distribution of variations on Tyndale's original translation of the New Testament. Parliament's regulatory law of 1542–1543 controlled the publication of the Bible. The law stated:

There shall be no annotations or preambles in Bibles or New Testaments in English. The Bible shall not be read in English in any church. No women or artificers, prentices, journeymen, servingmen of the degree of yeomen or under, husbandmen, nor labourers, shall read the New Testament in English. . . . anything contrary to the King's instructions . . . shall be thereof convict . . . his first offense recant, for his second abjure and bear a fagot, and for his third shall be adjudged an heretick, and be burned. (Neal 1855)

Up through the reign of Queen Elizabeth, control was strict and rationalized on the belief that maintaining peace required the suppression of all opinion critical of the Crown. Elizabeth did allow criticism of her predecessor, "Bloody Mary," but she oversaw the implementation of numerous decrees and orders on licensing, including the 1586 Star Chamber decree on printing. There would be no criticism of her rule or of the established Church of England. Elizabeth's Proclamation of 1570 offered rewards to those who helped identify writers critical of the monarchy.

The English Court of Star Chamber, a notorious secret tribunal, prosecuted these writers with zeal. The Star Chamber was not bound by traditional legal procedures, and it operated separately from other courts. Furthermore, the Star Chamber had a wide range of indictments and punishments available, including levying unlimited fines, imprisonment, the pillory, flogging, mutilation, and branding, but excluding execution (Scofield 1900). Summary proceedings were common and included private hearings with no protection against self-incrimination. For example, John Stubbes, author of a pamphlet criticizing the Queen, had his right hand "cut off by the blow of a Butcher's knife" under orders of the Star Chamber.

Generally the Tudors, the royal family in control of Britain between 1461 and 1603, successfully suppressed most dissenting opinion. During their reign, there was negligible resistance from Parliament, printers, or the public (Siebert 1952). Not all monarchs were as effective in suppressing dissent. The early Stuarts, who succeeded the Tudors, had far more difficulty controlling printed information (Siebert 1952). Increasing tension between the Crown, Parliament, and ecclesiastical leaders raised questions about the Crown's scope of authority. The Crown responded to the growing suspicion and mistrust of its authority by increasing prosecutions for dissent. Through the use of the Privy Council and an expanded mandate of the Star Chamber, the seventeenth century became one of the most repressive periods for expressive freedoms. In 1630 the Star Chamber sentenced Alexander Leighton for his publication *An Appeal to Parliament,* in which he claimed the preeminence of scripture over monarchal authority. Leighton was taken to Westminster, where he was "whipped, [had] one of his ears cut off, his nose slit, and one side of his face branded." (Siebert 1952, 122). One week later the mutilation was repeated on the other side.

The Star Chamber continued to interpret seditious libel quite broadly. William Prynn published a book in which he disparaged the theater and other "public amusements" (cited in *New York Times v. Sullivan,* 1963, 12). Because the Queen enjoyed the theater, the Star Chamber determined that Prynn had libeled the Queen. Prynn was fined, sentenced to an unlimited prison term, and lost his ears. The severity of punishment that accompanied prosecutions for seditious libel resulted in public outrage and contributed to the dissolution of the Star Chamber (1641), as well as royal control of printing during the Puritan Revolution. However, the most common form of press restrictions—licensing and seditious libel laws—remained, and prosecutions continued under English common law through the seventeenth century.

PARLIAMENTARY CONTROL OF LICENSING

Because of the general political and religious turmoil surrounding the transition from monarchal to parliamentary control of England, printing restrictions were inconsistently enforced. Parliament's lax enforcement was not the result of any decision that the press ought to be free; it came about because other matters occupied Parliament's attention at the time and the old institutions that implemented press restrictions were gone or in a mess. For example, the judicial arm of printing restrictions, the Star Chamber, had been abolished. The Stationers' Company, once filled with royal appointees and responsible for the regulation of printing, entered a state of disarray as authority switched to the Parliament. A flood of pamphleteering resulted that was difficult to contain later on. No longer suppressed, dissident printers attacked the king and Parliament and freely published works without the authority of the author or licenser.

When Parliament finally addressed free and uninhibited printing, it concerned itself with the "elimination of chaos and piracy in the printing trade, suppression of sedition, protection for religion, control of news of Parliamentary activity, and last, a program of active propaganda in defense of the Parliamentary position" (Siebert 1952, 179–180). Parliament's efforts culminated in the 1643 Ordinance for the Regulation of Printing. Sharply regressive in tone, the objectives of the ordinance were twofold: "to protect the property rights of the [Stationers] company and its membership from piracy and counterfeiting by the host of printers which had sprung up since the abolition of the Star Chamber" and "to assist the government by way of repayment in suppressing dangerous and seditious publications" (Siebert 1952, 176). The ordinance effectively re-created the harsh conditions of suppression that existed under monarchal rule.

PLEAS FOR THE ABOLITION OF LICENSING

Many of the prosecutions described above were in response to publications that were critical of the Crown's authority. By the mid-1600s, more writers were making impassioned arguments specifically for the abolition of printing restrictions. John Milton remains the most famous advocate of press freedoms during this period, but other pleas for expressive liberties preceded his. In the late 1500s, Peter Wentworth argued for freedom of discussion for Parliament at a time when Queen Elizabeth resisted parliamentary discussion on issues of religion. He asked, "How can Truth appear and conquer until falsehood and all subtleties that should shadow and darken it be found out?" For this, of course, Wentworth went to prison.

The distinct focus of Wentworth's argument, authored more than sixty years before Milton's *Areopagitica,* was to secure freedom of speech for Parliament, not to secure expressive rights for everyone, and despite language similar to that of Milton's later work, Wentworth did not advocate for freedom of the press specifically.

During the Puritan Revolution, more printers spoke out against Parliament's restrictions. Henry Robinson and William Walwyn, contemporaries of Milton, each published material that attacked press restrictions from various perspectives. In his unlicensed, anonymously published pamphlet *The Compassionate Samaritane,* Walwyn argued that while some regulation of printing was necessary and in the interest of the state, not all dissenting opinion should be subject to licensing. He said that licensing "stopt the mouthes of good men, who must either not write at all, or no more than is suitable to the judgments or interests of the Licensers" (Walwyn 1644, A5). He was not advocating complete religious toleration or complete freedom of the press; rather, he focused on the increasing difficulty and impracticability of maintaining an onerous licensing system. His hope was to extend, within reason, printing freedom for materials that were "not highly scandalous or dangerous to the state" (Walwyn 1644 as cited in Siebert 1952, 194).

Pamphleteer Henry Robinson anticipated the ultimate marriage of free expression with the value of individualism and free market ideology when he wrote, "No man can have a natural monopoly of truth, and the more freely each man exercises his own gifts in its pursuit, the more of truth will be discovered and possessed" (Haller 1934, 69).

At this time John Milton also penned his infamous tract, *Areopagitica,* in which he hoped, he later said,

> to deliver the press from the restraints with which it was encumbered; that the power of determining what was true and what was false, what ought to be published and what to be suppressed, might no longer be entrusted to a few illiterate and illiberal individuals, who refused their sanction to any work that contained views or sentiments at all above the level of vulgar superstition. (Milton 1957, 831)

As with Walwyn, it was the licensing mechanism, the remnant of the Puritan Revolution, that Milton attacked in *Areopagitica.* Milton, one of several great libertarians of the seventeenth century, felt that an unrestrained press was necessary and vital if "Truth" were to emerge. Men, he argued, must have the freedom to publish their thoughts and ideas, and those ideas that are true would emerge victorious in their competition with false ideas. He wrote, "For who knows not that Truth is strong, next to the Almighty?" (Milton 1992, 41). This belief in the ultimate victory of truth has come to be known as the self-righting principle. It operates most efficiently in the open marketplace of ideas. Licensing of the press undermines this efficiency. Milton was by no means advocating for a completely free press. His pleas did not extend to ideas that he abhorred. Milton held Catholicism and royalty in disdain, and at the end of *Areopagitica* and his lengthy argument against licensing, he supported the sanction of the press if it was printing material that was found "mischievous and libelous" (Milton 1992, 44).

Other key libertarians of the time held similar views on licentious expression. Roger Williams exempted from his libertarian arguments "scandal[s] against the civil state, which the civil magistrate ought to punish" (Williams as cited in Levy 1966, xxi). John Locke, in his 1689 *Letter Concerning Toleration,* did not include toleration of the intolerant: "No opinions contrary to human society, or to those moral rules which are necessary to the preservation of civil society, are to be tolerated by the magistrate" (Locke 1689 as cited in Levy 1966, xxi). According to historian Leonard Levy, Locke "regarded the opinions of atheists and the political implications of Catholic doctrine as seditious" (Levy 1966, xxii).

In spite of these published pleas to relax licensing laws, Parliament passed its most detailed Printing Act in 1649, five years after Milton's essay and shortly before the execution of King Charles I. This act and the subsequent Printing Acts of 1653 and 1662 harkened back to the kinds of control that existed during the time of the Star Chamber. Additionally, the law of seditious libel, the foundation of Star Chamber prosecutions, survived the abolition of the Star Chamber. Prosecutions of defendants charged with seditious libel, while occurring in the common law courts, proved more merciless and now included the death penalty.

One notable prosecution was that against John Twyn in 1663. Twyn published a book (he did not write it, and he refused to reveal the author's identity) arguing that the monarchy must be accountable to the people, particularly when the decrees of the king violated the law of God. In 1663 these words were nothing short of revolutionary and, in the eyes of the court, heretical. Twyn received the following sentence:

> [Y]ou shall be hanged by the neck, and being alive, shall be cut down, and . . . shall be cut off, your entrails shall be taken out of your body, and, you living, the same to be burnt before your eyes; your head to be cut off, your body to be divided into four quarters and your head and quarters to be disposed of at the pleasure of the king's majesty. And the Lord have mercy upon your soul. (*Rex v. Twyn*, 1664)

The pleasure of the king's majesty, it turned out, was to have each of the four quarters of Twyn's body nailed to a different gate to the city as a warning to others inclined to publish similar ideas.

In 1683, Algernon Sydney was executed for controversial writings on the government. However, these writings were never published; they were simply found in his home. His claim that they were never intended for publication made little difference.

In 1684, sixteen trials for seditious libel took place over a seven-month period (Siebert 1952). Prosecutions for seditious libel remained a very effective control on the press during the latter half of the seventeenth century. For more than 150 years, then, after the Proclamation of 1538, England's control of the press, whether from licensing or the threat of seditious libel prosecutions, was ever present and always brutal, yet its scope varied widely, depending on the political impulses of the Church, the Crown, or Parliament.

English Common Law Protection from Prior Restraint

Eventually, the licensing system started to fall apart. The dissolution of control of printed materials did not emanate from any decision based on a philosophical commitment to the value of free and uninhibited discussion of public issues. What began as a royal prerogative and then transformed into licensing by Parliament ultimately became too institutionally cumbersome and administratively unmanageable, and it had a negative impact on freedom of trade. Under the rule of William and Mary, the Printing Act expired in 1694, and the press was finally free of regulatory prior restraint. No more licensing; no more *preventing* the press from publishing.

Yet the press was far from free. Prosecutions under common law and through parliamentary citation, especially for seditious libel, remained an ominous form of control (Siebert 1952). English common law at the time indicated only that there was to be no prior restraint on the press; the threat of subsequent punishment remained a powerful muzzle on printers and publishers. The principle of prior restraint was set out in Blackstone's *Commentaries on the Laws of England* and fully reflected the tenuous status of press freedoms:

The liberty of the press is indeed essential to the nature of a free state; but this consists in laying no *previous* restraints upon publications, and not in freedom from censure for criminal matter when published. Every freeman has an undoubted right to lay what sentiments he please before the public: to forbid this is to destroy the freedom of the press: but if he publishes what is improper, mischievous, or illegal, he must take the consequences of his own temerity. (Blackstone 1818, 151)

Given that this was the legal extent of press freedom in England when the American colonies became established, naturally the principle of prior restraint was the extent of protection in colonial America prior to the American Revolution.

Colonial Debates over Freedom of the Press

The American colonies were on the cusp of formalizing their own ideas about free expression. Still, they drew on the traditions with which they were familiar: the legacy of licensing, the doctrine of prior restraint, the writings of seventeenth-century libertarian theorists, and a long-standing practice of subsequent punishment for speech deemed licentious or scandalous. As a result, the early British colonies restricted expression in ways similar to the motherland. Despite the fact that some of the American colonies were founded as a refuge from religious persecution, there were restrictions—some very harsh—on the ability to speak out against Christianity. Governor Thomas Dale's Virginia Code (1610) imposed the death penalty for such an act. Pennsylvania, home of the Quakers, promised freedom of religious practice as long as it involved "one God." The 1649 Maryland Act of Toleration protected the religious practice of Christians, but Maryland also allowed for the execution of anyone who denied the existence of God. As with some of the earlier struggles in England, challenges to prevailing religious practices or criticisms of religious authority exceeded the bounds of acceptable expression.

Although there appeared to be more tolerance for expression outside the realm of religion and seditious libel, colonial newspapers were regulated in a manner consistent with British policy at the time. The Press Restriction Act required that the printer's name and the place of publication be included on each printed document. A 1662 Massachusetts law forbade printing except by license. The Massachusetts governor and his council used this law to shut down the first colonial newspaper, Benjamin Harris's *Publick Occurences Both Foreign and Domestick.* The three-page, six-by-ten-inch printed paper published its first and only issue on September 25, 1690, reporting on how Indian allies of the British Army tortured French soldiers during skirmishes preceding the French and Indian War.

By the early 1700s, with the English licensing system gone and the colonial population reaching 250,000, newspapers began to appear. The first successful newspaper in America was John Campbell's *Boston News-Letter* launched in 1704. Its circulation was small, but it survived because of colonial government subsidies. Andrew Bradford's *American Weekly Mercury* began publication on December 22, 1719. William Bradford's *New York Gazette* began publication on November 16, 1725. In 1729 Benjamin Franklin started the *Pennsylvania Gazette,* which eventually became the most popular colonial newspaper. Low literacy rates, the hardships of colonial life, limited schooling opportunities, distribution challenges, nonpaying subscribers, and a shortage of locally available paper affected the development of colonial newspapers more than any form of government restriction. In the early 1700s, colonial newspaper circulations were low; the largest circulation approached 350 copies per issue.

With all remnants of prior restraint gone, colonial newspapers discussed freedom of the press, but generally from a Blackstonian perspective. For example, an article in the April 1734 issue of the Philadelphia-based *American Weekly Mercury* stated:

> We must carefully distinguish between liberty and licentiousness [for] the extreams that separate liberty from license are closer than most men imagine.... [B]y freedom of the press, I mean a liberty, within the bounds of law, for any man to communicate to the public, his sentiments on the important points of religion and government; of proposing any laws, which he apprehends may be for the good of his country, and of applying for the repeal of such, as he judges pernicious.

Another article in the *American Weekly Mercury* stated a proposal to start a magazine by two men, Andrew Bradford and John Webbe. This 1740 article included an assurance to prospective subscribers that the magazine would adhere to freedom of the press. Its pages would be open to all contenders, but it "would carefully avoid contributing to the licentiousness of the press."

The *New York Weekly Journal*, the paper that led to John Peter Zenger's seditious libel prosecution, wrote about the importance of press liberties in its second issue:

> The loss of liberty in general would soon follow the suppression of the liberty of the press; for it is an essential branch of liberty, so perhaps it is the best preservative of the whole. Even a restraint of the press would have a fatal influence. No nation ancient or modern has ever lost the liberty of freely speaking, writing or publishing their sentiments, but forthwith lost their liberty in general and became slaves.

Embracing the Blackstonian common law practice of disallowing prior restraint on the press, many newspapers went further, arguing that the need for religious toleration or stamp taxes on newsprint were a restraint of trade (Siebert 1952). None of these early writings explicitly suggested that seditious libel be decriminalized, possibly because there were far fewer prosecutions for seditious libel in the colonies than in England. Thus, although the press introduced ideas embracing press liberties, there was a sense that seditious libel exceeded the umbrella of protection. This view, of course, was a direct inheritance from Britain. Libel was still a punishable offense in England. And what constituted libel was broad based. One could be charged with blasphemy (denying the existence of God or religious doctrine), private libel (attacking someone's reputation), obscene libel (corrupting the morals of the king's subjects), and seditious libel (expression critical of the government). Seditious libel in particular was of concern to the press. Up through the early 1700s, it made no difference whether one's criticism of the government was true. In fact, true or justifiable criticism only made the libel worse, since it potentially exacerbated any scandals against the government.

It was in the 1730s that a shift emerged in the arguments for a free press. The eighteenth-century libertarians began to challenge the practice of seditious libel. The most famous writings were published as "letters" under the pseudonym Cato. The authors of these letters, John Trenchard and Thomas Gordon, were enormously influential in colonial America. Their writings on liberty were reprinted in pamphlets and newspapers and quoted liberally throughout the colonies. The most popular "letters" included writings on freedom of speech and libel. Cato argued that government and freedom of the press lived or died together. Even the potential of libelous statements was a risk worth taking in order to preserve the freedom of the press. Cato did not advocate unfettered, false rantings of the press. Rather, he argued that truthful criticism of government should not be subject to punishment. Thus, it was Cato who first introduced the idea that truth be a defense against libel charges, even though common law up to that time dictated otherwise.

Cato's writings were just that—writings. It was John Peter Zenger, a German immigrant printer, who lived Cato's ideas, defending seditious libel with truthfulness of the statement. In 1735, Zenger's trial changed the libel landscape in the colonies. Zenger primarily published religious pamphlets, but he agreed to print an oppositional weekly newspaper criticizing the administration of New York Royal Governor William Cosby. After repeated efforts to convince the grand jury that the *New York Weekly Journal*'s contents constituted seditious libel, Cosby successfully had Zenger arrested. Zenger's trial was a cause célèbre and attracted enormous public attention. Zenger was represented by one of the most successful and respected attorneys of the day, Andrew Hamilton. The challenge Hamilton faced was significant. He had to convince the jury to ignore existing law stating that proof of libel requires only that a jury agree on the identification of the author. The judge determines the libelous nature of the content. Since Hamilton stipulated in court that Zenger was the author, he had to convince the jury to nullify the judge's order of a guilty finding because, he argued, it was essential to allow the press to truthfully or justifiably criticize government leaders. These were Cato's ideas in action.

Hamilton anticipated the enormous implications of the decision when he stated to the jury in his closing arguments:

But to conclude: The question before the Court and you, Gentlemen of the jury, is not of small or private concern. It is not the cause of one poor printer, nor of New York alone, which you are now trying. No! It may in its consequence affect every free man that lives under a British government on the main of America. It is the best cause. It is the cause of liberty. And I make no doubt but your upright conduct this day will not only entitle you to the love and esteem of your fellow citizens, but every man who prefers freedom to a life of slavery will bless and honor you as men who have baffled the attempt of tyranny, and by an impartial and uncorrupt verdict have laid a noble foundation for securing to ourselves, our posterity, and our neighbors, that to which nature and the laws of our country have given us a right to liberty of both exposing and opposing arbitrary power (in these parts of the world at least) by speaking and writing truth. (Linder 2001)

The jury nullified the judge's guilty ruling in relatively short order, finding Zenger not guilty. It is important to understand precisely the significance of the Zenger trial with respect to press freedoms. The trial is often cited as a key moment for freedom of the press. It did have a great deal of significance. It did provide a forum for Hamilton's impassioned extension of Cato's ideas. Practically speaking, truth became an effective defense against libel charges even though the judge did not accept Hamilton's argument for truth as a defense. However, there was no formal change in the common law as a result of this case, as no formal precedent was established. Truth was not codified as a defense against libel for another fifty years. Furthermore, Hamilton did not argue against seditious libel. Finally, as historian Leonard Levy has noted, the truth as a protection against libel charges did not, in practice, extend to criticisms of the legislature, which continued to use a variety of means and rules to control the press (Levy 1966). After the Zenger trial, libertarian arguments for press freedoms waned. For some time thereafter, formal protection for the press in the colonies did not extend beyond the British common law protection against prior restraint.

Still, the foundational events leading to the Revolutionary War were unfolding, and some of them involved the press and press freedoms. Tension grew in the 1760s over taxes applied to the colonies by the Crown. The 1765 Stamp Act taxed all printed material, including newspapers and pamphlets. Although the Stamp act was repealed a year later, subsequent efforts to tax colonial goods became one of the triggers of the Revolutionary War. Newspapers, of which about two dozen were in circulation by the eve of the war, played a significant role in shaping public support for independence.

The war itself brought no immediate changes in press freedoms. The early position of the new states was the classic Blackstonian perspective, protecting the press from prior restraint but allowing punishment after publication. The Articles of Confederation contained no mention of press freedoms. A few states expanded the protection for the press in their own constitutions by including the principle articulated in the Zenger trial that truth is a defense against libel. The Virginia Declaration of Rights (1776) stated, "The freedom of the Press is one of the greatest bulwarks of liberty, and can never be restrained but by despotick Governments." The Maryland Declaration of Rights (1776) stated that the "liberty of the press ought to be inviolably preserved." The Pennsylvania legislature, in 1790, wrote the most detailed protection for the press but, like the legislatures in Virginia and Maryland, left the prosecution of seditious libel intact. Thomas Jefferson, who included the protection of truthful publication in the Virginia Constitution, encouraged James Madison to consider it in the federal constitution. In a letter to Madison from France, Jefferson wrote, "A declaration that the federal government will never restrain the presses from printing anything they please, will not take away the liability of the printers for false facts printed."

FREEDOM OF THE PRESS AND THE BILL OF RIGHTS

During the sweltering Philadelphia summer of 1787, delegates to the Constitutional Convention hammered out the terms of a new federal constitution. Federalist delegates supported a strong set of centralized federal powers, whereas the Anti-Federalist delegates remained concerned that a strong federal government would replicate the conditions and control associated with English rule. These opposing viewpoints manifested themselves in debates about protection for the press. Federalists saw no need for such protection, since common law protection against prior restraint was well established. Furthermore, Federalists intended to use the constitution solely to articulate the specific powers of the federal government. If the constitution did not explicitly give the federal government the power to regulate the press, the government could not do so. By extension, there was no need to create laws protecting the press from congressional actions that the legislative body simply had no power to do.

For example, a South Carolina delegate, Charles Pinckney, suggested that the constitution include the phrase "the liberty of the Press shall be inviolably preserved," but his proposal did not survive the Federalist argument and was defeated. It has been suggested that the language of the First Amendment was not to clarify a limitation on congressional power as a means of preserving an individual liberty, but rather to preserve the state power to regulate press freedoms (Levy 1966). The First Amendment explicitly prevented only Congress from creating regulations on the press. In fact, until 1925, the First Amendment did not limit the ability of states to place limits on free expression.

Anti-Federalists wanted specific protections for a range of individual rights in order to limit the power of the federal government over both individuals and states. One Anti-Federalist, writing under the pen name Centinel, made impassioned arguments for freedom of the press and other dangerously underprotected rights in the federal convention. The newspapers were replete with the writings of Anti-Federalists, under numerous pseudonyms, arguing for individual rights, including press freedoms. The public attention was captured, and the success of a federal constitution increasingly looked tenuous.

Through a compromise process, the Anti-Federalists agreed to support a federal constitution with the promise that a Bill of Rights would follow. James Madison proposed two possible amendments addressing freedom of expression. The first read, "The people shall not be deprived or abridged of their right to speak, to write, or to publish their sentiments; and the freedom of

the press, as one of the great bulwarks of liberty, shall be inviolable." Madison's second version read, "No State shall violate the
equal rights of conscience, or the freedom of the press, or the trial
by jury in criminal cases." This version specifically limited the
power of the states to enact restrictions on the press. But after
more compromises, the final version that Congress adopted as
part of the Bill of Rights on December 15, 1791, specifically limited Congress's ability to pass laws regulating speech or press. As
the states rewrote their own constitutions, some clarified their
ideas about freedom of the press (Sloan and Stovall 1989). Pennsylvania's new state constitution read:

> That the printing-presses shall be free to every person who undertakes
> to examine the proceedings of the legislature, or any branch of gov-
> ernment, and no law shall ever be made to restrain the rights thereof.
> The free communication of thoughts and opinions is one of the in-
> valuable rights of man; and every citizen may freely speak, write, and
> print on any subject, being responsible for the abuse of that liberty. In
> prosecutions for the publication of papers investigating the official
> conduct of officers or men in a public capacity, or where the matter
> published is proper for public information, the truth thereof may be
> given in evidence; and in all indictments for libels the jury shall have a
> right to determine the law and the facts, under the direction of the
> court, as in other cases. (Pennsylvania Constitution, 1790, Art. IX,
> Sec. 7)

With the First Amendment's meaning and intent shaped by the
interactions of common law, libertarian philosophical treatises,
Federalist and Anti-Federalist debates over protection of rights
and the power of states, historical limits on seditious libel, Cato's
writings, and the Zenger trial, it is not surprising that debates continue today about its original intent and contemporary meaning.
In the late 1700s there was one notable plea to dramatically extend
the protection of the press. Robert Hall's "An Apology for the

Freedom of the Press and for General Liberty" argued that men should have the freedom to discuss anything. The government should have no power to punish anyone for the expression of political opinions *regardless of the truthfulness* of the opinions. He wrote, "Publications, like everything else that is human, are of a mixed nature, where truth is often blended with falsehood, and important hints suggested in the midst of much impertinent or pernicious matter; nor is there any way of separating the precious from the vile, but by tolerating the whole." Here Hall takes up the early libertarian argument for the abolition of licensing—the discovery of truth while enmeshed with falsehood—and emphasizing that the discovery of truth cannot be assured without the protection of all expression, regardless of whether it is true or false or a mixture of both.

THE SEDITION ACT OF 1798

For the first seven years after the ratification of the Bill of Rights, things went relatively smoothly for the First Amendment. There was little change in press practices until things shifted abruptly with the Congress's passage of the Sedition Act in 1798. The events leading to the passage of the Sedition Act had as much to do with political maneuvering as with security issues. The country was on the cusp of war with France, but loyalties were divided between the Federalists—in power and unable to negotiate a peaceful resolution with France—and the Republicans, who had strong sympathies and ties with France. The Sedition Act empowered President John Adams, a Federalist, to punish Republican dissent of his administration by making it a federal crime to criticize high government officials. The Federalists were tired of being attacked by the Republican press and feared that public opinion might swing against the Federalist government. When Jefferson challenged the Sedition Act on First Amendment grounds, the Federalist government fell back on the Blackstonian meaning of the

First Amendment, saying that it was intended only to protect against prior restraint of the press (Bergh 1905). Furthermore, the Federalists argued that the government has an inherent right to protect itself (a position taken by the government during World War II and the 1950s Red Scare). Only about twenty-five arrests were made under the Sedition Act, with about ten convictions—eight of them involving Republican newspapers. After winning the presidential election, Jefferson allowed the Sedition Act to expire and pardoned all those who had been prosecuted under the act and were still in jail.

Freedom of the Press in the Nineteenth Century

At the start of the 1800s, although the Sedition Act had expired (1801), little headway had been made in clarifying what fell under the protective scope of the First Amendment's freedom of press clause. After the Sedition Act experience, the federal government shied away from sedition charges for about thirty-five years. Few press cases appeared before the U.S. Supreme Court during the century as a whole. As a result, the nineteenth century is often glossed over in histories of press freedoms. Yet state governments freely regulated expression, not bound by the First Amendment, and prosecuted those deemed offenders. Most such prosecutions were for criminal charges of personal libel, as opposed to blasphemy (about two dozen for the entire century) or obscenity. There was still a sense that freedom of the press did not apply to ideas that were abhorrent to those in power. A case in point was the new Republican president, Thomas Jefferson. Right at the turn of the century, Harry Croswell printed a federalist newspaper that regularly attacked Jefferson's new administration. Jefferson—a leading proponent of press freedoms and a critic of the Sedition Act—sued Croswell, saying the criticisms were licentious. The charges stated:

Harry Croswell did . . . wickedly, maliciously, and seditiously, print and publish, and cause and procure to be printed and published, a certain scandalous, malicious, and seditious libel, in a certain paper or publication, entitled "The Wasp"; containing therein, among other things, certain scandalous, malicious, inflammatory, and seditious matters, of and concerning the said Thomas Jefferson, Esq., then and yet being President of the United States of America. (*People v. Croswell* [1804])

Alexander Hamilton defended Croswell by advancing the argument Andrew Hamilton had made in the Zenger trial seventy-one years earlier. Hamilton argued that truth should be a defense against libel. Croswell did not win the case, but the result led to the New York legislature's passing a law establishing truth as a defense to a libel charge. This defense spread to other states. Furthermore, states began to establish laws protecting journalists from contempt charges for criticizing a judge's decision. The federal government soon matched that protection.

TECHNOLOGICAL INNOVATION AND THE RISE OF SPECIALTY PRESS

Legal and judicial activity related to press freedoms tapered during the eighteenth century, as did government involvement in the press. Government printing contracts—a lucrative catch for any printer, who would then be unlikely to "rock the boat"—died off with the establishment of the U.S. Government Printing Office. In the early part of the 1800s, over 500 papers were being printed. Although by 1820 twenty of these papers were published daily, the vast majority were weeklies (Emery and Emery, 1992). As labor interests developed, the first labor paper, the *Journeyman Mechanic's Advocate*, appeared in 1827. Although the paper lasted only a year, other labor papers emerged and drew impressive circulations (one-third to one-half the circulation of the biggest New

York daily newspaper). These papers clearly served the interests of labor, but, according to historians Michael Emery and Edwin Emery, they tended to be accurate, factual, and well-written (1992).

Increased literacy rates, the development of faster printing presses, and the rise of the penny press—a reduction of the cost of a newspaper from six cents an issue to a penny—resulted in a dramatic increase in newspaper readership and sales. It also stimulated fierce competition among newspapers. Out of the competition came the pressure to beat or "scoop" the competition. Journalists turned out stories more quickly, and more "spot" or on-the-spot news made its way to press. Technology fed the growth of national and foreign news reporting. The eighteenth century began with news delivery via sailing ships, the Pony Express, and even carrier pigeons. By the mid-1800s, those distribution systems were replaced by steamships and telegraph technology. It was the telegraph in particular that provided the distribution boost needed to eventually establish the Associated Press wire news service.

Thus, economic indicators and technological innovations boded well for press freedoms. However, other extralegal pressures affected freedom of the press in significant ways. Just because news had become easier to gather, produce, print, and disseminate, that did not mean that all ideas were welcome or that all newspapers distributed copies freely. Key areas of censorship through the mid–nineteenth century had to do with the abolitionist press, wartime censorship, prosecution for criminal libel, and the rise of obscenity prosecutions.

THE ABOLITIONIST PRESS

The public debate over slavery, an enormously contentious issue dividing the Union, also became a flash point for division within state and federal governments. Beginning in 1829, Southern states started to pass laws—in addition to the already established slave codes—punishing any expression that might incite slaves to insurrection. In part, this was a response to the North's resistance to censoring abolitionist publications. Virginia was one of the few Southern states that publicly discussed the slavery issue. That openness was largely due to a strong antislavery and well-to-do bloc of citizens. Virginia newspapers published handbills about emancipating slaves (Dickerson 1990). In the end, Virginia did restrict the publication of material that advocated slave rebellions. In fact, in 1849 the state enacted a law to punish anyone who denied the right to own slaves (Savage 1968). But the abolitionist movement, even though it had been around since the Revolution, became dramatically more active in the early 1830s, and its growth in turn contributed to the growth of abolitionist publications. The increase in activities led to a surge of vigilante antiabolitionist groups, who harassed antislavery publishers and burned abolitionist papers. According to communication historian Donna Dickerson, efforts to limit the distribution of antislavery material included:

> Prohibiting circulation or publication of incendiary publications calling for the arrest and punishment of any abolitionists carrying incendiary material with them; . . . seizing shipments of publications as they arrived at the post office; and demanding that Northern states pass laws to prohibit publication of incendiary materials. (Dickerson 1990, 86)

Because much of the debate over the distribution of abolitionist ideas had to do with its distribution through the postal system, there was some discussion of creating a federal law preventing the sending of incendiary abolitionist material by mail. Positions on such a move were highly divided. John C. Calhoun vigorously protested the distribution of abolitionist material. However, he did not want federal restrictions, because they would be reminiscent of the Sedition Act and could be used to restrict the flow of other information and ideas. After much congressional debate among the different factions, no law was passed that restricted the distribution of antislavery material through the mail. The bill that did pass, in fact, mandated the fining of postmasters who unlawfully held up the delivery of letters, pamphlets, and newspapers. Calhoun did not have the same concern about state restrictions on the dissemination of abolitionist material.

Although state laws resulted in arrests for possession of abolitionist material or for expressing sympathy for the abolitionist movement, prosecutions were often unsuccessful, for two reasons. First, many of the Southern laws written at this time specifically targeted *members* of abolitionist societies. Often those who were prosecuted were sympathetic to the abolitionist cause but not members of any abolitionist society. Second, most laws required a showing of criminal intent—often difficult to prove.

In 1837 an event occurred that shifted the public debate in a way that tied together the abolitionist movement and freedom of expression. Reverend Elijah Lovejoy, editor of the Alton, Illinois, *Telegraph,* publisher of the abolitionist newspaper the *Observer,* and a tireless advocate for the abolitionist movement, was killed during what was the third mob attempt to seize and destroy his printing press. Lovejoy became a martyr for the abolitionist movement, but his death also triggered public debate in the newspapers about freedom of the press (Dickerson 1990). For example, the *New Hampshire Herald of Freedom* proclaimed, "Not only has an editor been murdered for publishing his opinion, but the press throughout the country has had an outrage committed on it, and the rights which every editor possesses have been rudely and ruthlessly violated" (quoted in Dickerson 1990, 128).

The role of the slavery issue in the run-up to the Civil War is well known. But it was during the Civil War that the press ran up against a new form of censorship.

MILITARY CENSORSHIP OF THE
PRESS DURING THE 1800s

While the journalism profession was getting its bearings on emerging communication technology, local papers followed the War of 1812 and the exploits of General Andrew Jackson. Newspapers received their information from a range of sources, including journalists' dispatches from the front and from the War Department. The idea of a war correspondent had not yet emerged, and thus no system had been established to control or censor journalists covering wars. Newspapers near the military zones covered events. If reporters "stepped over the line," they were banished from the military camps (Dickerson 1990). The only confrontation between the military and the press worth noting involved the editor of the *Louisiana Gazette* and an article saying that Jackson had received word of a peace agreement between England and the United States. Jackson ordered the editor to get permission before publishing anything else. The editor's rather sharp and sarcastic retraction created a public uproar. Jackson instituted martial law and then used it—first to imprison a state legislator who criticized the law and then to expel the judge who ordered the legislator released. Ultimately, the courts caught up with Jackson and forced him to pay civil damages (Mott 1969).

The Civil War was the first military action in which formal press censorship rules were instituted. The military censored the press for the obvious reasons of protecting military secrets and strategy. Yet it also censored the press to limit the dissemination of critical opinions. For example, New York newspapers were closed down for criticizing Union loyalists (Dickerson 1990). The Northern presses had their use of the telegraph, postal services, and other distribution means limited by the government. The commander of the Union forces, Irwin McDowell, restricted reporters' dispatches relating to the army without his staff's review

(Crozier 1956). Correspondents and editors were arrested. Newspaper offices were sacked by the military. The military tried at one point to institute "ground rules" under which use of the telegraph would continue unrestricted. These rules included a ban on reports of troop movements or prediction of troop movements, information about munitions, and reports of troop mutinies or riots (Crozier 1956). Within nine days the agreement was violated and the telegraph was off limits (Cutler 1955). A second attempt at reaching voluntary censorship agreement in exchange for unrestricted use of the telegraph also failed (Nelson 1967).

Even with these restrictions in place, the press caught the flavor of the war, the division of opinions, and many details regarding the multitude of battles. For the most part, newspapers complained about their own restrictions and remained more silent about opposition newspapers (Dickerson 1990). Finally, when the *Chicago Times* was shut down in 1863, a unified voice of the press emerged to protest military censorship.

The South faced similar forms of censorship from the Confederate army. They had voluntary censorship guidelines in place throughout the Civil War, and telegraph restrictions were also added. In addition, the South suffered from the problem of newsprint scarcity.

The century rounded out with the Spanish-American War in 1898. By then, the telegraph was well established. Messages to and from South America could be transmitted in less than half an hour. Censorship began even before the war started. The Signal Corps handled key cable offices and intercepted messages. This was the beginning of censorship based on controlling the means of communications. Reporters on Navy ships were easily controlled because they were stuck on the ship and dependent on the Navy for information and access to the telegraph.

One particular incident led to a backlash of harsh censorship. A small steamer was deployed to deliver supplies to Cuban insurgents waiting near Havana. The newspapers used dispatch boats to send to their papers information about the progress of the delivery. Once information about the steamer's trip was published, Spanish troops learned of it and met the boat to send it back. Newspapers criticized the failed military drop harshly, and the military responded to the news leak and subsequent criticism with a strict new censorship policy. There would be no reports of ship military movements, and the Florida telegraph offices were censored. The press was still able to get some of the story to the public along with a mix of speculation and rumor. Nevertheless, at the close of the 1800s, the message to the press and the public was brought home: Military censorship of some sort was likely, was to be expected, and was necessary.

THE VEXING PROBLEM OF CRIMINAL LIBEL

As mentioned earlier, Thomas Jefferson fought against the Sedition Act and its criminalization of seditious libel, yet he also successfully sued a Federalist printer for libel. Although these may seem contradictory, the distinction is that Jefferson was not opposed to common law prosecution. A bigger issue was at stake in these matters, however—namely, whether the federal government or the states had jurisdiction over libel. The test came early in the century with *United States v. Hudson and Godwin* (1812). In that case, the U.S. Supreme Court ruled that the federal government could not prosecute for libel under common law. State governments, however, were free to deal with libel under common law. State libel actions peaked at the end of the century with over 100 cases between 1890 and 1900 (Nelson 1967). Nevertheless, by the end of the 1800s, the protection for the press against libel charges had expanded. Truth became a more potent defense against a libel charge. Reporters enjoyed qualified privilege (protection from libel suits) for their reports on official government proceedings. The right of the press to comment on issues, both political and nonpolitical, as well as the conditions for issuing retractions and corrections and for determining damages started to become standardized across states (Dickerson 1990).

OBSCENITY LAW AND
PROSECUTION OF PUBLISHERS

Although obscenity laws did not specifically involve the news media, it is worth noting their role in the distribution of printed material. Freedom of the press, while certainly encompassing within its scope the activities of journalists, also included the activities of printers and publishers more generally. Although journalists did not collide with obscenity laws, publishers and printers did. The development of obscenity law over the centuries and its impact on publishers, authors, filmmakers, and even Web site operators all bump up against freedom of the press.

Simply put, the nineteenth century was not a good one for publishers of sexually explicit material. Restrictions on distribution and punishment for publication were implemented at both the state and federal levels. In the years before the Civil War, as during the colonial period, relatively few arrests were made for obscenity. Those that occurred tended to be at the state level. For example, in 1815, Jesse Sharpless was charged and convicted in Philadelphia under the common law (no state or federal statutes yet) for exhibiting "for money, to persons . . . a certain lewd, wicked, scandalous, infamous, and obscene painting, representing a man in an obscene, impudent, and indecent posture with a woman." Six years later the Supreme Court of Massachusetts upheld the common law conviction of Peter Holmes for publishing John Cleland's *Memoirs of a Woman of Pleasure* (a conviction overturned by the U.S. Supreme Court). About this time, obscenity laws began to appear in the statutes; in 1821, Vermont was the first state to enact such laws. Eventually, the federal government became involved. In 1842, Congress passed the first federal obscenity statute as part of the Tariff Act. The law barred the importation of all indecent and obscene prints, paintings, lithographs, engravings, and transparencies into the United States.

The mid-1800s crusade of a young puritanical clerk reshaped the way the government handled sexually explicit materials. Anthony Comstock, a veteran of the Civil War who worked in a dry goods store, became extremely upset with the reading material being passed around by his coworkers. Comstock proceeded to track down one of the suppliers of the materials and had him arrested. Motivated by his success, he made it his mission to rid the country of sexually explicit materials. At age twenty-eight, he founded New York's YMCA Committee for the Suppression of Vice. With the support of wealthy benefactors, such as J.P. Morgan and Samuel Colgate, Comstock successfully lobbied Congress for a statute prohibiting the mailing of obscene publications or any materials concerning birth control or abortion. Comstock even worked without pay as a postal inspector to help enforce the law.

Although the "Comstock Act," as it came to be known, criminalized the mailing of obscene materials through the postal system, the post office also had wide discretion to bar what it thought to be obscene materials without ever invoking criminal prosecution. But what was obscene? For that determination, the U.S. Supreme Court announced in 1896 (*Rosen v. United States* [1896]) that it would use England's Hicklin rule of 1868, a remarkably broad but probably historically appropriate definition of obscenity. The Hicklin rule is named after Benjamin Hicklin, who heard the appeal of an outspoken anti-Catholic, Henry Scott, once convicted of distributing immoral publications (an anti-Catholic pamphlet called, for short, *The Confessional Unmasked*). Hicklin concluded that the pamphlet was not obscene. Yet the Court of the Queen's Bench disagreed, and Lord Chief Justice Cockburn announced the Hicklin rule: "The test of obscenity is this, whether the tendency of the matter charged as obscenity is to deprave and corrupt those whose minds are open to such immoral influences, and into whose hands a publication of this sort may fall" (*Regina v. Hicklin,* 1868, cited in Tedford and Herbeck 2001, 129).

With a free rein to restrict mailings, criminal prosecution for attempting to mail obscene materials, and a definition of obscenity based on the standard of what was appropriate for a child, the federal government restricted many publications from entering the country or the postal system. For example, the 1873 Comstock Act, along with the 1842 Tariff Act, banned such books as Daniel Defoe's *Moll Flanders,* Voltaire's *Candide,* Walt Whitman's *Leaves of Grass,* James Joyce's *Ulysses,* D.H. Lawrence's *Lady Chatterly's Lover,* and Hemingway's *For Whom the Bell Tolls.* State governments also used legislative power to punish the sale of "obscenity." These collective state and federal efforts to suppress vice continued well into the 1900s.

CONCLUSION

To capture the origins of the freedom of press clause, a story that spans several centuries, is a major endeavor. However, some threads through the centuries help tie the spread of years together in meaningful ways. First, the philosophical foundations of the freedom of press clause have never left the debate and dialogue about the importance of a free and unfettered press. The words of Milton and Mill and the ideas of Locke were echoed again and again as England struggled with the licensing system. Those libertarian ideas found a place in the rhetoric of the American constitution-making process as well as in the Anti-Federalist arguments for protecting state power and establishing a Bill of Rights.

When the federal government flexed its muscle to silence political opponents at the end of the eighteenth century, opponents of the Sedition Act found their strongest arguments in the ideas of the early English libertarians. The idea of a free press expanded in scope as early American printers, publishers, and lawyers extended these ideas into the area of criminal libel and sedition. If truth was to emerge triumphant, to paraphrase Milton, then truth must be protected from government prosecution. But the path of articulating, securing, and expanding rights is never smooth. The rise of obscenity prosecutions during the 1800s illustrates the impact of cultural values, norms, and social practices on the meaning and scope of liberty and freedom. It is an excellent precursor to understanding the historical context of the twentieth-century political prosecutions for dissident expression.

These ideas and struggles for press freedoms helped carve out a sphere of protection from the federal government, but as the events of the nineteenth century reveal, numerous other pressures on the press translated into explicit as well as more subtle forms of censorship. The stage was set for the next century, one marked by tremendous judicial activity, and the most significant century for the clarification and expansion of America's press freedoms.

References and Further Reading

Altschull, J. Herbert. 1990. *From Milton to McLuhan: The Ideas Behind American Journalism.* New York: Longman.

Anderson, Daniel A. 1983. "The Origins of the Press Clause." *University of California at Los Angeles Law Review* 30:455–541.

Bergh, Albert E. 1905. "Resolutions Relative to the Alien and Sedition Laws," in *The Writings of Thomas Jefferson,* Vol. 17, edited by Albert E. Bergh and Andrew A. Lipscomb, 381–382. Washington, DC: Thomas Jefferson Memorial Association.

Berlin, Isaiah. 1969. *Four Essays on Liberty.* New York: Oxford University Press.

Blackstone, Sir William. 1818. *Commentaries on the Laws of England,* Vol. 4. Boston: T.B. Wait and Sons.

Crozier, Emmet. 1956. *Yankee Reporters, 1861–65.* New York: Oxford University Press.

Curtis, Michael Kent. 2000. *Free Speech: "The People's Darling Privilege."* Durham, NC: Duke University Press.

Cutler, J. Andrew. 1955. *The North Reports the Civil War.* Pittsburgh: University of Pittsburgh Press.

D'Ewes, Sir Simonds. 1682. *Journal of All the Parliaments During the Reign of Queen Elizabeth.* London.

Dickerson, Donna. 1990. *The Course of Tolerance.* New York: Greenwood Press.

DiStefano, Christine. 1991. *Configurations of Masculinity: A Feminist Perspective on Modern Political Theory.* Ithaca, NY: Cornell University Press.

Dunn, John. 1969. *The Political Thought of John Locke.* New York: Cambridge University Press.

Emerson, Thomas I. 1970. *The System of Freedom of Expression.* New York: Random House.

Emery, Michael, and Edwin Emery. 1992. *The Press and America,* 7th ed. Englewood Cliffs, NJ: Prentice Hall.

Farrand, Max, ed. 1966. *The Records of the Federal Convention of 1787.* New Haven, CT: Yale University Press.

Fiss, Owen. 1996. *Liberalism Divided: Freedom of Speech and the Many Uses of State Power.* Boulder, CO: Westview Press.

Frank, Tenney. 1927. "Naevius and Free Speech," *American Journal of Philology* 48:105–110.

Haller, William. 1934. *Tracts on Liberty in the Puritan Revolution,* Vol. 1. New York: Columbia University Press.

Jaggar, Alison M. 1988. *Feminist Politics and Human Nature.* Totowa, NJ: Rowman and Littlefield.

Levy, Leonard W. 1960. *Legacy of Suppression.* New York: Harper and Row.

Levy, Leonard W. 1985. *Emergence of a Free Press.* New York: Oxford University Press.

Levy, Leonard W., ed. 1966. Introduction to *Freedom of the Press from Zenger to Jefferson.* New York: Bobbs-Merrill.

Linder, Douglas. 2001. "The Trial of John Peter Zenger: An Account." Available at www.law.umkc.edu/faculty/projects/ftrials/zenger/zengeraccount.html.

Locke, John. 1990 (orig. 1689). *A Letter Concerning Toleration.* Amherst, NY: Prometheus Books.

McDonald, Forrest. 1985. *Novus Ordo Seclorum: The Intellectual Origins of the Constitution.* Lawrence, KS: University Press of Kansas.

Mill, John Stuart. 1947 (orig. 1859). *On Liberty.* Edited by Alburey Castell. New York: F.S. Crofts and Co.

Milton, John. 1992 (orig. 1644). *Areopagitica.* Edited by S. Ash. Santa Barbara, CA: Bandana Books.

Milton, John. 1957. "Second Defense of the People of England," in *John Milton: Complete Poems and Major Prose*, edited by Merritt Hughes, 831–837. New Haven, CT: Yale University Press.

Momigliano, Arnaldo. 1942. "Review of Laura Robinson's Freedom of Speech in the Roman Empire." *Journal of Roman Studies* 32:120–124.

Mott, Frank L. 1969. *American Journalism, A History: 1690–1960.* Toronto: Macmillan and Co.

Neal, Daniel. 1855. *The History of the Puritans*, Vol. 1. New York: Harper and Brothers.

Nelson, Harold L. 1967. Introduction to *Freedom of the Press from Hamilton to the Warren Court*, edited by Leonard Levy. New York: Bobbs-Merrill.

Okin, Susan M. 1979. *Women in Western Political Thought.* Princeton, NJ: Princeton University Press.

Phillips, Anne. 1991. *Engendering Democracy.* University Park: Pennsylvania State University Press.

Radin, Max. 1927. "Freedom of Speech in Athens." *American Journal of Philology* 48:215–220.

Robinson, Laura. 1940. Freedom of Speech in the Roman Republic. Ph.D. diss., Johns Hopkins University (Baltimore).

Savage, W. Sherman. 1968. *The Controversy over the Distribution of Abolition Literature, 1830–1860.* New York: Negro Universities Press.

Schwartz, Bernard, ed. 1980. *The Roots of the Bill of Rights.* New York: Chelsea House.

Scofield, Cora L. 1900. *A Study of the Court of Star Chamber; Largely Based on Manuscripts in the British Museum and the Public Record Office.* Chicago: University of Chicago Press.

Siebert, Fredrick S. 1952. *Freedom of the Press in England, 1476–1776.* Urbana: University of Illinois Press.

Sloan, W. David, and James Glen Stovall. 1989. *The Media in America: A History.* Worthington, OH: Publishing Horizons.

Smith, Jeffrey A. 1988. *Printers and Press Freedom.* New York: Oxford University Press.

Storing, Herbert J., ed. 1981. *The Complete Anti-Federalist.* Chicago: University of Chicago Press.

Tedford, Thomas, and Dale Herbeck. 2001. *Freedom of Speech in the United States*, 4th ed. State College, PA: Strata Publishing Co.

Trenchard, John. 1994. *The English Libertarian Heritage: From the Writings of John Trenchard and Thomas Gordon in the Independent Whig and Cato's Letters.* San Francisco: Fox and Wilkes.

Walwyn, William. 1644. *The Compassionate Samaritane.* London.

3

TWENTIETH-CENTURY ISSUES

Any attempt to encapsulate the freedom of press issues of the twentieth century is an ambitious undertaking. It was a busy century, with the federal court system actively shaping the meaning of a free press by clarifying unresolved issues lingering from the nineteenth century and expanding press freedoms into new realms as broadcasting technology emerged. In the latter part of the century, the courts continued to grapple with new, expanded notions of the "press" as a result of technological innovation and convergence of ownership as well as the shifting economic, cultural, and social practices of the press.

Understanding press freedoms during the twentieth century is not a simple matter of tracing key judicial decisions, although there were numerous landmark cases whose impact significantly reshaped the meaning of a free press. Often Supreme Court decisions were intertwined with larger forces—economic, technological, and cultural—and a solid understanding of press freedoms in the twentieth century should include a sense of that overall context.

The mere fact that press freedoms in the twentieth century include new forms of media complicates the way the courts address the First Amendment rights of the press. Although some press freedoms stand independent of technology, different media face different judicial interpretations of press freedoms.

Let us begin by reiterating that "the press" is a broad concept and encompasses different media. In addition to journalistic icons such as the *New York Times* and the *Wall Street Journal,* the press also includes hometown newspapers and even those grocery checkout counter tabloids whose headlines catch our attention: "Does Osama Bin Laden and Saddam's Gay Marriage Count?" (*Weekly World News,* October 7, 2003). The press includes high school newspapers, nightly broadcast network news, local television and radio news, Sunday morning talk shows, cable news networks, and Internet versions of all the above as well as stand-alone Internet news Web sites such as the Drudge Report. And, of course, the press includes the journalists themselves, who create the content for the various media.

This chapter begins with a discussion of general press freedoms that shape the news media. The discussion is driven by three overriding questions:

1. When can the government prevent the press from publishing?
2. Under what conditions is a government regulation that infringes on press freedoms constitutional?
3. When can the government punish the press for publishing, either through criminal means (prosecution) or by permitting civil recourse (lawsuits)?

The responses to these questions will cover the major topics associated with freedom of the press, but it is important to understand that these topics are not categorically distinct. The complex ways in which press freedoms evolved over the twentieth century subvert any neat categorization of topics and thus leave plenty of overlap. For example, discussions of prior restraint and of freedom of press versus the right to a fair trial are dealt with as separate topics because they are complex issues warranting in-depth discussion. Yet gag orders and judicial limiting of pretrial publicity are forms of prior restraint. General discussions of national security issues run the gamut from publishing top-secret documents to the more complicated questions of whether secrecy oaths are a justifiable prior restraint on publishing. However, the issue of press restrictions during military conflicts, although also a prior restraint in the name of national security, is complex enough to be addressed separately.

Finally, toward the latter part of the twentieth century, technological innovation, economic growth, deregulatory trends, and shifts in cultural norms all played nonlegal but noticeable roles in shaping the practice of press freedoms. I will touch on this topic toward the end of the chapter and address it more fully in Chapter 4.

When Can the Government Prevent the Press from Publishing? Modern Prior Restraints on the Press

There are not many prior restraints on the press. As we saw in Chapter 2 in the discussion of the British licensing system in the eighteenth century, the meaning of prior restraint was clarified by William Blackstone when he wrote that freedom of the press meant no prior restraint. His summary of British common law— one of the foundations of American legal traditions—duly noted that preventing prior restraint by no means excluded the possibility of subsequent punishment for acts of "temerity." A similar principle applies to the press today. In the United States, it is extremely difficult to place a prior restraint or injunction on the press, and, fortunately, it is reasonably difficult to punish the press after publication. In fact, the U.S. Supreme Court clearly articulated the importance of protecting the press against prior restraints in an important 1931 decision involving a Minnesota state law that permitted authorities to shut down a "malicious, scandalous, and defamatory newspaper" by declaring it a public nuisance (*Near v. Minnesota* [1931]). In this instance, the *Saturday Press* printed numerous articles charging that Minneapolis law enforcement officials, especially the police chief, were doing little to counter the illegal activity of gangsters involved in gambling, bootlegging, and racketeering. The Supreme Court overturned the lower court's decision to uphold the ban on publication. The Court drew on the ideas of James Madison, Blackstone, and the *Schenck v. United States* (1919) decision to argue that prior restraints on the press are almost always unconstitutional. The only case of prepublication prior restraint of the press permitted, according to the decision in *Near v. Minnesota,* was in matters of national security.

What constitutes a legitimate injunction on publication in the name of national security then became the subject of future cases. In general, an injunction or prior restraint is a last resort, the only choice when the alternative—subsequent punishment—will not provide an adequate remedy to the harm resulting from publication. Thus, if publication of sensitive material would cause irreparable harm to national security, an injunction against publication might be possible.

The question of what constitutes irreparable harm to national security was raised in 1971 when the *New York Times* published three articles in a series of investigative stories based on secret Pentagon documents about the Vietnam War. The research for the story relied on a voluminous amount of material from a Pentagon study that was surreptitiously copied and delivered to the *Times* by Daniel Ellsberg, a former analyst for the U.S. Department of Defense. The bulk of the documents were classified, and thus it was a federal crime for Ellsberg to remove them from the department—a crime for which he was prosecuted separately. However, much of the content was historical, and some of it was embarrassing to the administration because it revealed that the government had lied about its Vietnam War policy.

While the first few stories were coming out in the *Times*, the government requested an injunction against future publication in federal district court. This marked the first time that the government attempted to use the federal court system to prevent publication of information (Tedford 2001). After a full hearing two days later, the request for an injunction was denied. Meanwhile, the *Washington Post* began publishing stories based on the same documents. A government request for an injunction against the *Post* was denied in district court. The federal government, pushing its request through the judicial appeals process, found a sympathetic ear in the federal appellate court system. The appeals court ruled that both newspapers had to temporarily stop publication of the stories until there could be a full hearing. Each newspaper had its own hearing in its own regional appellate court. One court ruled in favor of the *Post* and the other ruled against the *Times*. An appeal went to the Supreme Court, which combined the cases to hear them together. All of this unfolded very quickly, within the course of days. Yet, during this time other newspapers were publishing stories based on some of the Pentagon documents. Government efforts to enjoin publication by these newspapers were inconsistent. Six days after the petition to the Supreme Court, the Court ruled that the *Post* and the *Times* had the right to publish material from the Pentagon documents (*New York Times v. United States* [1971]).

This case, which came to be known as the "Pentagon Papers" case, represented an important victory for the press. Nevertheless, in separate opinions issued by several of the justices, it was clear that a majority of the Court did not support an absolute ban on prior restraint. Five of the justices stated that they either would have supported censorship in this particular case or would have allowed sanctions to be imposed on the press for publishing the documents.

Eight years later, the lower courts viewed the publication of sensitive material quite differently. Freelance journalist Howard Morland researched and prepared an article for the *Progressive* magazine entitled "The H-Bomb Secret: To Know How Is to Ask Why." A scientist who had been asked by the magazine to review the story for accuracy alerted the government about its pending publication. At the government's request, a federal district court issued a temporary restraining order and then a temporary injunction on publication. The injunction was issued on March 16, 1979, and a court hearing was scheduled for early September. Before the case could be heard or any decision appealed, several other newspapers published similar information based on the research of another journalist. As a result, the government dropped the case. In the end, there was no decision on the prior restraint, despite the *Progressive*'s plea for the appellate court to rule on the constitutionality of the federal government's actions. The court did not engage the constitutional question before it, but it did suggest that the outcome might not have been as favorable for the *Progressive* as it had been for the *Times* and the *Post* eight years earlier.

Specifically, the court indicated that there were several facts that distinguished the *Progressive* case from the Pentagon Papers case. First, the publication of the *Progressive* article appeared to be a violation of the Atomic Energy Act (1946), which prohibited the communication of restricted information connected to atomic energy. Second, the Pentagon Papers case involved historical material that was classified but the publication of which would not present an immediate threat to national security. The *Progressive* article contained current information involving ongoing national security concerns. Yet none of the material used in Morland's article involved classified information. His information was gathered through interviews and from publicly available documents. This fact, however, did not appear to alleviate the court's concern about national security, because the information was now packaged in a form that might assist other countries in the development of thermonuclear weapons. Finally, there was a significant difference in clout between the *New York Times* and the *Progressive*. The *Times* case came before the Supreme Court within a week of the original effort to enjoin publication. The first hearing for the *Progressive*, in district court, was scheduled almost six months after the injunction was placed on publication. The willingness of district court judge Robert W. Warren to impose a prior restraint on the press on the mere possibility of harm is the most chilling legacy left by this case. He stated in his opinion:

> A mistake in ruling against the *Progressive* will seriously infringe cherished First Amendment rights. If a preliminary injunction is issued, it will constitute the first instance of prior restraint against a publication in this fashion in the history of this country, to this Court's knowledge. . . . A mistake in ruling against the United States could pave the way for thermonuclear annihilation for us all. In that event, our right to life is extinguished and the right to publish becomes moot. (*United States v. The Progressive* [1979], 996)

Another way in which national security concerns have led to injunctions on publication occurred in the 1970s with an attempt by a former agent of the Central Intelligence Agency (CIA), Victor Marchetti, to publish a book on his CIA experiences. Marchetti had voluntarily signed a secrecy agreement when he was hired by the CIA, but he refused to abide by it for the purposes of his book. After a series of court hearings and two refusals by the Supreme Court to review the case, the government's request to remove material from the book was upheld (*United States v. Marchetti* [1972]). Knopf published the book with sections deleted by the government left as blank spaces in the book. Another ex–CIA employee, Frank Snepp, published a book without permission, after signing a termination agreement reaffirming his secrecy oath. The government successfully sued in district court for breach of contract seeking an injunction against further publication and asking the court to turn over the book's profits to the government. Even though there was no evidence that secret information was included in the book, Snepp lost his appeal before the Supreme Court (*Snepp v. United States* [1980]). Both Snepp and Marchetti are permanently enjoined from discussing their CIA experiences without the agency's permission. Furthermore, the courts have made it clear that secrecy contracts are binding in spite of First Amendment rights and regardless of whether the information in question is sensitive.

In the end, the courts have looked carefully and skeptically at prior restraint requests. Although the Pentagon Papers case offers, at one level, a good degree of protection for journalists, the lack of consensus among the justices and the distinctions made about the ruling in the *Progressive* case eight years later, along with the unsettling decisions in the CIA cases, leaves a sense of unease about precisely when the government can censor the press.

War Coverage and National Security

Press freedoms during times of war have varied through the country's history, and an ongoing tension between press freedoms and national security remains. Part of the problem is defining what is an adequate accommodation for the press under the First Amendment and what is a justifiable limit on press freedoms because of real national security concerns. The *Near* decision in 1931, which specifically mentioned preventing the reporting of troop locations as an example of an acceptable prior restraint, did not provide guidance on the more subtle areas of press freedoms during wartime. It is unlikely that the press would challenge such a clear national security concern. But the history of press censorship during wartime involves other forms of information control. It is this history that demonstrates the complexity and the unresolved nature of the issue and explains much of the antagonism between the press and the military.

Prior to the Civil War, there was no notable wartime censorship of the press. The shift during the Civil War was precipitated by technological innovation. With the development of the telegraph, there was no longer a geographical and time barrier to reporters' getting sensitive information into print. The Confederate press, however, faced strict official censorship as well as shortages of reporters and newsprint. The Union press was not as aggressively censored, but some papers were prosecuted, were forbidden from using the mail system, were barred from the front lines, or had their telegraph transmissions monitored. The military also temporarily shut down three papers for printing sensitive material and for criticizing the administration (Dennis et al. 1991).

This early tension between the military and the media persisted in military conflicts that followed. From the Spanish-American War through World War I, the military restricted the press with little challenge. Censorship during World War I expanded dramatically with the creation of the Committee on Public Information, headed by former journalist George Creel. The committee set press censorship regulations that focused primarily on the publication of sensitive information. Most newspapers followed the regulations voluntarily. In combat areas, the military established a second censor, former journalist Frederick Palmer. His job was to censor dispatches from the front. Add to this the punch provided by the Espionage and Sedition Acts of 1917 and 1918, which called for severe sanctions against the publication of any information that might aid the enemy, journalists covering World War I faced the most extensive censorship of any military conflict up to that point (Dennis et al. 1991).

The negative reaction by journalists and scholars to the military censorship of World War I translated into less direct censorship during World War II. Some limitations did go into place a year before the attack on Pearl Harbor, however. When the United States formally entered the war, the Office of Censorship was established. It developed the Code of Wartime Practices, which called for *voluntary* compliance with censorship guidelines. Additionally, the military made an explicit commitment to avoid holding up news stories without justification. However, military commanders, particularly in the Pacific arena, delayed the release of news and pressured journalists to write positive stories about the troops under their command (Dennis et al. 1991).

With the erratic application of censorship guidelines at the start of the Korean War, journalists probably longed for the well-planned, evenhanded, and consistent guidelines from World War II. The voluntary censorship was abandoned once it became evident that the war would not end quickly. All press communications were reviewed in the field or in Tokyo before being forwarded to the States. The Korean War represented a low point for press freedoms.

The Vietnam War marked a distinct shift in press-military relations. The military wanted the press to cover the conflict in an effort to bolster public support for the war. The military was also acutely aware of its inability to control press movements in and out of Vietnam because it was not in control of civilian population movement. Journalists and their stories, film footage, and photographs moved freely between the States and the Saigon airport. Journalists who wanted to reach the interior of Vietnam could simply rent a plane. There was no enforced censorship; security guidelines remained voluntary and were largely successful. Only six of the 2,000 or so American journalists working in Vietnam had their press credentials revoked for violating the guidelines (Dennis et al. 1991).

What makes Vietnam such an interesting story of press-military relations is the lingering impression that news stories—not ones that compromised national security, but rather stories that questioned policy and revealed the horrors of the protracted fighting—eventually played a role in turning the tide of public opinion against the war. That memory shaped press-military relations for the next U.S. military action: the Grenada invasion. Since technological advances in communication by then made it nearly impossible to control the flow of information, the military banned the press altogether from Grenada. There is no independent documentation of what occurred when U.S. military forces landed on the island. The reaction of the media was understandably strong, but the strategy proved successful for the military, because it created a willingness on the part of the press to consider military censorship a compromise between a total ban on press access and unrestricted access in future military operations. A panel that included key media representatives devised recommendations for handling future military-media relations. The Sidle panel—named for the panel's chairman, Gen. Winant Sidle—encouraged voluntary compliance with security guidelines, an arrangement reminiscent of World War II policies. However, the panel made a new recommendation. After seeing how successfully Prime Minister Margaret Thatcher controlled the British press when Britain invaded the Falkland Islands, the panel recommended a similar press pool structure. Press pools involve taking a selected group of journalists into the key conflict areas and letting them gather information and distribute it to all other news sources. The first attempt at using press pools failed when delays prevented any meaningful press access to the 1989 invasion of Panama City, Panama. As a result, little independent documentation exists of the events leading up to General Manuel Noriega's arrest.

In 1991, as U.S. troops were deployed to the Middle East for Operation Desert Storm, extensive negotiations took place between the press, the secretary of defense, and the Saudi government about the presence of the media on Saudi soil. The resulting compromise was a set of guidelines detailing twelve categories of information on which the press would not be permitted to report and how violations would be handled. Furthermore, the press pool system was fully deployed. Reporters in the war zone were assigned a military escort, for their own safety, according to officials. The press objected, concerned that it would be hard to gather information with a public affairs officer present at all times. All information gathered by the press pools would go through a security review. If the military restricted press pool stories, the media had several venues for appeal. Once all appeals were exhausted, the press retained the right to publish, enabling the government to claim that there was no prior restraint on the press. However, after the time it took to work through the appeal process, stories had lost their newsworthiness. As one study of press coverage of the 1991 Gulf War concluded, "[T]he outcome of the security review process, if a journalist chose to challenge it, would likely be a kind of *de facto* censorship" (Dennis et al. 1991, 18).

During the Gulf War, journalists in the pool system complained about press pools. Journalists excluded from the pool system complained about press pools. Still other journalists circumvented the pool system and entered Kuwait on their own. Some were taken into custody by the U.S. military, allied forces, or the Iraqis. Others managed to report successfully from outside the pool system.

Several news outlets (*Harper's, Mother Jones, Nation,* and the *Village Voice*) launched a lawsuit shortly before the start of the Desert Storm ground offensive. These organizations argued that any restrictions beyond those voluntary guidelines in place during the Vietnam War constituted an excessive prior restraint on the press. The Agence France-Presse news wire, also excluded from the press pool, sued, challenging the constitutionality of the military's decision to include the Associated Press and Reuters news wires but to exclude the French news service. These lawsuits were combined, but before a hearing could take place, the active phase of the war ended and the Department of Defense moved to dismiss the case. The news outlets objected, asking the court to evaluate the pool system before it was used in future military actions. The court ultimately dismissed the case, indicating that it would not rule on the Department of Defense's press restriction policies, so the constitutionality of the press pool system or the reporting guidelines was never determined.

The press pool system was deemed a failure by the media, who, in a highly competitive news environment, had to depend on pooled information and visuals in addition to official sources. The military concluded that the system was highly successful in terms of shaping the news without controlling or censoring the press in a potentially unconstitutional manner. But the use of the press as a public relations tool and a way to counter enemy propaganda remained elusive with the press pool system. As discussed in the next chapter, the military developed another framework for press coverage when the United States invaded Iraq in 2003. It blended public relations appeal, the persuasive impact of instantaneous visual imagery, and the power of personal relationships into a reporting framework that, although still problematic, is generally agreed to be an improvement over the pool system.

Nevertheless, in hindsight, the press pool model remains an illustrative example of the gray areas associated with censorship. The hypothetical example of national security of the *Near* case—the reporting of troop locations—is an easy call. Discerning when a complex organizational framework, such as the pool system, unduly limits freedom of the press is far more difficult.

The Judiciary

Although censorship of the press during wartime remains an unresolved issue for free press advocates, a groundswell of concern about press coverage of the judicial process cannot be far behind. The challenges to the press are manifested in several ways. The overriding concern is how to best balance the press's First Amendment rights and a defendant's Sixth Amendment right to trial before an impartial jury. Of particular concern to the judiciary is the ever-present pretrial publicity associated with high-profile trials and court hearings. With the judiciary's effort to offset pretrial publicity and ensure a fair trial, the press now faces difficulties in gaining access to the courtroom and a growing use of gag orders by judges.

Pretrial Publicity

With the growth of cable television, satellite television, and the Internet, the demand for content to fill space is virtually insatiable. Add to the mix an increasingly fragmented audience spread over more and more news options, and the media face growing pressure to scoop the competition in an effort to preserve their diminishing market shares.

The press is not bound by rules of evidence, and, as a result, defendants in high-profile cases increasingly face two trials: one in the courtroom and one in the media. For example, a confession made before trial might be suppressed at trial for any number of reasons, but the press can report at length that the accused had confessed to the crime. In one case, Wilbert Rideau confessed to a murder under duress and without legal representation. The court refused to admit the confession. However, his filmed confession was broadcast on television and seen by about 100,000 viewers. On appeal, the Supreme Court overturned his conviction (*Rideau v. Louisiana* [1963]).

The results of some tests, such as lie detector tests, DNA tests, blood tests, and so on, as well as a refusal to take such tests may not be admissible in court but may be reported by the press. Prior criminal records generally are not admissible evidence in court but are reported in the media. Likewise, comments made by family members, neighbors, ex-spouses, employers, and the like are generally not admissible in court but are basic fodder for the broadcast media. For example, in August 2002, as police dug under the concrete slab patio in Ward Weaver's backyard looking for the bodies of two missing teens, Miranda Gaddis and Ashley Pond, the local media stood in front of the house interviewing various emotional bystanders, including Weaver's ex-wife, who believed that Weaver had killed the teens. In an ABC News *Good Morning America* interview, Pond's stepmother accused Weaver of the murders and put a sign on Weaver's front yard saying "Dig Me Up." The content of the many television interviews surrounding the investigation of Ward Weaver for rape and murder would not be admissible at trial. Yet they painted a grim public picture of the man, increasing the possibility that Weaver might not find an impartial jury in Clackamas County, Oregon—where the bodies were in fact discovered, one in his shed and one under his patio.

There were numerous cases in the twentieth century, in addition to the *Rideau* case, in which defendants sought to have convictions overturned because of pretrial publicity. The Supreme Court's approach has been to balance First and Sixth Amendment rights on a case-by-case basis, keeping at the forefront two overriding concerns: protecting against jury bias and maintaining an atmosphere in the courtroom that does not undermine the judicial process. It is certainly possible that press coverage can preclude a fair trial. But in coming to that determination the Court has recognized that it is not essential that juries have *no* prior knowledge of the case in order for a trial to be fair; it is only crucial that potential jurors are able to consider the evidence presented in court without outside influence or preconceived notions of guilt or innocence (*Murphy v. Florida* [1975]).

It is not easy to prove jury bias resulting from media publicity. Courts ask jurors if they are capable of considering the evidence in an unbiased manner or if they have formed an opinion about the defendant's guilt or innocence. Courts may but are not required to ask potential jurors what information they already know about a defendant. Thus, it remains difficult to demonstrate that mere knowledge of information presented in the media would bias a juror. The Supreme Court established that convictions may be overturned if there is substantial evidence that the jury was biased (*Irvin v. Dowd* [1961]) or that pretrial publicity was so intense that the court can assume that the jury was prejudiced (*Estes v. Texas* [1965]).

The Court has concluded on at least one occasion that the overwhelming publicity and "carnival-like" atmosphere in the courtroom undermined a fair trial without the defense introducing evidence of prejudice. In the famous case of *Sheppard v. Maxwell* (1966), which spawned the television series and the movie *The Fugitive*, the press focused intensely on Sam Sheppard, whose wife had been murdered. The press went too far, the Court determined. The press demanded Sheppard's arrest, called him a liar, printed crime scene photos, and revealed Sheppard's refusal to take a lie detector test. The Supreme Court overturned the guilty verdict, saying that Sheppard did not receive a fair trial. However, the Court did not admonish the press for its obsessive focus on the trial (although it danced around the possibilities of future sanctions), but instead chastised the trial judge for not doing more to ensure that Sheppard received a fair trial.

What can a trial judge do to balance freedom of the press while protecting a defendant's right to a fair trial? When media attention is particularly intense, a change of venue is a common request. The trial of Timothy McVeigh, the militia member who bombed the Murrah Federal Building in Oklahoma City, was moved to Denver, Colorado. Although the events associated with McVeigh's trial were known throughout the country, the concern was to remove him from a media environment filled with personal stories of the tragedy. Outside of Oklahoma City, coverage tended to be more fact based and less emotionally driven. The Washington, D.C., sniper defendants, Lee Boyd Malvo and John Allen Muhammad, received a change of venue that moved them 200 miles from the nation's capital. Scott Peterson, on trial for the December 2002 murder of his wife and their unborn child, was granted a change of venue from Stanislaus County to San Mateo County after his attorney reported survey results suggesting that the residents of Peterson's hometown have a "lynch-mob mentality," as evidenced by the fact that 98 percent of the people surveyed in the county were aware of the case, and 75 percent have formed an opinion about the case (Coté 2004).

Gag Orders

Although a change of venue may be a reasonable accommodation between freedom of the press and a fair trial, courts also have employed another strategy to control pretrial publicity: the gag order. A 2000 study tracked gag orders for a three-month period in twenty-six states and the District of Columbia. The study noted that most of the forty-three orders were not accompanied by a hearing to determine whether less drastic options were available. Almost half of the orders were imposed in civil, not criminal cases (Reporters Committee on Freedom of the Press 2000).

Gagging the press is a prior restraint. It requires a hearing in which significant evidence is presented that no lesser measures will preserve a fair trial and that leaving the press unrestrained is a threat to the judicial process. In 1976, the Supreme Court ruled that any court thinking about a gag order on the press faces a heavy burden of showing that a fair trial would not otherwise be possible (*Nebraska Press Association v. Stuart* [1976]). Justice Burger looked at three factors to determine whether pretrial publicity poses a serious threat to a fair trial: the degree of pretrial publicity, other possible measures to handle the concern, and the likelihood that the gag order would diminish pretrial publicity (Middleton et al. 2004). On several occasions, gag orders against the press have not been successfully challenged on First Amendment grounds. In 1990, a federal court ordered CNN not to air taped conversations involving General Manuel Noriega, the former leader of Panama, and his attorneys until the court could determine whether the release of the conversation would violate Noriega's right to a fair trial. The Supreme Court ruled in 1984 that the *Seattle Times* could be enjoined from publishing information it obtained through the discovery process as a defendant in a libel suit (*Seattle Times Co. v. Rhinehart* [1984]).

But the press is not the only party that can be subject to a gag order. The Supreme Court explicitly recognized that the use of gag orders on trial participants is a reasonable strategy for a trial judge concerned about the integrity of the judicial process (*Sheppard v. Maxwell* [1966]). However, there are no clear guidelines for applying gag orders on trial participants and attorneys. Different states require different burdens of proof.

Gagging the jury after the trial is also a growing trend, but the justifications for doing so are dubious—after all, the trial is over. Gag orders on the whole remain a potentially abused mechanism that can limit public access to the judicial process. For example, a federal judge in Texas entered 219 gag orders in two years, blocking the flow of information to the public in nearly all of his cases (Reporters Committee on Freedom of the Press 2000).

Access to the Courtroom

With the *Nebraska* decision in place and judges largely powerless to gag the press, some language in that same decision suggests that judges could close courtroom proceedings to the press. However, in 1980, the Supreme Court held that the public and the press have a right of access to criminal trials (*Richmond Newspapers v. Virginia* [1980]). Drawing on precedent, the Court wrote:

> [T]he historical evidence demonstrates conclusively that at the time when our organic laws were adopted, criminal trials both here and in England had long been presumptively open. This is no quirk of history; rather, it has long been recognized as an indispensable attribute of an Anglo-American trial. (569)

Furthermore, the Court admonished the lower court for not considering other alternatives to closing the courtroom to the press.

The Supreme Court has required that trial courts meet a similar burden before closing to the press the jury selection process in criminal trials (*Press-Enterprise Co. v. Riverside County Superior Court* [1984]). Chief Justice Warren Burger wrote that judges must show that there is an overriding interest in protecting a defendant's Sixth Amendment right to a fair trial or a need to protect the privacy of a juror "when interrogation touches on deeply personal matters that [the] person has legitimate reasons for keeping out of the public domain" (511). Furthermore, judges must demonstrate that there was no other way to accomplish this overriding interest. Two years later, the Supreme Court extended this right to preliminary hearings (*Press-Enterprise Co. v. Riverside County Superior Court* [1986]). Again Chief Justice Burger wrote of the importance of having an independent eye on the proceedings, especially when there is no jury.

Access to the courtroom is not absolute. It is well protected for jury selection proceedings, pretrial hearings, and the trial itself— in *criminal* trials. The trial court bears a heavy presumption against closing the courtroom to the public or the press. The Supreme Court has not formally extended this press freedom to civil trials, although most trial courts handle civil proceedings similarly. Finally, the Court has made it quite clear that the presumption of openness does not extend to grand jury proceedings. Without a judge or the traditional rights of counsel, cross-examination, and so on, the Court has maintained that publicity of those secret hearings would undermine the trial process (*Press-Enterprise Co.* [1986]).

Cameras in the Courtroom

Although the press is allowed to attend most judicial proceedings, the courts have been less open to press technology invading the courtroom. The Supreme Court has yet to recognize a First Amendment right to televise judicial proceedings. Hostility to cameras in the courtroom may be rooted in the 1935 high-profile trial of Bruno Hauptmann, accused of kidnapping and killing the infant son of Charles Lindbergh, who was already known world-wide as the first man to fly solo across the Atlantic. The trial was a media sensation and was disrupted by the flood of journalists and photographers. Afterward, the American Bar Association rec-ommended banning cameras (Middleton et al. 2004). That recom-mendation stuck until the 1950s, when Colorado began to let cameras in the courtroom. Texas followed suit a decade later. It was the 1962 televised trial of Billie Sol Estes in Texas that resulted in a Supreme Court review of cameras in the courtroom. Justice Clark described the Texas courtroom as follows:

> [A]t least 12 cameramen were engaged in the courtroom throughout the hearing taking motion and still pictures and televising the pro-ceedings. Cables and wires were snaked across the courtroom floor, three microphones were on the judge's bench and others were beamed at the jury box and the counsel table. It is conceded that the activities of the television crews and news photographers led to considerable disruption of the hearings. (*Estes v. Texas* [1965], 536)

Several justices noted that the mere presence of cameras vio-lated Estes's right to a fair trial. Justice John Marshall Harlan stated that, at the very least, cameras should not be allowed for high-profile criminal trials. The majority concluded that there was no First Amendment right of the media to have cameras in the courtroom. The federal district courts also do not allow cameras. The Ninth and Second Circuit Courts have allowed cameras on a limited basis (Reporters Committee on Freedom of the Press 1996). It does not appear likely that any television stations will soon be broadcasting Supreme Court oral arguments, as evi-denced by Justice David Souter's comment to the congressional appropriations subcommittee, "The day you see a camera come into our courtroom, it's going to roll over my dead body" (Reporters Committee on Freedom of the Press 1996).

However, there is no constitutional barrier to state courts' allowing cameras (*Chandler v. Florida* [1981]). In the state court system, the decision to allow cameras in the courtroom rests with the courts themselves. State courts seem more open, and many states leave it up to the trial judge. As of 2003, forty-three states allowed television coverage of trial and appellate court proceedings. Other states allow some coverage but still ban cameras in certain circumstances, such as cases involving minors or sexual abuse, or when one of the parties objects to cameras (Middleton et al. 2004).

Court Records

There is a long tradition in common law of providing journalists access to court records. Appellate courts have suggested such access is constitutionally protected, but the Supreme Court has yet to explicitly guarantee media access to court records under the First Amendment. The media's right to documents and materials introduced as evidence is even less clear. Access varies from court to court. The Third Circuit allowed broadcasters to copy tapes that had been introduced as evidence in one of the trials resulting from the Federal Bureau of Investigation's "Abscam" sting, arguing that it allowed those not physically present at the proceeding to follow an important trial (*In re NBC* [1981]).

Courts are also divided on whether discovery proceedings are open. Furthermore, some sealed court documents are not necessarily available to the press. Several statements and motions were sealed in the Timothy McVeigh Oklahoma City bombing trial. The Tenth Circuit Court of Appeals ruled that evidence that is not admissible at trial need not be made available to the press or the public (*United States v. McVeigh* [1997]). Finally, some states statutorily limit access to certain court cases involving sensitive or private matters or involving minors. Nevertheless, the Supreme Court has made it clear that if the news media legally acquires information, it can be published without fear of subsequent punishment (*Cox Broadcasting Corp. v. Cohn* [1975]; *Smith v. Daily Mail Publishing* [1979]; *The Florida Star v. B.J.F.* [1989]).

Open Meetings, Open Records, and the Freedom of Information Act

Although it is not a particularly long-standing practice, nor one explicitly provided for in the Constitution, journalists extensively use public records. Access to government records is not guaranteed through the courts, although the courts have been involved in interpreting applicable statutes. Instead, access to records is facilitated through "sunshine laws" or "open meeting acts." The Government in Sunshine Act (1976) opens official meetings of about fifty federal agencies and commissions to the public. There are some exceptions, such as federal advisory bodies, whose job is advisory only. There also are circumstances in which an otherwise public meeting might be closed. For example, a 1979 meeting of the Nuclear Regulatory Commission (NRC) to discuss the reopening of the Three Mile Island reactor was closed to the public. When the decision to close the meeting was challenged, the court of appeals ruled that the NRC had to delineate carefully the aspects of the meeting that justified excluding the public and to ensure that all other topics related to restarting the reactor be open to the public (*Philadelphia Newspapers v. Nuclear Regulatory Commission* [1984]). It is an ongoing struggle to compel compliance with the Government in Sunshine Act (Pember 2003). As one government watch group reported, "Some agencies have been accused of changing the names of meetings—that is to say, calling them something else (such as staff discussions)—or of using telephone conference calls to avoid the intent of this Act" (OMB Watch 2002).

Sunshine laws exist in every state, although their specific provisions, including the sanctions they impose for violations, vary extensively. Legislative proceedings, parole board sessions, military agencies, and medical agencies are generally exempt from state open-meeting laws (Pember 2003). Most open-meeting acts require that the press be notified of meeting schedules and that records or minutes be kept of all official meetings. There are times when meetings can be closed to discuss personnel or sensitive subjects or to conduct negotiations. Even in these executive sessions, minutes are kept and eventually must be made public. Furthermore, one federal district court ruled that the public may raise personnel matters, normally reserved for executive session meetings, during the public comment portion of government meetings. In this particular instance, the Battle Creek, Michigan, City Commission stopped two residents from criticizing Police Chief Jeff Kruithoff's conduct during the public comment portion of the city commission meeting. According to an American Civil Liberties Union (ACLU) press release, "At the April 6 meeting, Gault and Mitchell wanted to comment on a police detective's sworn testimony in federal court that Kruithoff authorized an illegal wiretap on a subordinate to monitor him while Kruithoff was having a sexual affair with the subordinate's wife" (ACLU 1999). Mayor Dearing stopped the comments because they constituted personal attacks and because the matter was under litigation and was more "appropriate" for closed executive session. At the next open city commission meeting, Gault and Mitchell were again stopped from speaking, this time threatened with arrest. At the request of Mayor Dearing, police escorted Gault from the meeting. Gault successfully sued, arguing that the mayor's censorship of public comments violated the Michigan Open Meetings Act. The federal court ruled that the public could comment on the activities of executive session during public comment portions of public meetings (*Gault v. City of Battle Creek* [1999]).

Even with open-meeting laws in place, journalists have to be vigilant about their right to cover a public meeting. The reasons for closing public meetings should be scrutinized carefully and skeptically. Sanctions for state agencies violating the open meetings acts are typically outlined in the statute and may include criminal as well as civil remedies.

Taxation

The American disdain for taxation of the press extends all the way back to colonial times. After the English licensing system ended, the British taxed publications and advertising until 1855. Although taxation is not a direct prevention of publication like the licensing system or the current ability to block publication in the name of national security, it can have a similar effect if the tax is unduly burdensome. Aversion to this form of revenue generation reached its apex in the colonialists' objections to the Stamp Tax, a trigger for the American Revolution. The English imposed "taxes on knowledge" intended to "[curtail] the circulation of newspapers, and particularly the cheaper ones whose readers were generally found among the masses of the people..." (*Grosjean v. American Press Co.* [1936] 246).

Contemporary courts have looked at taxation issues carefully, recognizing the ways in which selective taxation can be used to unfairly burden some media over others. The courts also have recognized that the government needs taxes to operate and thus that a blanket ban on taxation of the media would be excessive.

Several cases over the last seventy years have articulated the middle ground on taxation of the press. In 1936, the Supreme Court struck down a selective state tax on newspaper and magazine advertising receipts for media with circulations over 20,000 copies per week. This selective tax effectively singled out

Louisiana's thirteen largest newspapers, twelve of which opposed the current governor. The Court concluded that the tax was a prior restraint because it cut into advertising revenue and potentially restricted media circulation (*Grosjean* 1936). Not all tax constitutes a prior restraint—only selective or targeted taxes against specific media. Accordingly, the Supreme Court has declined to review lower appellate court decisions holding that the media, as businesses, are not exempt from routine business-related taxation, but are exempt only from taxation that attempts to control or punish them.

Almost fifty years later, the Supreme Court struck down a Minnesota tax on newspapers that used large amounts of ink and paper. Although the tax did not directly target large-circulation papers, the Court still found it unconstitutional (*Minneapolis Star and Tribune Co. v. Minnesota Comm'r of Revenue* [1983]). The Court concluded that the state did not demonstrate a compelling governmental interest that would justify targeting newspapers with such a tax. Likewise, the Court struck down an effort by the State of Arkansas to add a sales tax to general-circulation magazines but not special-interest magazines. The Court again reasoned that the tax selectively discriminated against certain types of magazines (*Arkansas Writer's Project v. Ragland* [1987]). The Court's view seems to be that taxes that penalize some media organizations but not others within the same medium (intra-media-based tax—some newspapers, but not others; some magazines, but not others) are unconstitutional. Furthermore, the Court seems to be saying that some compelling interest must be demonstrated before any tax is justified.

In the late 1990s, the Court seemed to head in a different direction. When a tax encompasses one medium completely, even if it does not cover other media (inter-media-based tax—cable, but not television; radio, but not newspapers), the Court tends to view the tax as nondiscriminatory. *Leathers v. Medlock* (1991) is an example that has raised the question among some scholars of whether the Supreme Court is moving in two conflicting directions on the issue of media taxation (Graefe 1993; Packer and Gower 1997). In this 1991 case, the Court ruled that sales tax on one medium—cable and satellite television—was constitutional, even though the tax was not applied to print media.

The Court has not clarified why an intramedia tax is suspect but an intermedia tax seems acceptable. In this age of converging technology, the issue is bound to become more complex. In the meantime, the Court seems to have identified a set of general conditions that need to be met before a tax on the media can survive constitutional scrutiny:

- The tax must not interfere or appear to interfere with First Amendment activities of the media (this issue will be revisited below, in the discussion of newsracks).
- The tax may not single out a specific media (intramedia discrimination).
- The tax may not be content based (e.g., a tax that targets sports magazines but not news magazines) (Packer and Gower 1997).

Under What Conditions Is a Government Regulation That Infringes on Press Freedoms Still Constitutional?

Although prior restraints on the press bear a presumption of unconstitutionality, the government may be able to justify regulating—but not censoring—the press in other ways. Regulation is a form of prior restraint, but in this case the message is not censored but rather "channeled" in some manner. With sufficient justification, the government can use what are referred to as time, place, and manner restrictions to limit the time that the expression takes place, the location of the expression, or the manner in which parties express themselves.

Regulations that impinge on the First Amendment are not easy to justify. Most time, place, and manner restrictions start from the initial position that the expression should not be limited in any way and that the burden of proof is on the government to demonstrate that a given regulation (say, one requiring a permit for a parade) is based on a compelling government interest (such as traffic control); that the regulation is content neutral, meaning it is not intended to limit certain ideas and not others (e.g., if the government granted a permit for a Columbus Day parade but not a Native American parade); and that there are other options for dissemination of the message. Furthermore, most time, place, and manner restrictions involve speech more often than they do the press. Thus, although it is valuable to recognize that the government has means of controlling expression other than outright censorship, time, place, and manner restrictions are not commonly employed against the press. The few ways in which they are used against the press are the focus of the next section.

THE REGULATION OF NEWSRACKS

At first glance, this may appear to be a minor press issue, but with the plethora of print media available, cities are seeing a dramatic increase in the number of newsracks along sidewalks and street corners. Across the country it is becoming a trigger for litigation between publishers and communities. Cities and other urban jurisdictions, maintaining that these mushrooming newsracks affect pedestrian traffic and public health and safety, have responded with regulations. The courts, in turn, have appropriately scrutinized the constitutionality of any limits placed on the distribution of printed material.

Two Supreme Court cases made it clear that regulations affecting newsracks may not be based on the content of printed material. Specifically, an attempt to limit the Cleveland *Plain Dealer*'s efforts to place newsracks on the public sidewalks of suburban Lakewood was remanded for rehearing with the clear message that Lakewood's regulations must be content neutral and not arbitrarily limit certain newspapers over others (*City of Lakewood v. Plain Dealer Publishing Co.* [1988]). In 1993, the Court expanded the requirement to commercial media, saying that a city cannot deny permission for the placement of newsracks for commercial publications, such as free real estate magazines or auto trading magazines, if they allow newspapers to place newsracks on city sidewalks (*Cincinnati v. Discovery Network* [1993]).

These two cases raise the question of how a city can control the unfettered proliferation of newsracks up and down city streets—a location long recognized by the courts as a historical public forum and subject to a higher level of protection of expressive activities. This battle has taken place at the appellate court level. The appellate courts have recognized a city's interest in avoiding too much clutter on public sidewalks and upheld a lottery system for newsrack placement as a content-neutral solution that satisfies time, place, and manner requirements (*Honolulu Weekly v. Harris* [2002]).

On the other hand, an appellate court upheld a ban on newsracks in the historical Beacon Hill district of Boston as part of an overall "street furniture policy" (intended to maintain the integrity of the historical area) (*Globe Newspaper Company v. Beacon Hill Architectural Commission* [1996]). The First Circuit Court of Appeals ultimately was sympathetic to the argument that the street furniture policy served an important interest in maintaining the historical quality of Beacon Hill. The policy did not regulate on the basis of the content of the media in the newsracks. All newsracks were to be removed from the streets, not just newsracks for some papers. Finally, the court concluded that other venues were already in place for distributing the media, including store sales and subscription sales.

But newsracks are not placed only on public streets. Airports often have large numbers of newsracks, and airports arguably function much like a public space. Additionally, many airports are owned and operated by the government. However, Chief Justice William H. Rehnquist wrote in a Supreme Court opinion,

> The government need not permit all forms of speech on property that it owns and controls. Where the government is acting as a proprietor, managing its internal operations, rather than acting as a lawmaker with the power to regulate or license, its action will not be subjected to the heightened review to which its actions as a lawmaker may be subject (*International Society for Krishna Consciousness v. Lee* [1992], 678).

In other words, there are some government facilities, such as airports, that do not fall under the public forum doctrine. Accordingly, a narrowly split Supreme Court ruled that airports are not a traditional public forum, like streets, sidewalks, and parks. In this particular case, involving the Krishna religious movement, the Court banned solicitations by the Krishnas at airports but allowed leafleting. Removing airports from a public forum designation opened the door to potentially significant control over expression within such facilities. However, one appellate court struck down a total ban on newsracks in airports even though airports are not considered a public forum (*Multimedia Publishing Co. v. Greenville-Spartanburg Airport Dist.* [1993]).

In blending the *Krishna* decision and a desire to create an attractive environment in anticipation of the 1996 Olympics, an appellate court judge upheld the right of the City of Atlanta to require newspapers to rent city-owned newsracks at the Hartsfield International Airport at a for-profit price. The court also upheld the right of airport officials to determine which printed material would be placed on the newsracks, although it required that safeguards be in place to protect against the possibility of airport officials discriminating against some newspapers on the basis of content or viewpoint. In the same decision, the court struck down the city's attempt to include advertising for other nonmedia on these newsracks (in this particular case, Coca-Cola ads) (*Atlanta Jour-*

nal and Constitution v. City of Atlanta Department of Aviation
[2003]).

Issues surrounding newsrack placement and control remain unsettled. Many cities, including Kansas City, Missouri, San Francisco, Boston, and New York, continue to grapple with strategies
to balance control of newsrack placement and potential First
Amendment challenges to any limitations (*Yank Magazine* 2002).
For example, on July 12, 2004, New York Mayor Michael R.
Bloomberg signed a law allowing the city to regulate the placement, installation, and maintenance of newsracks, stating that
"The goal is to balance the right to disseminate information with
the safe and orderly use of the city sidewalks that we all share"
(New York City Department of Transportation 2004). The New
York Newspaper Publishers Association is fighting the new law,
arguing that it is unnecessary given previous agreements between
publishers and the city. Also, the association believes that the law
unduly "restricts ownership of multiple-vending newsracks, bans
single-publication newsracks, and fails to clarify the selection process for inclusion in multiple-vending newsracks" (Reporters
Committee on Freedom of the Press 2002, 17).

The Supreme Court is likely to uphold any city's right to regulate newsracks in a narrowly tailored, content-neutral manner.
Similarly, it is likely to continue to carefully scrutinize regulations
for viewpoint discrimination and tendencies to be overreaching in
scope and to ensure that other venues are available for newspapers, such as store vendors and subscription sales.

WHEN CAN THE GOVERNMENT PUNISH THE PRESS FOR PUBLISHING?

Having reviewed the ways in which the government can prevent
the press from reporting or distributing its message and the conditions under which the government can pass regulations that affect freedom of the press, we can now turn to the question of

when the government can apply "subsequent punishment," that is, when it can prosecute the press for the content of a message that has already been disseminated. The tests used to determine when the government might punish a person or organization for the content of a printed message arise from a standard developed for criminal prosecution of individual speech. Thus, the early cases involved political speech as well as the distribution of printed material.

The Seeds of Contemporary Protection against Criminal Subsequent Punishment: World War I and the Bad Tendency Standard

It might be best to preface a discussion of subsequent punishment of the press in the twentieth century by noting that some lessons are hard to learn. With the memory of the Sedition Act of 1798 dimmed by a century of enormous growth and change in the United States, the launching of World War I in Europe and fears of communism at home led to the creation of the 1917 Espionage Act and the 1918 Sedition Act. These laws, which included passages strikingly similar to the 1798 Sedition Act, reinvigorated government powers to squelch dissent under the guise of national security. It was on this stage that the first series of cases calling for First Amendment protection for politically dissenting speech reached the Supreme Court.

These key World War I–era cases were not "press" cases in the obvious sense. Some involved the distribution of antiwar leaflets, and some involved speeches. Nevertheless, the language of the Court in its decisions addressed expression generally and jump-started the metaphorical, philosophical, and judicial framework of press freedoms for the rest of the century. In other words, these World War I–era speech cases held crucial implications for the press.

The first set of cases heard by the Supreme Court in 1919 resulted from political protests associated with the war. Charles

Schenck, general secretary of the Socialist party, was prosecuted under the Espionage Act for supervising the printing and distribution of antidraft leaflets to young men lined up outside a Philadelphia military recruitment office. By the time Schenck's appeal reached the Supreme Court, the war was over. While upholding Schenck's conviction, Justice Oliver Wendell Holmes Jr. laid the judicial framework for a new standard protecting free expression: the "clear and present danger" test. Holmes argued that the Court must consider "whether the words used are used in circumstances and are of such a nature as to create a clear and present danger that they will bring about the substantive evils that Congress has a right to prevent" (*Schenck v. United States* [1919] 52).

Arguably, this was a departure from the Court's previous standard of "bad tendency," inherited from English common law. The bad tendency standard guided the Court to suppress or punish speech that *might* lead to some undesirable result. Yet, although Holmes argued for a more vigorous protection of speech, he concluded that Schenck's message satisfied the clear and present danger test.

Such was the outcome for the other socialists and anarchists charged under the Espionage Act. Jacob Frohwerk, the owner of a German immigrant newspaper, went to prison for printing twelve articles criticizing the war (*Frohwerk v. United States* [1919]). Eugene V. Debs, a socialist candidate for the presidency, was indicted for an antiwar speech he gave (*Debs v. United States* [1919]). They and others all lost their First Amendment appeals and went to prison.

However, during these 1919 Supreme Court espionage cases, a crucial shift in the Court's voting pattern could be seen after these initial decisions. Until that point, all of the convictions were upheld by a unanimous Court. In a case appealing the conviction of Russian immigrant anarchists who distributed leaflets calling for a general strike on the heels of the U.S. decision to send troops to Russia, the Court split its vote 7–2. Justice Holmes, with the support of Justice Louis D. Brandeis, continued his argument for a clear and present danger standard but did not agree with the majority that Abrams's leaflets constituted such a threat. In his dissent, Holmes argued that "the best test of truth is the power of the thought of the idea to get itself accepted in the competition of the market" (*Abrams v. United States* [1919] 630). Holmes's introduction of a new doctrinal standard for speech laid the seeds of a major shift in the Court's position on free expression over the next forty years but did not help the antiwar protesters and socialist activists during World War I—they all served time in prison. In fact, over 2,000 political dissenters faced prosecution under the Espionage Act of 1917. Among them were people like filmmaker Robert Goldstein, who went to prison because the Court believed his motion picture *The Spirit of '76*, which depicted the American Revolution and some of the atrocities committed by the British, might "question the good faith of our [World War I] ally, Great Britain" and cause insubordination—a violation of the Espionage Act (*United States v. Motion Picture Film "The Spirit of '76"* [1917] 948).

In addition to the World War I prosecutions for seditious speech, the courts dealt specifically with press activities that ran afoul of the Espionage Act in two key cases. The Espionage Act contained a provision denying publications access to the postal system if they violated any of the act's provisions. In the first case, Judge Learned Hand's eloquent argument for balancing the Espionage Act against the commitment to free expression came as a result of the prosecution of *The Masses*, a radical intellectual monthly journal containing political criticism, satire, and commentary. The postmaster general refused to accept the August 1917 issue for mailing, claiming that several cartoons and other text, including some poetry, violated the Espionage Act.

Judge Hand, under consideration for promotion to the U.S. Court of Appeals for the Second Circuit, courageously enjoined the postmaster, requiring that he allow *The Masses* access to the postal system. Judge Hand found that the material in the magazine did not constitute a "direct advocacy" of the specific illegal activities detailed in the act and thus remained protected by the First Amendment (*Masses Publishing Co. v. Patten* [1917]). Judge Hand's decision, one that anticipated Justice Holmes's clear and present danger test, was promptly overturned by the Second Circuit Court (*Masses Publishing Co. v. Patten* [1917]). Judge Hand did not receive his promotion. Barred from the mail, *The Masses'* circulation dropped, and its staff was quickly indicted under the Espionage Act. The publication went out of business within months (Stone 2003).

In the second case, the *Milwaukee Leader,* a socialist newspaper, was denied its second-class mailing privilege because "in its newspaper frequently, often daily, [were] articles which contained false reports and false statements, published with intent to interfere with the success of the military operations of our Government, to promote the success of its enemies, and to obstruct its recruiting and enlistment service" (*Milwaukee Social Democratic Publishing Co. v. Burleson* [1921] 412).

EXTENDING THE FIRST AMENDMENT TO THE STATES

The text of the First Amendment specified only that *Congress* could make no law abridging freedom of the press. An earlier draft of the First Amendment introduced by James Madison included broader protections, but subsequent negotiations and drafts narrowed the language in part because Anti-Federalists did not want to limit state power. Their concern was limiting the scope of federal power. With the implementation of the alien, espionage, and sedition laws and subsequent prosecutions in the late 1700s and early 1800s, the protections of the First Amendment, however unevenly or weakly applied, did not apply at all to state-level prosecutions of individuals and the press. The Supreme

Court even reaffirmed that the Bill of Rights was not intended to intrude on states' rights—in this case the Fifth Amendment protection against the taking of private property for public use without proper compensation (*Barron v. Baltimore* [1833]).

Ultimately, it took a little-known socialist agitator from upstate New York to significantly broaden the reach of the First Amendment. Benjamin Gitlow and several other socialists were arrested in 1919 under a New York state criminal anarchy law for publishing and distributing copies of the *Left Wing Manifesto,* a political tract calling for the establishment of a socialist state through strikes and mass struggle. The New York law defined criminal anarchy as "the doctrine that organized government should be overthrown by force or violence, or by assassination of the executive head or of any of the executive officials of government, or by any unlawful means" (New York Penal Laws § 160). Gitlow's conviction was upheld by both New York appellate courts. On appeal to the U.S. Supreme Court in 1925, Gitlow argued that the First Amendment protected his expressive activities. Up to this point, the Supreme Court had made rulings on the premise that the First Amendment protection did *not* limit state law. However, in this case, the Court shifted direction, accepting Gitlow's argument that the Fourteenth Amendment further safeguarded a citizen's liberties—including First Amendment rights—from state prosecution. Thus, state laws could be found unconstitutional under the federal Bill of Rights. Although the Court dramatically expanded the protection of civil liberties in this case, it also found that Gitlow's activities extended beyond the scope of the First Amendment and let his conviction stand (*Gitlow v. New York* [1925]).

SUBSEQUENT PUNISHMENT: CRIMINAL RECOURSE FOR PUNISHING SPEECH

Two principal features marked the history of speech freedoms from 1919 to the early 1950s. First, with striking consistency, the

Supreme Court upheld conviction after conviction for expressive activities, even after it extended the Bill of Rights to state laws. Second, starting with the 1919 *Abrams* decision, each conviction was marked by eloquent dissents arguing that expression should remain protected unless there was an immediate, realistic, and likely threat of harm. Furthermore, those arguments were placed in a rhetorical context that paved the way for one of the most powerful metaphors signifying the American system of free expression: the marketplace of ideas. The marketplace of ideas was mentioned in the *Abrams* decision when Holmes said, "The ultimate good desired is better reached by the free trade in ideas— that the best test of truth is the power of the thought to get itself accepted in the competition of the market" (*Abrams v. United States* [1919], 630), and again in the 1927 *Whitney* decision when Holmes and Brandeis said, "If there be time to expose through discussion the falsehood and fallacies, to avert the evil by the processes of education, the remedy to be applied is more speech, not enforced silence" (*Whitney v. California* 274 U.S. 357 [1927] 377). It is worth noting that the Court never directly addressed the constitutionality of the Espionage and Sedition Acts under which the World War I–era prosecutions occurred. It was not until the *Dennis* case (*Dennis v. United States* [1951]) that the court finally upheld the constitutionality of the newest variation of the sedition laws: the Smith Act of 1940. As a result, the Smith Act became a powerful prosecutory weapon during the 1950s Red Scare.

The importance of these early cases for general protections for the press must not be underestimated. The press's role as a watchdog of government almost demands the regular critical analysis of government policies, decisions, and practices. Determining when such criticism reaches the level of sedition is highly subjective and depends on the historical context. The World War I–era Supreme Court decisions on seditious speech may seem almost absurd by today's standards. But the historical political and cultural context explains much of the reasoning. It was, simply put, a fearful time.

As we will see in the next chapter, the fearful climate associated with the "War on Terror" raises serious questions about the context in which free expression cases will be adjudicated. But political times do change, and these early speech cases helped set the stage for an activist court to insist on a very high level of protection for politically dissenting speech—protection essential to the function of a free press.

THE BRANDENBURG INCITEMENT STANDARD

A higher level of protection for the press was articulated in 1957 when the Supreme Court, entering one of its most politically progressive and activist eras, overturned the conviction and ordered new trials for Oleta Yates and numerous others because their communism education activities were the advocacy of abstract theory, not the advocacy of concrete action (*Yates v. United States* [1957]). Our contemporary standard for speech protection (against criminal prosecution by the government) was further clarified in a 1969 case in which the Court, in response to the lower court conviction of Clarence Brandenburg, a Ku Klux Klan (KKK) leader with a penchant for publicity, established that speech was protected unless it advocated imminent illegal action and was effective or persuasive enough to be likely to produce such action (*Brandenburg v. Ohio* [1969]). The standard is high and provides an enormous amount of protection to individuals and the press when criticizing the government, advocating for change, or voicing extreme ideas. This standard is relevant to press activities, both as a real barometer of protection for advocacy press and as an envelope of protection against abuses of the national security exception for press freedoms. But more recent cases illustrate how the *Brandenburg* standard has been applied. In one example, Paladin Enterprises published a book titled *Hit Man: A Technical Manual for Independent Contractors*—literally a how-to manual for killers. In the introduction, the author states that "the professional hit man fills a need in society and is, at times, the only alternative for 'personal' justice." The case arose from a contract murder committed by hired hit man James Perry, in whose apartment a copy of the book was found. The relatives of the victims sued the publisher for aiding and abetting Perry in the commission of a crime. The court distinguished between *Brandenburg*'s finding that the First Amendment protects the teaching of abstract advocacy of illegal activity (historically involving the teachings of Marxist doctrine) and what they viewed as the teaching of illegal activity, with nothing abstract about it. A multitude of newspapers, networks, and publishers jointly submitted an amicus brief arguing that "allowing this lawsuit to survive will disturb decades of First Amendment jurisprudence and jeopardize free speech from the periphery to the core. . . . No expression—music, video, books, even newspaper articles—would be safe from civil liability" (*Rice v. Paladin Enterprises* [1997] 265). In the end, the court concluded that the First Amendment did not bar civil liability against the publisher for aiding murder. The Supreme Court refused to review the decision, and Paladin settled out of court.

As it now stands, the *Brandenburg* standard provides a high level of protection for the press. It remains unclear whether the courts will continue to finely distinguish between the advocacy of abstract illegal doctrine and the advocacy of illegal activity. As we pick up this discussion in Chapter 4, we will closely examine the implication of the *Brandenburg* standard for Internet communication.

OBSCENITY AND THE MODERN PRESS

Until midcentury, the United States relied on the Hicklin rule (see Chapter 2) as a guide for adjudicating obscenity cases. During the nineteenth century, numerous books that later came to be acknowledged as American classics were prosecuted for obscenity.

In the mid-1950s, with a progressive Supreme Court in place, a new standard giving extraordinary protection for publication of sexually explicit material was established.

In *Roth v. United States* (1957), the Court established a multi-part test to determine whether material was obscene (which the Court agreed was not protected under the First Amendment). In order for expression to be obscene, it must be

1. Worthless (utterly without redeeming social value) and
2. Sexually lewd (which is defined as follows):
   a. whether to the average person;
   b. applying contemporary community standards;
   c. the dominant theme, taken as a whole; or
   d. appeals to the prurient interest.

Numerous cases followed, most of which helped clarify the elements of the *Roth* test. For example, in a case involving the book *Fanny Hill*, the Court clarified "worthless" as meaning that the work in question must have absolutely no redeeming social value (*Memoirs v. Mass.* [1966]). Any remotely literary merit would preclude a declaration of "obscene." This made it *extremely* difficult to successfully prosecute an obscenity case. Even with exceedingly explicit material, in print or film, it was possible to argue there was artistic merit in the dialogue, the lighting of a film set, the musical score, and so on.

The expanding protection of sexually explicit expression reflected a larger trend toward adopting a "consenting adults" approach to pornographic material. The 1970 Report of the Commission on Obscenity and Pornography recommended abolishing any censorship of sexual material for adults. The U.S. Senate, President Nixon, and numerous religious leaders successfully pressured Congress to reject the commission's recommendations. Meanwhile, the tenor of the Court was beginning to shift, and in 1973 a new obscenity case appeared before the justices. In this case, Marvin Miller was convicted of "knowlingly distributing obscene matter" when he mass-mailed unsolicited advertisements for sexually explicit books (*Miller v. California* [1973]). Using his appeal from a lower court conviction as a catalyst, the Court substantially weakened First Amendment protection of explicit materials by rewriting the test for obscenity as follows:

1. Whether an average person, applying contemporary community standards of the state or local community, would find that the work as a whole appeals to the prurient interest;
2. Whether the work depicts or describes in a patently offensive way sexual conduct specifically defined by the applicable state law; and
3. Whether the work lacks serious literary, artistic, political, or scientific value (called the SLAPS test). (Miller v. California [1973])

The *Miller* test allows individual communities to set their own standards for "the prurient interest." It also replaces the *Roth* standard of "utterly without redeeming social value" and replaces it with the SLAPS test, a significantly easier standard for a prosecutor to demonstrate. The result is that communities are more successfully and aggressively prosecuting sexually explicit material. The one balance to the expanded ability to prosecute for obscenity is that the Court ruled in 1969 that individuals may possess, in the privacy of their homes, sexual material that would be illegal to distribute or sell in public (*Stanley v. Georgia* [1969]).

There is one area of sexually explicit material on which the Court has not wavered in its willingness to support prosecution: child pornography. In a consistent departure from reliance on the *Miller* test, the Court has upheld a ban on any sexual material involving children as models or actors. The Court found that the state's interest in protecting children was strong enough to ban the materials in hopes of drying up the market (*New York v. Ferber* [1982]). Eight years later, the Court took it a step further when it banned possession of child pornography even in the privacy of one's home. Thus, producing child pornography, watching child pornography, and possessing child pornography, even in one's home, is illegal and may be vigorously prosecuted.

Why would obscenity be of concern to the press? In addition to being able to adequately cover the growing number of stories emerging about obscenity and pornography in the age of the Internet (see Chapter 4), a journalist needs to understand the differences between legal terms, such as obscenity, and social terms, such as pornography. The two are often mixed in the media, yet very little pornography is legally obscene. Additionally, the press encompasses a variety of media, including sexually explicit publications such as *Playboy, Hustler,* and *Penthouse.* Writers for these publications are journalists. In fact, *Playboy* often features in-depth interviews of high-profile individuals in the magazine. One of the more notable *Playboy* interviews featured Georgia Governor Jimmy Carter in November 1976, on the cusp of his election to the presidency. Other famous political interviews in *Playboy* include Malcolm X (1963), Fidel Castro (1967), Ralph Nader (1968), George McGovern (1971), Lech Walesa (1982), Yasser Arafat (1988), and Vladimir Zhirinovsky (1995).

During the latter part of the twentieth century, numerous unsuccessful attempts were made to prosecute offensive musical lyrics as obscene. One of the most notable examples was the attempt to prosecute Two Live Crew for production of an album titled *As Nasty as They Wanna Be,* which included the targeted song, *Me So Horny* (*Luke Records v. Navarro* [1992]). In Chapter 4 we will examine the focus of much of the current litigation over sexual material: Internet pornography.

SUBSEQUENT PUNISHMENT CIVIL RECOURSES FOR PUBLICATION OF MATERIAL THAT CAUSES HARM

Civil torts punishing speech are far more common than criminal prosecutions and fill the dockets of the federal court system. A civil tort does not involve the government except to provide a neutral forum for hearing the complaint. The government is not party to the complaint. A lawsuit involves the mediation of a dispute between two parties. The solution tends to be an assessment of damages, typically in the form of money; jail time is not an option in such cases (except when one of the parties violates judicial procedure and order and thus draws jail time for contempt of court, or fails to follow through on a court judgment). In the sections that follow, several major topics of media law are presented. Although they are discussed separately, keep in mind that a lawsuit may involve more than one of these areas.

LIBEL

As discussed in Chapter 1, the origins of defamation date back to the earliest experiments with free expression. From ancient Greek and Roman times through the evolution of English common law to the contemporary meaning of free expression, there remains an understanding that an individual has a right to protect his or her reputation against injurious comments, whether written or spoken. Someone who makes a false statement that injures another's reputation may be subject to a defamation lawsuit.

However, defamation law, which includes both slander (spoken injury) and libel (printed injury), looks quite different today than it did in ancient times. Early English libel common law did not factor in, as a defense, the truthfulness of the statement. A truthful criticism of the government or the Crown or the Church could result in a punishment as severe as, and possibly more severe than, a false statement. Furthermore, English common law recognized four basic types of libel: 1) blasphemous libel, defined in part as any speech that denied the existence of God or ridiculed any Christian doctrine; 2) seditious libel, or criticism of the government, its leaders, or policies; 3) obscene libel, which was the English forerunner of obscenity laws; and 4) private libel, defined as speech or publication that injured the reputation of another person.

Those four forms of libel have been dramatically altered in modern American libel law. Blasphemous libel is not recognized in the United States. Obscenity is dealt with as a separate criminal action at the state level. Seditious libel, although reinvigorated under the Espionage and Sedition Acts in the early twentieth century, is largely dormant in modern free speech doctrine because of the wide berth given to the right to criticize the government as long as the expression does not rise to the *Brandenburg* standard. The English tradition of private libel is most similar to contemporary American libel law. It is almost always a civil action in the United States, although some states have criminal libel laws on the books, which allows the state to criminally prosecute a defendant for libeling someone else; such laws are rarely used, however (see Chapter 4 for a discussion of a recent attempt to prosecute for criminal libel).

There are two types of libelous statements: libel per se and libel per quod. Libel per se statements are defamatory on their face, meaning that the statement is automatically libelous. The courts simply assume that such a statement is injurious to another's reputation. For example, it may be libelous per se to *falsely* 1) accuse another person of a crime (e.g., "Susan stole a coat from the department store"); 2) state that a person carries an infectious or offensive disease (e.g., "John contracted syphillis"); make injurious statements about a person in relation to his or her business (e.g., "Chris falsifies the expiration dates on the meat at his butcher shop"); and make statements that a person is sexually immoral (e.g., "Shelly works as a prostitute to make extra money").

Libel per quod statements may or may not be defamatory, depending on the context. For these kinds of statements, evidence must be presented to the jury, and the jury then decides whether the statements injured the plaintiff's reputation.

Libel suits are among the most litigious areas of press law. Although one individual can sue another for libel, the focus here will be on lawsuits against the press. Almost all libel suits are civil actions, which are distinctly different from criminal actions, in which the state prosecutes defendants and the level of proof for a conviction must be "beyond a reasonable doubt." In a civil suit, the party injured by a libelous statement sues the party who made the statement. The standard of proof is substantially lower in a civil suit, and a plaintiff has to prove his or her case with a "preponderance of the evidence," except in occasional instances in which the plaintiff has to meet a slightly higher standard of "convincing clarity."

The difference between standards of proof in civil and criminal trials can be crucial, as we saw in the O.J. Simpson cases. Simpson was acquitted in the criminal prosecution for the 1994 murder of his wife, Nicole Brown, and Ronald Goldman, because the state was not able to prove his guilt beyond a reasonable doubt. However, he lost in the civil suit brought by the Brown and Goldman families for wrongful death. Jail sentences cannot be imposed in civil suits, but there can be substantial monetary awards. In Simpson's case, the jury, concluding that Simpson was responsible for the two deaths, awarded Brown's family $33.5 million dollars.

How might the press become a defendant in a libel suit? Several basic conditions have to exist. First, the press must publish something that appears to be insulting or harmful to the plaintiff. In one case, for example, a radio station referred to a magazine distributor (who distributed, among other publications, nudist magazines, which are perfectly legal), as a "smut distributor" and "girlie book peddler" (*Rosenbloom v. Metromedia* [1971]). Second, the information must be published or broadcast. Technically, this means that the information must be communicated to a third party. However, a plaintiff does not have to prove that someone actually read the newspaper story or listened to the radio or television broadcast in question. The mere fact that it was published or broadcast satisfies the requirements of publication. Finally, the article in question has to identify the plaintiff. A general statement about government employees would not allow Joe Johnson, an Oregon state controller, to file a libel suit. However, a person does not necessarily have to be named in a story in order to file a libel suit. If the details of the story would enable a reasonable person to identify the person, then the story may be libelous.

The question of fault became a component of libel cases after the mid-1960s. Fault—that is, that the defendant was at fault—is the most challenging element to prove in a libel suit, and the standard of proof applied in determining fault varies with the type of plaintiff. Before the 1964 decision in *New York Times v. Sullivan,* the press could lose a libel suit on the basis of the outcome of the first three conditions outlined above. The *Sullivan* decision significantly shifted the landscape of libel law, sweeping defamatory statements against public officials under the protection of the First Amendment. In this case, heard during the heat of the civil rights movement, the *New York Times* published a full-page advertisement the contents of which suggested that police officials in the South, including those in Montgomery County, Alabama, were participating in an "unprecedented wave of terror" against African-American students. Sullivan, a Montgomery County commissioner who was responsible for police supervision, sued for libel. The Supreme Court ruled that a public official could not recover damages for defamation "unless he proves that the statement was made with 'actual malice'—that is, with knowledge that it was false or with reckless disregard of whether it was false or not" (*New York Times v. Sullivan* [1964], 279–280).

After this landmark decision, a series of Court decisions extended the actual malice standard to a wider range of people and articulated how the actual malice standard may be applied to private aspects of a public official's life. For example, on hearing the appeal of a libel suit initiated by a man named Baer, a supervisor of the Belknap County recreation and ski area, against Rosenblatt, a journalist who reported mismanagement of revenues from the facility, the Court expanded the actual malice standard to include nonelected officials, such as government employees or people in appointed government positions (*Rosenblatt v. Baer* [1966]).

Over the years the courts have included a wide variety of people as public officials: police officers, social workers, school administrators, judges, candidates for public office, and most public employees who are in positions of substantial responsibility. A few years after the *Rosenblatt v. Baer* ruling, the Court again expanded the actual malice standard in a review of two cases. The first case involved Wally Butts, the athletic director at the University of Georgia. He sued the *Saturday Evening Post* after it published a story claiming that he had fixed a football game; the Court upheld the lower court's award of damages to Butts. The second case involved an appeal by the Associated Press (AP) after it lost a libel suit filed by retired Army General Edwin Walker. The AP distributed a wire story that provided an eyewitness account of how Walker led a violent riot at the University of Mississippi over the court-mandated enrollment of the first African-American student; the Court overturned the award to Walker, claiming that the AP error was an innocent mistake given the pressure of events. The significance of these decisions lies in the Court's extension of the actual malice standard to public figures (*Curtis Publishing Co. v. Butts* [1967]). Their effect was to dramatically increase the ability of the press to report on the activities of celebrities and other public figures without fear of lawsuits.

There is no clear formula for determining whether someone is a public figure, however. Courts have looked carefully at whether the plaintiff has voluntarily thrust him- or herself into the public eye over some issue. Over time, the courts have further attempted to distinguish between types of public figures. One category the Supreme Court identifies is the all-purpose public figure. This is someone who is consistently in the public eye, with the corresponding influence. The courts have specifically ruled that former late-night talk show host Johnny Carson and columnist William F. Buckley Jr. qualify as all-purpose public figures (*Carson v. Allied News* [1976]; *Buckley v. Little* [1976]).

The second type of public figure defined by the Supreme Court is a limited-purpose public figure. This is a person who has become publicly active for a limited time or for a specific issue. An individual who speaks out on the environment and an author who hits the talk show circuit to promote a book are examples of people who would be considered limited-purpose public figures, assuming they were not otherwise publicly known.

Still unresolved was the question of what level of fault could be applied in libel cases involving private figures. Up to this point, protection for the media from libel suits was consistently expanding. The courts had extended the public official requirement to prove actual malice to include public figures. Furthermore, the courts had recently suggested that private persons may have to prove actual malice if the subject matter of the suit was one of public interest (*Rosenbloom v. Metromedia* [1971]). Applying the actual malice standard to any story of public interest could conceivably apply that standard of fault to everybody mentioned in a news story (and, one could argue, the act of publishing the story itself is sufficient evidence that it is a story of public interest).

The Court then issued a ruling that backed off the *Rosenbloom* implication that the actual malice standard might, by extension, apply to everyone libeled in the media. The case involved attorney Elmer Gertz, who was representing a family in a civil suit against the Chicago police officer who shot and killed their son. The police officer had already been convicted of murder in the case. The publisher of *American Opinion,* a magazine for the politically conservative John Birch Society, published an article that falsely stated that Gertz had a criminal record and was a "Communist fronter" (*Gertz v. Welch* [1974] 326). Gertz sued for libel. When the case came before the Supreme Court, Justice Lewis Powell clarified crucial aspects of the public figure category. It appeared that Gertz, thrust into the public eye because of the *American Opinion* article, would have to show that the magazine acted with actual malice. However, the Court backed off the actual malice standard for private individuals even if the subject matter was of public interest.

The Court also has recognized that a private person does not become a public person if he or she is involuntarily thrust into the public eye. For example, a research scientist who had federal grant funding became the target of Senator William Proxmire's Golden Fleece Award, given monthly to government agencies that sponsored work Proxmire believed to be a waste of taxpayers' dollars. Proxmire criticized the research of Ronald Hutchinson, a scientist studying animal aggression, in staff conferences, in a newsletter sent to more than 100,000 of his constituents, and on the Senate floor, where he said, "Dr. Hutchinson's studies should make the taxpayers as well as his monkeys grind their teeth. In fact, the good doctor has made a fortune from his monkeys and in the process made a monkey out of the American taxpayer" (*Hutchinson v. Proxmire* [1978] 116). Hutchinson filed a libel suit claiming that he "has suffered a loss of respect in his profession, has suffered injury to his feelings, has been humiliated, held up to public scorn, suffered extreme mental anguish and physical illness and pain to his person. Furthermore he has suffered a loss of income and ability to earn income in the future" (*Hutchinson* 1978, 118). Clearly the elements necessary to bring a libel suit had been met. There was defamation, publication, and identification. But in order to determine fault, the Court had to consider whether Hutchinson was a public or a private figure. That decision would determine whether Hutchinson had to demonstrate that Proxmire acted with actual malice or negligence. The Court concluded, "Hutchinson did not thrust himself or his views into public controversy to influence others" on the issue of federal expenditures, and therefore was a private figure for the purposes of the lawsuit (*Hutchinson* 1978, 135).

One limit the Supreme Court did place on libel suits by private plaintiffs is a restriction on the kind of damages plaintiffs may seek against the press. Libel actions might trigger four types of damages that apply to private or public figures. Nominal damages are awarded to plaintiffs who win their suits but have not suffered a compensable loss. They have the vindication that comes with a judgment against the defendant, but do not receive large monetary awards. Carol Burnett sued the *National Enquirer* for publishing a photograph and text suggesting that she was a drunk. Burnett became the first person to win a libel suit against the tabloid, but on appeal her damages were reduced from $1.6 million to $200,000 (*Burnett v. National Enquirer* [1983]). Although this amount is not quite nominal damages, Burnett stated, "If they had given me only one dollar plus carfare, I'd have been happy because it was the principle" (Pressman 2004). She donated $100,000 of the award to the University of Hawaii journalism program to establish the Carol Burnett Award for Responsible Journalism.

Compensatory damages address the actual injury to reputation, humiliation, pain and suffering, or mental anguish. Special damages compensate for the out-of-pocket expenses—legal costs, loss of work, medical bills, and so forth. In the O.J. Simpson civil trial, the initial compensatory award was $8.5 million. These first three types of damages—nominal, compensatory, and special—are the only types of damages a private plaintiff may seek without proving that the press acted with actual malice. Presumed damages are assumed to have occurred if the conditions of the libel cases are met. If damages are awarded, the jury sets the amount.

The big awards against the press come from punitive damages. Burnett's original award of $1.6 million was largely punitive damages. Of the $33.5 million verdict in the O.J. Simpson case, $25 million was punitive damages. At least four states, Oregon, Michigan, Massachusetts, and Washington, do not recognize punitive damages in any libel suits. The *Gertz* decision made it clear that even private persons must show actual malice if they hope to be awarded presumed or punitive damages against the press.

How does the press defend itself in a libel suit? There are several well-established defenses for the press, which can be broken down into two types: constitutional defenses and common law defenses. Constitutional defenses are rooted in the First Amendment guarantee of a free press. Hesitation on the part of the press to cover controversial issues out of fear of costly judgments against them can have a chilling effect on news-gathering activities. The Supreme Court specifically addressed this concern in a libel case against the *Philadelphia Inquirer.* Justice Sandra Day O'-Connor wrote that a private plaintiff involved in an issue of public concern not only had to show fault but also had to prove that the allegedly defamatory statement was false (*Philadelphia Newspapers v. Hepps* [1986]). Shifting the burden of proving falsity to the defendant, Justice O'Connor argued, helped stave off a chilling effect on the press. The press would not have to bear the burden of proving that its statements were true and hence would not be inclined to avoid publishing information that might be difficult to satisfactorily verify. Furthermore, the plaintiff bears the burden of proving that the media was at fault—and when the standard of fault is actual malice, the plaintiff must go beyond the preponderance of evidence common in standard litigation and instead show convincing clarity or proof.

One specific constitutional defense the press maintains against libel suits is the neutral reportage defense. This principle developed out of a case involving a story published at the height of the DDT pesticide controversy in the 1970s. A *New York Times* article suggested that representatives of the Audubon Society had referred to several scientists who they claimed misinterpreted Audubon Christmas Bird Count data to conclude that bird populations were increasing, as paid liars for the pesticide industry. Three of the scientists criticized by the Audubon Society filed a lawsuit against the *New York Times* for publishing an obviously defamatory statement. Although the Supreme Court refused to hear the case, the appellate court released the *Times* from a lower court libel judgment, saying that a reporter using good professional journalistic judgment and practice in preparing a story will not be held liable for reprinting a defamatory statement by a reliable source about a public figure (*Edwards v. National Audubon Society* [1977]).

The Court also suggested that journalists are protected if their reporting is accurate, objective, and responsible but they doubt the truth of what they are reporting. Critics of this new level of protection suggest that it protects journalists who publish with actual malice. Supporters believe it is important to insulate the press from liability when repeating a false defamatory claim as part of a story. On the basis of the *Edwards* decision, the courts appear to look for the following criteria before applying the neutral reportage defense:

- The statements must be newsworthy and associated with a public controversy.
- The statements must come from a responsible person or organization.
- The statements must refer to a public official or public figure.
- The statements must be reported accurately and in an impartial manner.

The neutral reportage defense, in combination with the actual malice standard, provides enormous protection to the press from libel actions (Smolla 1999). However, it has not been adopted everywhere. Currently the Second and Eighth Circuit Courts, along with several federal district courts and several state courts (e.g.,

Florida, Wyoming, Ohio, and Vermont) have incorporated the neutral reporting defense (Middleton et al. 2004). A few states have rejected the defense (e.g., Kentucky, South Dakota, and Michigan). Without a ruling by the Supreme Court, use of this defense will continue to vary among districts and states.

Another constitutional defense is the reporting of opinion. Since defamation law turns on the truth or falsity of information, and since libel plaintiffs have to prove that a statement was false, pure opinion, which by definition cannot be proven true or false, is an effective defense. The Supreme Court said as much in the *Gertz* decision when Justice Powell wrote, "There is no such thing as a false idea" (*Gertz v. Welch* [1974] 339–340). The opinion defense protects book, movie, and restaurant reviewers from libel suits. If a movie reviewer wrote that Jack Nicholson's latest performance was canned, stiff, and uninspiring, and as a result of the review, box office receipts dropped and Nicholson wasn't hired for another film, neither the producers nor Nicholson could sue for libel, because the review was protected opinion.

However, the protection of opinion is not absolute. A movie reviewer cannot state, for example, that Nicholson's performance was stiff and uninspiring because, in the reviewer's "opinion," he was drunk on the set every day. If Nicholson had proof that he was not drunk on the set every day, he could file a libel suit and possibly win. Hence an important limitation to the opinion defense is that a false statement of fact cannot be protected under the guise of opinion. However, it is difficult to navigate the differences between fact and opinion. In 1984, the D.C. Circuit Court attempted to develop a test to differentiate opinion from fact. The test looks carefully at the common usage and meaning of the words in question, at the context of the statement within the article, and at the broader social context. The test also seeks to determine whether the statement includes provable fact (*Ollman v. Evans* [8th Cir. 1986]). The *Ollman* test did not fare well at the

Supreme Court level, which in 1990 decided that a statement is protected as opinion unless it can be proven factually false (*Milkovich v. Lorain Journal Co.* [1990]).

Similar to the concept of opinion, but derived from common law instead of constitutional law, is the concept of fair comment and criticism. Although the constitutional protection of opinion might be a more frequently used defense, journalists can call on this common law tradition if their comment was opinion, was focused on something of legitimate public interest, and was based on facts presented in the article.

Another kind of statement protected under the opinion defense is rhetorical hyperbole. Rhetorical hyperbole is a false statement that is so outrageous that no reasonable person would believe it to be true. The Supreme Court established this defense in 1970 when a local newspaper published an article on a pending real estate deal and mentioned that some people thought the real estate developer's negotiations constituted blackmail. The Court concluded that no reasonable reader would believe the developer had actually blackmailed the city council. The Court stated, "Even the most careless reader must have perceived that the word was no more than rhetorical hyperbole, a vigorous epithet used by those who considered the negotiating position extremely unreasonable" (*Greenbelt Publishing Association v. Bresler* [1970] 14). Another example involved a television station general manager who appeared on the local newscast to present an editorial. In his statement, he compared a local politician who had voided a city council election that removed him from office, to the deposed leader of Panama, Manuel Noriega, who also had voided an election. The editorial added that the local politician was a thief because "he stole the most precious right this democracy has" (*Maholick v. WNEP TV* [1992]). Thus, the courts have clarified that even falsely accusing a person of being a criminal—say, a blackmailer or a thief—normally defamatory on its face, may be defended under the rhetorical hyperbole defense.

One of the most important and absolute defenses against a libel suit is the truth defense. Libel requires that the defamatory statement be false. The burden of proof is on the plaintiff. However, if the defendant shows that the statement is true, the libel suit will be dismissed. As mentioned in Chapter 1, truth was not always a defense against libel. In England, before the mid–eighteenth century, it was thought that a truthful criticism of government would be more damaging than a false one, and hence truthful seditious statements were actually punished more severely. Since the *Zenger* decision in 1735, truth has been an effective libel defense in the United States, and it is an absolute defense today. Furthermore, a defense of truth does not require that the information be completely true, only substantially true. That leaves some wiggle room, as the Supreme Court affirmed in a case involving a journalist's fabrication of quotes:

> [S]ubstantial truth ... would absolve a defendant even if she cannot justify every word of the alleged defamatory matter; it is sufficient if the substance of the charge be proved true, irrespective of slight inaccuracy in the details. ... Minor inaccuracies do not amount to falsity as long as the substance, the gist, the sting, of the libelous charge be justified. ... [T]he statement is not considered false unless it would have a different effect on the mind of the reader from that which the pleaded truth would have produced. (*Masson v. New Yorker Magazine* [1991] 516–517)

An essential defense for journalists who cover the government is that of privilege, which can take several forms. Privilege is rooted in the idea that the press is a watchdog of the government. As discussed in Chapter 1, the value of robust debate and the discovery of truth are believed to be essential to maintaining a healthy democracy. In order to meet its watchdog responsibility, the press needs the freedom to report, analyze, and critique the activities of the nation's government representatives without the threat of subsequent punishment.

Absolute privilege attaches to a wide range of communication that involves the actual business of governing. Any communication by a government official that is part of their official duties is privileged—that is, protected by privilege. This would include, for example, government officials' comments in official meetings as well as statements of witnesses testifying before governmental committees. If persons who speak in an official capacity are granted absolute immunity from libel suits, then it makes sense that journalists reporting on their communications would also be protected from libel suits.

A reporter's privilege is not absolute; it is qualified or conditional. Privilege protects a journalist reporting on privileged communications even if those communications are defamatory, provided the reporter presents the information in a fair, balanced, and accurate manner. The courts have applied a reporter's qualified privilege in legislative settings (from the U.S. Congress to city council meetings), judicial proceedings (e.g., testimony, depositions, and attorney statements, but not closed proceedings), and executive actions (e.g., by mayors, department or administrative supervisors, and the president). A journalist's conditional privilege may be at risk if a plaintiff demonstrates that an otherwise fair and balanced report (normally protected from libel suits) is intended to harm the target of the defamation.

Another common legal defense against libel suits is consent. Simply stated, if the plaintiff consented to the publication of the defamatory material, he or she cannot sue for libel. Consent is not a simple matter, because clear consent is rare. The courts have grappled with the notion of *implied* consent. If a plaintiff comments to a journalist about a defamatory charge, for example, it may be considered implied consent to publish the defamatory statement (*Pulverman v. A.S. Abell Co.* [1956]). Implied consent is difficult to prove, however, and not many courts have accepted it as a defense.

Finally, newspapers often include material that is not created by staff reporters. For example, letters to the editor might contain defamatory language. Generally, these letters are considered opinion, and the courts usually protect the press in an effort to preserve an important public forum.

Libel is a complex area of media law and one of the main sources of pressure on press freedoms. The pressure is not from government efforts to censor, but from the chilling effect of concerns about having to pay large monetary awards if a media organization or agent loses a libel suit. Some judicial procedures work in the press's favor. In about half the states, libel suits must be filed within a year, and the longest window to file a libel suit is three years (in New Mexico, Arkansas, Vermont, New Hampshire, Maine, and Rhode Island). Furthermore, a substantial majority of libel suits are dismissed with summary judgment in favor of the press. When libel cases do go to a jury trial—an expensive undertaking—the press tends to lose, with juries awarding large actual and punitive damages. On appeal, however, the press tends to prevail, either by having the lower court's decision reversed on one of the constitutional defenses mentioned above or by having monetary damages reduced.

In sum, journalists have a tremendous amount of protection from libel suits. Although the requirement of publication is self-evident in most cases, the burden of proof for identification, falsity, fault, and harm rest on the plaintiff. Furthermore, journalists have a variety of constitutional and common law defenses against charges of libel. The threat of libel suits with increasingly large jury awards remains one of the biggest threats to freedom of the press. The best insurance, besides actual libel insurance, is responsible journalism. In general, courts appear to look for evidence of responsible journalism in determining the outcome of libel suits. That is why fair, balanced, and accurate reporting is critical to protecting a journalist from libel charges. When potentially defamatory statements are published, often retractions, apologies, and corrections are enough to ward off a lawsuit, weaken the plaintiff's demonstrable harm, reduce jury awards, and, if the statement is made in one of the thirty or so states with retraction statutes, even eliminate the possibility of punitive damages.

INTENTIONAL INFLICTION OF EMOTIONAL DISTRESS

In the past three decades a new threat to press freedoms has emerged. With the tremendous difficulty of successfully suing the press for libel, plaintiffs have found some judicial sympathy in lawsuits for intentional infliction of emotional distress. This tort has been around for a long time, and since the mid–twentieth century it has contained two key parts:

- The conduct of the defendant was intentional or reckless, extreme, and outrageous.
- The conduct of the defendant caused the plaintiff severe emotional distress.

In the context of press freedoms, a journalist may act in such an outrageous manner or print such outrageous content about someone as to cause that person severe emotional distress. Even with its growing popularity, this type of lawsuit is very difficult to win, and the Supreme Court has made it clear that public officials and public figures have to show that the content was a false statement of fact (not opinion) and that the journalist acted with actual malice. In essence, the standard of proof is as high as with libel.

INVASION OF PRIVACY

A right to privacy is a broad-based right that intersects and sometimes conflicts with a range of other rights, including freedom of the press. However, the right to privacy has not been a recognized right for very long, and in media law it is a relatively new legal concept. It was introduced in an 1890 *Harvard Law Review* article written by Samuel Warren and future Supreme Court justice Louis Brandeis out of frustration over the practice of journalists intrusively reporting on people's private lives. Warren and Brandeis argued that citizens should have legal recourse for unwarranted intrusions and publication of private information (Warren and Brandeis 1890). A few years after publication of the article, in 1903, New York became the first state to recognize a right to privacy by prohibiting the commercial exploitation of a person without consent. This area of litigation has grown over the years but is not universally recognized. A few states do not recognize the right to privacy, and many others do not recognize parts of the four-part privacy tort. Even though the number of privacy lawsuits filed is growing, the specifics of what is actionable varies from state to state. Over the past century the right of privacy has taken on four specific wrongs or torts, which are discussed in turn below.

Appropriation

Consider the following hypothetical story: A local publisher who wants to increase the number of readers for the People and Places section of her newspaper runs an ad campaign featuring a photograph of Britney Spears. Under the photo is the text, "Britney Spears reads our paper, shouldn't you?" Britney Spears's manager, passing through town, sees the advertisement on a billboard. Shortly thereafter, the publisher receives notice that she is being sued for invasion of privacy. Why? Because the publisher appropriated Britney Spears's image or likeness and used it for commercial gain without Spears's permission.

In promoting their product, media enterprises need to be careful not to trigger an appropriation lawsuit by linking their product to an individual without permission. If the person whose image or likeness is appropriated is a private individual, then the cause of action is typically the right to privacy. However, if the person is famous, then the cause of action is typically the right to publicity. These rights are similar but have some key differences. A right to privacy action addresses the humiliation and embarrassment that results when one's image or likeness is appropriated. Here, a personal right has been violated. A right to publicity is a property right. It addresses the fact that there is economic value in a celebrity's image or likeness. Appropriation of that image is like stealing. Another difference between the two causes for action is that a person's right to privacy dies when the person dies. As with libel, it is not actionable after death. No one can sue on behalf of the estate of the deceased person. However, a right of publicity is a property right, and in some states it survives the plaintiff's death. The heirs can start or continue a lawsuit on behalf of the deceased person.

Laws protecting the right to publicity are made at the state level. In spite of encouragement by the American Bar Association, no federal law has been passed to protect the right to publicity, and, as a result, the bite of the law varies from state to state. It should not be surprising, then, to see that many of the right to publicity cases emerge from the key entertainment states: New York and California. California and Tennessee (the original home of Elvis Presley) have some of the most celebrity-friendly right to publicity laws, protecting the estates of celebrities for seventy years in California and forever in Tennessee. Although many of these cases are heard in federal court because they involve parties from different states, the applicable state law is that of the state in which the lawsuit is filed.

The risk of an appropriation lawsuit extends beyond the obvious use of a person's image. The courts have supported lawsuits against "look-alikes" and "sound-alikes." Jacqueline Kennedy Onassis successfully enjoined a magazine from using a Christian

Dior advertisement featuring Barbara Reynolds, a Jackie look-alike. The court said that although imitators are permitted to simulate features of celebrities in noncommercial settings (parties, television appearances, and so on), they may not "trade on another's name or appearance" in commercial advertisements that are intended to suggest, deceptively, that the person is the actual celebrity (*Onassis v. Christian Dior–New York* [1984] 261). Johnny Carson, host of NBC's *Tonight Show* for thirty years, successfully sued the manufacturer of "Here's Johnny Portable Toilets." The company admittedly capitalized on Ed McMahon's nightly introduction of Carson with the phrase "Here's Johnny" (*Carson v. Here's Johnny Portable Toilets* [6th Cir. 1983]).

The courts also have upheld the commercial value of how a celebrity sounds. After singer Bette Midler turned down a request by Young and Rubicam, an advertising agency, to use her song "Do You Want to Dance" for a Ford Motor Company advertisement, a sound-alike (a former back-up singer for Midler) was hired to do the song. Midler successfully sued Ford under a California law that prohibits appropriation of a person's likeness or voice for commercial use without permission. The court recognized that "to impersonate her voice is to pirate her identity" and awarded Midler $400,000 (*Midler v. Ford Motor Co.* [9th Cir. 1988] 463). Other sound-alike cases followed. For example, Tom Waits successfully sued Frito-Lay under the federal Lanham Act, which prohibits unfair competition, for using a sound-alike and received a $2.5 million award (*Waits v. Frito-Lay* [1992]).

The courts have to grapple with how far the right to publicity can be pushed. Vanna White, the hostess of *Wheel of Fortune*, successfully sued Samsung Electronics for the use of her likeness (*White v. Samsung Electronics of America* [1992]). However, in this case the "likeness" was a well-dressed robot standing in front of a game board. After a series of appeals, White was awarded $403,000. Judge Alex Kozinski, sitting on the Ninth Circuit Court, known for its liberal position on free speech issues, objected to the appellate court's en banc decision to let the trial go forward. Kozinski wrote:

Something very dangerous is going on here. Private property, including intellectual property, is essential to our way of life. It provides an incentive for investment and innovation; it stimulates the flourishing of our culture; it protects the moral entitlements of people to the fruits of their labors. But reducing too much to private property can be bad medicine. . . . So too it is with intellectual property. Overprotecting intellectual property is as harmful as underprotecting it. Creativity is impossible without a rich public domain. Nothing today, likely nothing since we tamed fire, is genuinely new: Culture, like science and technology, grows by accretion, each new creator building on the works of those who came before. Overprotection stifles the very creative forces it's supposed to nurture. The panel's opinion is a classic case of overprotection. Concerned about what it sees as a wrong done to Vanna White, the panel majority erects a property right of remarkable and dangerous breadth: Under the majority's opinion, it's now a tort for advertisers to remind the public of a celebrity. Not to use a celebrity's name, voice, signature or likeness; not to imply the celebrity endorses a product; but simply to evoke the celebrity's image in the public's mind. This Orwellian notion withdraws far more from the public domain than prudence and common sense allow. . . . It raises serious First Amendment problems. It's bad law, and it deserves a long, hard second look. (*White v. Samsung Electronics of America* [1992] 1513–1514)

The Supreme Court has heard only one appropriation case. It involved the question of whether the newsworthiness defense, commonly applied by the media in invasion of privacy lawsuits, protected a television station from an appropriation lawsuit. In this case, Hugo Zacchini, who made his living as a "human cannonball," sued a television station for appropriation. Of course, it is not uncommon to show excerpts of a performance as part of a

news story on the subject, but in this case, footage of Zacchini's finale—a dramatic fifteen seconds of him being blown out of a cannon—was broadcast in its entirety. Zacchini claimed that broadcasting the finale undermined the economic value of the
performance. The Supreme Court agreed (*Zacchini v. Scripps
Howard Broadcasting* [1977]).

The *Zacchini* decision did not conclude that *any* appropriation
by the press is actionable. The Court's ruling was based in an effective argument that the news program broadcast the essence of
the performance—and that fact took precedence over how much
of the performance was broadcast. Most of the time, the right of
publicity tort is not actionable in newsworthy situations, even
though news is a commercial business and, one can argue, the
press profits from its coverage of celebrities. Furthermore, the
courts have interpreted newsworthiness very liberally, giving the
press wide latitude. The courts have protected news companies
that use images of celebrities previously covered as part of a news
story in the company's own advertising and promotion. Thus, for
example, if *Vogue* did a cover story on Tom Cruise with pictures
and then used one of those pictures in its subscription solicitation
materials, it would not be appropriation. But the *Zacchini* case
made it clear that it is possible to cross the line of newsworthiness
and violate a right to publicity.

Since *Zacchini,* other lawsuits have been filed against the press
for appropriation. Cher gave an interview to a freelance writer
who hoped to publish the interview in *Us* magazine. Instead the
story was published in two other magazines: *Forum* and *Star.* One
of the magazines, *Forum,* then used her name and likeness in an
advertisement suggesting that she read the magazine. Cher sued
both magazines. The Ninth Circuit Court of Appeals ruled that
Star magazine did not violate her right to publicity, because it
published a newsworthy article. However, the court said that *Forum* magazine went too far. Its publication of the article was fine,

but its use of her image as an apparent endorsement violated Cher's right to publicity (*Cher v. Forum International* [1982]).

Cher's case and a similar suit filed by football legend Joe Montana (who lost his case) relied on the Booth rule, which came from a court decision that allows the press to use images and material from news stories in advertising as long as they do not imply an endorsement (*Booth v. Curtis Publishing* [1962]). Among other examples of successful appropriation lawsuits are Dustin Hoffman's suit against *Los Angeles* magazine for the publication of a digitally altered picture of Hoffman's head on top of a female model's body (*Hoffman v. Capital Cities/ABC* [1999]). Clint Eastwood won an appropriation lawsuit against the *National Enquirer* after they published an "exclusive" interview that Eastwood claimed he never gave (*Eastwood v. National Enquirer* [1997]). Despite these successful examples, appropriation lawsuits are very difficult to win.

The News-Gathering Tort: Intrusion and the Intentional Infliction of Emotional Distress

A second invasion of privacy tort is intrusion, which is of special interest to the press. Intrusion does not focus on the content of publication but on how information is gathered. As technology develops, more and more intrusion lawsuits are filed because of reporters' using eavesdropping equipment and hidden cameras. But any intrusion into an area where a person had a reasonable expectation of privacy can trigger a lawsuit.

Generally the press has the freedom to gather information and images in public places for newsworthy stories. But what happens when the location is private and the journalist gains access or uses hidden devices to gather information? One of the early cases may sound a bit like the kinds of stories that now air regularly on prime-time television news magazines. In this case, two reporters for *Life* magazine posed as a patient and her husband at the home office of a man named Dietemann, who had no medical training and was suspected of practicing medicine without a license. They wore a hidden radio microphone for law enforcement agents and took photographs without Dietemann's knowledge. Dietemann sued for invasion of privacy. The court determined that although the pictures were newsworthy and *Life* had a right to publish them, the journalists did not have the right to gather the information the way they did (*Dietemann v. Time* [1971]).

In general, reporters can take pictures and gather information as they wish in public and quasi-public places. Journalists can photograph police publicly frisking suspects (*Prahl v. Brosamle* [1980]) and can photograph private property from public places (*Bisbee v. Conover* [1982]). Journalists can tape conversations or take pictures in places where there is no expectation of privacy, such as the front door of a person's home, a public part of a restaurant, or the public sections of a jail (*Deteresa v. American Broadcasting Co.* [1997]; *Dempsey v. National Enquirer* [1997]; *Holman v. Central Arkansas Broadcasting Co.* [1979]). On the other hand, it is not clear whether surreptitious information gathering by a journalist in a restaurant's private dining area or in an inmate's cell might be subject to an intrusion charge. California has passed a law that allows charges to be brought against a journalist for using a "visual or auditory enhancing device, regardless of whether there is a physical trespass," if the information could not have been gathered without otherwise trespassing (implying that the plaintiff had a reasonable expectation of privacy) (Reporters Committee on Freedom of the Press 1998).

The courts have been sympathetic to plaintiffs who have been harassed by aggressive journalists gathering information in public places. The aggressive practices of celebrity photographers—the paparazzi—have led to physical attacks by celebrities as well as lawsuits for intrusion when photographers continue to track and hound their subjects. One famous case involved Jackie Onassis and the Kennedy children. Celebrity photographer Ron Galella relentlessly trailed Onassis, using tactics such as faking his identity and blocking passageways, that the courts decided reached the level of harassment, assault, and intentional infliction of emotional distress. He was given a restraining order to stay at least twenty-five feet from Onassis. Galella's behavior reached a degree of intrusion far exceeding the practice of most journalists. Some may be aggressive in their style and even resort to ambush interviewing, but it is not common for members of the press to be formally accused of harassment.

With the exception of extreme examples, like the Onassis case, the courts seem to focus primarily on intrusion into private places, either physically or with electronic devices. It is the electronics that have complicated the tort. For example, police officers need a warrant to wiretap, eavesdrop, or hack into communications, and citizens, including journalists, are not allowed to do any of these. It is also illegal to intercept wireless point-to-point communications, such as those of cell phones, e-mail, and microwave and satellite transmissions (Electronic Communications Privacy Act of 1986, 1998). In an interesting twist, however, a journalist is protected under the First Amendment if he or she publishes illegally taped conversations, as long as the journalist broke no laws in acquiring the tapes (*Bartnicki v. Vopper* [2001]). In other words, if someone else stole them and gave them to the journalist to publish, the journalist can do so without threat of prosecution. However, other court decisions have suggested that this interpretation might not hold if the conversations contained proprietary information such as trade secrets (*Bartnicki* 2001). The courts generally support journalists' right to record their own telephone interviews, but whether the reporter must notify or needs the other person's permission varies among the states.

Journalists entering private property without permission are subject to trespassing charges. The courts remain unclear on whether journalists who misrepresent themselves to gain access to private areas may be liable. In one case, in order to gain access to a cataract clinic, ABC journalists agreed not to secretly record information or ambush-interview anyone. Nevertheless, ABC reporters posed as patients and used hidden cameras. A federal court ruled that the reporters did not trespass and noted that the facility should have remained skeptical about their investigative activities in spite of the reporters' agreement (*Desnick v. ABC* [1995]).

On the other hand, an appeals court upheld a judgment against ABC for misrepresenting itself when its journalists falsified job applications in order to secretly investigate food-handling policies at Food Lion grocery stores. The court said that ABC was liable for trespassing and for the reporters' fraudulently concealing their identities (*Food Lion v. Capital Cities/ABC* [1995]).

Because of the essential role the press plays in a democracy, the courts have generally maintained very broad protections for news-gathering activities. At the same time, however, a general fascination with the lives of the rich and famous has spawned an insatiable demand for celebrity stories and images. The more base practice of provoking celebrities in order to get shocking images represents the low point for information gathering practices. But the courts are careful not to become the arbitrator of values and, in this tort, they stay carefully focused on the manner in which information is gathered, not on the quality of the information. Judgments about the kind of information published are the focus of the remaining two torts: publication of private facts and false light.

Publication of Private Facts

The third invasion of privacy tort involves the publication of private facts. This is the type of invasion of privacy that prompted Warren and Brandeis's late–nineteenth century call for a "right to privacy." The kind of information that ends up in this lawsuit is the bread and butter of the tabloids and gossip columns. A majority of the courts in the country will hear this kind of case, but plaintiffs rarely win (Pember 2003). This is because handing a victory to the plaintiff would typically call for punishing the press for publishing truthful information acquired without breaking the law. Yet it remains the tort of last resort for people who have been embarrassed by the widespread publication of private information but can't sue for libel because the information is true. The plaintiff bears the entire burden of proof for *all* of the following key elements of a publication of private facts case:

- There must be publicity, not simply publication to private facts about a person.
- The publicity of this private information must be offensive to a reasonable person, not just to the plaintiff.
- The private information must not be newsworthy.

Publicity is distinct from publication—it goes much further. It requires that the private material communicated is literally becoming public knowledge. Thus, for example, private information transmitted to a limited list of e-mail addresses would constitute a far weaker case than publication in the *New York Times* or the *National Enquirer* or broadcast on the *CBS Evening News with Dan Rather*. Additionally, the private information really has to be private, not just something a person would rather not disseminate. If the report involved something embarrassing that happened in public, even if offensive, it is not private. Public records generally are not subject to this kind of lawsuit, because they are not considered private.

Two cases illustrate the way the courts conceive of public information. During a Pittsburgh Steelers game, an enthusiastic fan encouraged a *Sports Illustrated* photographer to take a picture of him. When the picture was published in the magazine, the fan realized that his fly was unzipped in the photograph. No doubt the photograph was widely published and embarrassing, but the court ruled that there was no expectation of privacy in a public place, so the information was not private (*Neff v. Time* [1976]). A second case involved Oliver Sipple, who struck the arm of would-be assassin Sara Jane Moore, who, as a result, missed her shot at President Gerald Ford. In the flood of stories that followed his heroic act, the *San Francisco Chronicle* printed a story suggesting that the reason President Ford never thanked Sipple might have been that Sipple was homosexual. Sipple sued for publication of private facts, but ultimately lost. An appeals court concluded that his sexual orientation was not a private fact, since he was actively involved in the political activities of the San Francisco gay community (*Sipple v. Chronicle Publishing* [1984]).

Is the publication of a juvenile's name publication of private facts? Is the publication of a rape victim's name publication of private facts? The Supreme Court has ruled that the press cannot be criminally punished for the publication of a minor's name. However, it did not preclude the possibility of civil remedies, such as invasion of privacy lawsuits, if the information did not come from a public document (*Smith v. Daily Mail* [1979]). Likewise, since a rape victim's name is generally part of a court record, it is not a private fact and the press is not liable if it publishes the name (*Florida Star v. B.J.F.* [1989]). However, there might be civil remedies if the name of the victim was obtained from sources that were not public. Ultimately, this is a hotly contested area because of the ethical issues associated with the decision of whether or not to publish juvenile offenders' and rape victims' names. Although it was routine to publish the names of rape victims fifty years ago, today it is usually a matter of editorial policy for newspapers and televisions not to do so.

Even more challenging than grappling with whether information is public or private is determining whether the material in question is offensive. One would expect that publication of the private material is offensive in the mind of the plaintiff who files a lawsuit. However, the courts do not rely on the plaintiff's assessment of offensiveness. The courts ask whether a reasonable person would find the dissemination of the private information offensive.

It is hard to overcome the courts' interest in protecting the press in such circumstances, but there have been cases in which the courts found that the dissemination of material was offensive to a reasonable person. For example, Dorothy Barber had a rare metabolic disorder. She ate constantly and still lost weight. While she was in the hospital, journalists entered her room and took pictures of her without permission. *Time* magazine published a story calling her "the starving glutton." Barber sued for publication of private facts and won. The court found that Barber has some expectation of privacy and that the particular story was offensive, presenting Barber as a freak. Furthermore, the court found that since this was a rare, noncontagious disease, the claim that there was a legitimate public interest was dubious (*Barber v. Time* [1942]).

Another case involved a woman visiting the fair with her children. While they were leaving the fun house, an air jet blew her skirt up over her head, exposing her from the waist down. As luck would have it, a photographer caught the moment, and the photograph, in which her face was hidden by the skirt, appeared in a local paper. The woman sued. Although her face was hidden, her children were in the picture, so she was easily identified. Even though the incident occurred in a public place where numerous people saw what happened, the court found that the photograph was an intimate revelation, highly offensive, and of little public value (*Daily Times-Democrat v. Graham* [1962]).

Determining whether information is of legitimate public concern is a key element in the publication of private facts tort. The two cases just mentioned might suggest that the courts do not necessarily assume that a voyeuristic interest on the part of the public justifies a legitimate public concern. However, in a number of cases, material most suited for the tabloids has been found to be of legitimate public concern. The courts have ruled, for example, that there was a legitimate public concern in cases involving publications revealing the involuntary sterilization of an eighteen-year-old girl (*Howard v. Des Moines Register* [1979]) and the reckless personal behavior of a well-known body surfer (*Virgil v. Time* [1975]). The courts typically assume that if the material is something people find interesting, then it is newsworthy and the lawsuit fails. How can one define newsworthiness? For the courts to make this determination in anything but the most obvious cases would put them in the position of imposing values on a public that purchases millions of tabloids a week. Is something newsworthy if it contributes to the democratic process? Is it newsworthy if lots of people pay to read the article? Is it newsworthy because an editor, acting in his or her professional capacity, determined that with the limited space or time available, the story was worth publishing over other stories? If that is the case, then how is newsworthiness determined on the Internet, which has no space limitation? Not surprisingly, the courts continue to grapple with the concept, and no clear guidelines have been formulated.

False Light and Fictionalization

If a publication of private facts lawsuit provides a remedy for the dissemination of true private facts, what recourse is there for the dissemination of false facts that are not defamatory? Plaintiffs in this situation can file a false light invasion of privacy lawsuit. This is a controversial tort, and some states don't recognize it at all. It permits a person to sue if he or she has been portrayed falsely in a manner that is highly offensive to a reasonable person. Furthermore, the publisher of the false, highly offensive material must be at fault in a manner that parallels the fault requirements in libel cases. As with libel, the plaintiff must show publication and identification. Also as with libel, constitutional defenses are applicable to false light lawsuits. The key difference between false light invasion of privacy lawsuits and defamation lawsuits is the nature of the harm. A false light suit addresses the emotional and psychological harm from the publication of false information. A defamation suit is the recourse for reputational harm from the publication of false information.

False light also addresses an increasingly common practice in publishing and dramatic works: fictionalization. Fictionalization is the dramatic presentation of a story that has its basis in true events or facts. The NBC network television production based on the rescue of Army private Jessica Lynch, "Saving Jessica Lynch," is an example of fictionalization, as is the CBS production "The Elizabeth Smart Story" (interestingly, the two were scheduled head-to-head during the November 2003 television ratings sweeps). Both productions were based on books; the Smart made-for-TV movie, which recounted the story of Elizabeth's abduction, months-long absence, and eventual return, was fully endorsed by her parents. The Lynch movie, on the other hand, was an unauthorized presentation of her capture and rescue in Iraq.

Although authorization is not required in a fictionalization, there is some level of risk in not having it. Intentional fictionalization or distortion of the truth may be subject to a false light suit. Even though some states do not recognize the tort, two cases have reached the Supreme Court. The first involved the Hill family, who were taken hostage by escaped convicts. There was extraordinary media coverage of the incident, and later a novel, a Broadway production, and film about the events appeared. Yet, it was an article in *Life* magazine that prompted a lawsuit. The article purported to tell the real story but used photos from the Broadway play, in which the story was greatly embellished. The family sued for invasion of privacy. The Supreme Court overturned a lower court's award to the family, noting that a false light lawsuit involving an issue of public concern requires that the plaintiff show actual malice.

It is not uncommon to see disclaimers at the beginning of television shows (e.g., *Law and Order*) and novels stating that the events in the work do not depict any actual persons. Such disclaimers will not protect against a lawsuit, however.

More directly affecting journalists is the fictionalization or distortion of quotations. Making up facts about a story or manufacturing quotes not only violates journalistic ethics but also can result in legal action. For example, Margaret Cantrell won an invasion of privacy lawsuit for the fictionalization of a follow-up feature story on her life after the bridge collapse that killed her husband. The story included excerpts of an interview with her. However, the journalist never interviewed Cantrell, who in fact was not at home when the journalist dropped by the house. Cantrell claimed that the deliberate falsifications humiliated and ridiculed her family, causing mental distress. The Supreme Court agreed that the journalist acted with actual malice because of a reckless disregard for the truth (*Cantrell v. Forest City Publishing Co.* [1974]).

Although the Cantrell case occurred some thirty years ago, fictionalization remains a problem with journalists. In 1981, *Washington Post* writer Janet Cooke won a Pulitzer Prize for a heart-wrenching story about "Jimmy," an eight-year-old heroin addict. The story spawned a citywide search for the boy after Cooke insisted on protecting her sources. Her editor, on discovering that her resume was falsified, challenged her story, and she admitted to having made it up. She resigned from the *Washington Post* and returned the Pulitzer Prize. Other respected media outlets have published fabricated work by their writers. Christopher Newton was fired from Associated Press for fabricating sources. Antoine Oman fabricated a piece for the *New Times LA.* Jay Forman, a writer for *Slate.com,* fabricated a story about fishing for monkeys with rotten fruit.

Arguably the most complex known efforts at fictionalization come from the recent trials and tribulations of two journalists working at highly prestigious media outlets: Stephen Glass, an associate editor at the *New Republic,* and Jayson Blair, a writer at the *New York Times.* Both journalists covered up their fictional stories with elaborate ruses. Glass compiled false meeting notes, fictitious Web sites, and phony e-mail accounts (Penenberg 1998). Blair submitted fake receipts for travel and plagiarized quotes from the published works of other journalists (Kurtz 2003). Recently Glass was back in the spotlight with *The Fabulist,* a novel about—not surprisingly—a journalist who fictionalizes his stories. Additionally, *Shattered Glass,* a movie based on his life, was released in 2003. Jayson Blair recently penned a tell-all book, *Burning Down My Master's House: My Life at the New York Times,* for which he received an advance of more than $100,000 (Arce 2003). In spite of the elaborate fictionalizations, neither of these journalists has, as of yet, been subjected to a libel or invasion of privacy lawsuit.

Distortion is a more common problem in journalism than the highly unethical practice of fictionalization. Distortion can trigger a lawsuit against the press if key information is omitted or used out of context. Docudramas, infotainment, and the use of file photos and video can be risky when the subject matter is sensitive. Such lawsuits are difficult for a plaintiff to win, but the courts are allowing some to go to trial. For example, a case went to trial that involved a story on herpes that showed a close-up of Linda Duncan as the voice-over stated, "For the 20 million Americans who have herpes, it's not a cure" (*Duncan v. WJLA-TV* [1984]). Another trial took place over the placement of an unrelated photo next to sexually suggestive text (*Braun v. Flynt* [1984]). Suits such as these suggest that it is not only journalists who need to be wary about practices that might lead to a lawsuit, but also editors, who can shape the contextual message conveyed by a set of facts.

Defenses in Invasion of Privacy Lawsuits

Although the burden of proof for all the invasion of privacy torts rests entirely on the plaintiff, the press does have some affirmative defenses. The First Amendment casts broad protections for press activities that encompass invasion of privacy lawsuits. As with libel suits, invasion of privacy lawsuits may require the plaintiff to show that the journalist acted with actual malice if the subject matter was of public concern.

Another important press defense against invasion of privacy lawsuits, straddling both constitutional and common law, is newsworthiness. If use of a likeness or image is part of a newsworthy story, it is not appropriation. If a story that includes legally obtained private information that is embarrassing to the plaintiff but the subject matter is of public concern, it would be difficult to win a lawsuit.

This protection is crucial if the press is going to cover stories of public interest. The courts give wide latitude to the newsworthiness defense, protecting tabloids (print and broadcast) and other media that focus on sensationalized and scandalous news. However, this protection is diminished if a story contains inaccuracies, especially if inaccuracies were introduced with actual malice. Again, however, intrusion lawsuits do not address the newsworthiness of the information. The intrusion tort focuses only on the information-gathering method used by the journalist.

One of the best defenses against any invasion of privacy lawsuit is consent—that is, voluntary agreement to publication or permission to enter a private place to gather information. The more explicit the consent, the better the protection for the press. Consent should also encompass all possible uses of information. Consent for one specific use of a photograph, for example, does not extend to other uses. A general consent for use, on the other hand, gives the press tremendous flexibility. For example, Brooke Shields attempted to stop publication of nude photographs taken of her when she was a child. Unfortunately, her mother had signed a general consent that allowed the photographer to sell the images, so Shields could not sue for appropriation (*Shields v. Gross* [1983]).

The warning conveyed by false light and fictionalization law-suits is that journalists in particular and the media in general need to be careful about the use of dramatic license when telling stories based on true events. Furthermore, journalists and editors have to be scrupulous in their attention to detail when reporting quotes or sensitive facts. The longtime journalistic practices of corroborating sources and recording interviews to ensure accurate quotes help minimize the risk of distortion in the news. The actions of Stephen Glass and Jayson Blair are an easy call: they made up their stories. But what if the stories or interviews are not made up but a plaintiff claims that the quotes are partially fabricated or taken out of context? A case involving the *New Yorker* and a well-known psychoanalyst illustrate the complexity of the problem journalists face when "cleaning up" quotes. In 1983, Janet Malcolm published a lengthy story about Jeffrey M. Masson, a prominent psychoanalyst and projects director of the Sigmund Freud Archives. The multipart article was based on notes and the transcriptions of extensive tape-recorded interviews with Masson. The article discusses, among other things, his tumultuous professional life, his conflicts with colleagues, and his firing from the Freud Archives. Masson sued for invasion of privacy and libel because of several misquotations in the article that falsely portrayed him as "egotistical, vain, and lacking in personal honesty and moral integrity" (*Masson v. Malcolm* [1987] 1397). Since there was no question that Masson was a public figure, either tort required a showing of actual malice. This case spent years in the courts. At one point the Supreme Court heard a petition from Masson requesting summary judgment that the alteration of quotes constituted actual malice. In other words, his claim was that the fact that Malcolm altered the quotes, intentionally, could only mean that she knew they were false when she published them. (Part of the difficulty lay in the fact that Malcolm could not locate some of her written notes.) The Court declined the request for summary judgment, writing, "We conclude that a deliberate alteration of the words uttered by a plaintiff does not equate with knowledge of falsity . . . unless the alteration results in a material change in the meaning conveyed by the statement (*Masson v. Malcolm* [1991] 517). The message from the Court is that alteration of quotes, in and of itself, is not proof of actual malice. The Masson-Malcolm dispute took eleven years to litigate, with multiple trials and appeals. Every time, the courts ruled in favor of Malcolm. In an interview, Malcolm confirmed that she would continue to repair quotes that were grammatically incorrect or "mangled." The one thing she would do differently? "[S]ave every piece of paper" (Carvajal 1991).

Generally, invasion of privacy lawsuits are difficult to win, but not impossible. As with libel suits, the cost of going to trial may have a chilling effect on aggressive press coverage, especially in sensitive situations.

Over the years, attempts have been made to mediate libel claims through news councils. News councils are designed to provide a forum for handling complaints about the media. News councils typically comprise a mix of media representatives and community representatives. They hold public hearings for complaints by community members who believe they were harmed by the media. No decisions are binding, and news councils have no authority. They simply act as a forum to facilitate dialogue and understanding and to mediate complaints. News councils are not that common, but the Minnesota News Council, started in 1971, is a successful example of how mediation can avert potentially expensive litigation. Another option to help address misunderstandings that can turn into lawsuits is for a media outlet to employ an ombudsman. The ombudsman has no authority but acts as a neutral arbitrator of complaints about his or her media outlet. The *Washington Post* has a long-standing tradition of using an ombudsman, who both handles complaints and independently calls the newspaper to task in a column whenever he or she believes the newspaper has acted unprofessionally. News councils and ombudsmen represent less litigious ways of mediating minor complaints before they become expensive, even if frivolous, lawsuits.

SHIELD LAWS AND CONTEMPT

One of the most precious commodities for a good investigative reporter is his or her sources. In sensitive news stories, it is not uncommon for sources to want to remain anonymous. *Washington Post* reporters Bob Woodward and Carl Bernstein relied in part on "Deep Throat," an anonymous source inside the Nixon administration whose information helped the journalists uncover the series of crimes collectively known as the Watergate scandal. These crimes included a break-in at the Democratic National Committee offices in the Watergate office complex and the burglary of a psychiatrist's office to gather information on Daniel Ellsberg, the Department of Defense analyst who leaked the Pentagon Papers to the *New York Times.* Woodward and Bernstein, with information provided by Deep Throat, linked the break-ins to a secret Republican fund used to spy on behalf of the Nixon reelection campaign. The stories that followed led to Nixon's resignation within a year of his reelection. It is likely that this story would not have been published without the corroborating information from Deep Throat. No court has compelled Woodward and Bernstein to reveal the identity of Deep Throat. But not all journalists have been so lucky. Many journalists who have been called before a grand jury or a judge to reveal confidential information have refused and as a result been cited by the court for contempt. A charge of contempt of court means that the journalist has interfered with the legal proceeding and may be fined or imprisoned. Many journalists have sat in a jail cell for refusing to reveal their sources.

The question at hand is whether a reporter has a constitutional "privilege" that protects him or her from having to testify about confidential sources of information. Attorneys, doctors, and priests have enjoyed this protection for centuries. Journalists' protection against revealing confidential information, on the other hand, is a twentieth-century phenomenon. The courts have not been entirely sympathetic to the idea of privilege for journalists. In 1958 an appellate court upheld a contempt charge against a journalist who refused to identify the CBS network executive who made insulting statements about Judy Garland. Garland needed that information for a libel suit. The journalist spent ten days in jail (*Garland v. Torre* [1958]).

Fourteen years later, three conflicting appellate court decisions on constitutional privilege for reporters were combined and heard before the Supreme Court. In all three cases, reporters had refused to answer grand jury questions about illegal activities they may have witnessed. The Court concluded, in a narrowly split decision (5–4), that there was no constitutional privilege for journalists (*Branzburg v. Hayes* [1972]). The opinion of the Court, however, suggested some wiggle room on the issue. Four of the five justices in the majority believed that a journalist was no different from any other citizen when it came to testifying before a grand jury. The fifth justice, Justice Powell, indicated that there might be times when a reporter's privilege would hold under the First Amendment, and the issue should be addressed on a case-by-case basis. One of the dissenting justices, Justice William O. Douglas, believed that journalists should never be made to testify about confidential information. The other dissenting justices believed that journalists should have a qualified privilege, with a heavy burden on the government to show an overriding interest in the information, that the information is relevant to an illegal activity, and that there is no other way to get the information.

Independent of the *Branzburg* decision, journalists take protection of confidential information very seriously. In one of the appellate cases leading to the *Branzburg* decision, Earl Caldwell, a reporter for the *New York Times,* interviewed members of the Black Panthers. When he was summoned to appear before a federal grand jury investigating militant groups, he not only refused to testify, he even refused to show up. Grand jury proceedings are secret, so if he had shown up, no one outside the grand jury would have known if he revealed anything. Still, he did not even want to risk the appearance of jeopardizing confidentiality (*United States v. Caldwell* [1970]).

Several appellate decisions since *Branzburg* have ruled in a manner that reflects the dissenting opinion in that case. Most have recognized a limited privilege for journalists. None have suggested that the privilege extends to grand jury investigations. However, one case recognized the privilege in a civil lawsuit (*Baker v. F&F Investment* [1972]). Furthermore, a qualified privilege was extended to documentary filmmakers (*Silkwood v. Kerr-McGee* [1977]). In a strong affirmation of privilege by the Ninth Circuit Court of Appeals, the court held that authors of investigative books share a reporter's privilege. Additionally, the court concluded that a journalist's notes are privileged if the journalist is subpoenaed to testify in a civil suit unless the information is essential to the suit and cannot be obtained anywhere else (*Shoen v. Shoen* [1995]). However, courts have consistently not recognized any privilege for journalists who are eyewitnesses to an event (*Dillon v. City and County of San Francisco* [1990]). In recent years, most federal courts and numerous state courts have recognized a qualified privilege rooted in a mix of the First Amendment, federal common law, and federal rules of procedure (Overbeck 2004).

Shield laws are a statutory protection on which journalists rely. Statutory protection has been legislated in at least thirty-one states for journalists. Many of these shield laws came in response to high-profile contempt charges against journalists. The protection these laws provide varies from a near-absolute privilege to privilege for information actually published to a qualified privilege with a variety of exceptions. Oregon's shield law, for example, protects journalists from having to reveal confidential information unless they are defendants in a lawsuit and the information is the basis of their defense or the information is vital to a criminal defense (O.R.S. 44.510–44.540 [1979]). Not all state shield laws fare well. The shield law in New Mexico was overturned by the state supreme court (*Ammerman v. Hubbard Broadcasting* [1976]) for unconstitutionally encroaching "on the information-seeking authority of the judiciary" (Overbeck 2004, 343). California incorporated its shield law into the state constitution to protect it from court challenges.

There are some notable examples of reporters refusing to reveal confidential information and paying heavily with contempt charges. Reporter Bill Farr published a story that included information from attorneys who were under a gag order. Over the next decade Farr battled several courts' efforts to extract the name of his source. He spent forty-six days in jail under a civil contempt charge that could have continued indefinitely. Finally the Supreme Court created a mechanism for shifting civil contempt charges to a criminal contempt (carrying a maximum sentence of five years) if it was clear that continued incarceration would not convince the reporter to comply with the court order and if the refusal to comply with the order was rooted in a moral principle (Overbeck 2004). Generally it is uncommon for journalists to serve jail time. Most media outlets do not have the resources to fund protracted litigation or to pay the fines that typically accompany a contempt charge. The press is more likely to negotiate a compromise, releasing a narrow range of information or information that is not critical to the preservation of confidential sources. The Reporters Committee on Freedom of the Press tracks the jailing and fining of reporters on contempt charges for refusing to testify. Their records show that fifteen journalists were incarcerated between 1984 and 2001, with time in jail ranging from a few hours to 168 days (Reporters Committee on Freedom of the Press 2004).

The most recent high-profile case of a journalist incarcerated on contempt charges involved Vanessa Leggett and her research for a book about a murder in Houston. She was subpoenaed by a federal grand jury (recall that the courts have not supported privilege claims for grand jury testimony). She refused to reveal the contents of her interviews with a murder suspect. The federal court system, up through the appellate court, upheld the contempt order. The Supreme Court refused to hear the case. Leggett was released when the grand jury adjourned without issuing any indictments. Her case started another discussion about passing a federal shield law. Disagreements about what constitutes a "journalist" and the extent of the privilege have undermined the effort (Dias 2002).

There has been an interesting recent development in the status of the most famous confidential source, Woodward and Bernstein's Deep Throat. The two reporters have maintained from the outset that they would not reveal the identity of Deep Throat until his or her death, and they have remained true to their word. Meanwhile, though, after several years of researching the Watergate story, the enterprising students of an investigative reporting class at the University of Illinois announced that Deep Throat is Fred Fielding, deputy counsel to President Nixon during the scandal. Fielding denies that he is Deep Throat (Gaines et al. 2003), and Bernstein chastised the University of Illinois professor, Bill Gaines, saying, "The last thing students in a journalism class should be doing is trying to find out who other reporters' sources are. They should be learning how to protect sources" (Eaton 2003).

To turn the tables on the question of privilege, what happens if a journalist backs off an agreement of confidentiality and publishes the identity of a source? The Supreme Court has ruled that breaking an agreement of confidentially is the same as obtaining information unlawfully. Therefore, it is not protected by a First Amendment right to publish truthful information about newsworthy events (*Cohen v. Cowles Media Co.* [1991]).

Finally, the Supreme Court has addressed the question of newsroom searches. One tactic a court might use when a journalist will not reveal sources is to search the newsroom. The press has argued that there is a First Amendment protection against newsroom searches. The Court ruled differently, however, concluding that a newsroom, like any other property, may be searched if a valid search warrant has been issued (*Zurcher v. Stanford Daily* [1978]). At the same time, the Court indicated that a lack of constitutional protection did not preclude the possibility of statutory protection. In response, several states passed laws prohibiting newsroom searches. Oregon's shield law, for example, states:

> No papers, effects or work premises of a person connected with, em-
> ployed by or engaged in any medium of communication to the public
> shall be subject to a search by a legislative, executive or judicial officer
> or body, or any other authority having power to compel the produc-
> tion of evidence, by search warrant or otherwise. The provisions of
> this subsection, however, shall not apply where probable cause exists
> to believe that the person has committed, is committing or is about to
> commit a crime. (O.R.S. 44.520(2) [1979])

COPYRIGHT

The right and ability to control and profit from one's intellectual property is rooted in a long-standing tradition in England (although more to censor than to protect authors), and it was codified in the United States shortly after the Constitution was enacted. The first U.S. copyright statute protected authors of books, maps, and charts for fourteen years. Protection for authors of other media was added later: musical compositions in 1831, photographs in 1865, and paintings in 1870. Further adaptations in the law were made with the advent of the motion picture, broadcasting, computers, photocopies, and so on. Today copyright is governed by the Copyright Act of 1976 (which preempted state laws) and the Digital Millennium Copyright Act of 1998.

Copyright law is extremely complex. A key starting point is to understand that *all* intellectual property is copyrighted. In addition to all the obvious works—books, CDs, artwork, and so on—copyright also covers less obvious creative work. For example, students' homework assignments, class notes, exams, and doodles are copyrighted. The contents of computer documents, Web pages, removable and permanent computer disks, and CD-ROMs are the copyrighted property of the author from the moment they are created. Thus, copying a Web page without the author's permission is not just bad "netiquette," it is also a violation of copyright. That said, it is important to understand what about the creative work is actually protected. Copyright protects expression, but not ideas or facts. Thus, for example, more than one person can write a story about a local fire, and each specific story is copyrighted, not the story idea and not the facts of the story.

Some authors register their work with the copyright office in Washington, D.C. This is not necessary to protect copyright. It simply provides official proof that the work is the original, along with extra leverage and larger damage awards if someone uses a registered work without permission.

The duration of copyright protection has been extended over the years. Most recently, in 1998, copyright holders were granted an additional twenty years of control. It has been speculated that pressure from the Disney Corporation drove the extension. Mickey Mouse was poised to enter the public domain in 2003, with Donald Duck and Goofy close behind. Now, works created after 1977 are copyright-protected for the life of the author, plus seventy years (Sonny Bono Copyright Term Extension Act P.L. 105-298 [1998]). Eric Eldred, owner of Eldritch Press, operated a Web site on which he placed the text of books as soon as they entered the public domain (such as A.A. Milne's *Winnie-the-Pooh*), with the goal of making them available to anyone. He challenged the new law before the Supreme Court, arguing that extending the term of copyright protection violates the First Amendment because it holds back even more creative material from the public domain where it can be freely used. However, the Court disagreed, arguing that "fair use" guidelines allow for that kind of creative use (*Eldred v. Ashcroft* [2003]).

Journalists are most likely to encounter copyright questions in a few areas: works made for hire, fair use limitations, and use of facts. Journalists freelancing on a specific job or on the payroll of a media firm typically do not hold copyright control over their work. While they are on the job, their productive output belongs to the employer. Journalists need permission from the publisher to use their stories in other ways. Journalists who use their own resources and materials to create a story and then sell it to a publisher may have the option of retaining copyright control, although a publisher may require that it be relinquished as part of the agreement to publish.

If a journalist gets an exclusive interview, other media outlets cannot rebroadcast it or print the transcripts. However, they can paraphrase what the interviewer said and relate facts from the interview (recall that copyright protects the expression, not the facts). Failure to give the original source credit will not cause trouble with copyright, but, in addition to violating professional ethics, it might lead to a plagiarism charge. A good case in point involved Gene Miller, an honored reporter for the Miami Herald. He spent an enormous amount of time researching and writing a book, *83 Hours Till Dawn,* about a highly publicized kidnapping. Universal City Studios made offers for the movie rights to the story, which he did not take. When the docudrama came out anyway, he sued for copyright violation. On appeal, the court ruled that Miller's research was not copyright protected, only his particular expression of that research, meaning the book (*Miller v. Universal City Studios* [1981]).

However, that does not mean that journalists can freely take from other news sources. A Pennsylvania broadcast station was sued for taking stories from the local newspaper and reading them over the air without acknowledging the source (*Pottstown Daily News Publishing v. Pottstown Broadcasting* [1963]).

The second area in which journalists may encounter copyright issues is in the fair use clause of the Copyright Act. Fair use allows journalists, scholars, students, and others to use limited excerpts of copyrighted material in limited ways, without having to secure prior permission or pay royalties to the copyright holder. It is intended to balance the right of the copyright holder to be compensated for his or her work against the public interest in the dissemination of ideas (*Triangle Publications v. Knight-Ridder* [1980]).

A variety of factors come into play in determining whether a journalist's use of copyrighted material falls under fair use. Especially important for journalists is being clear about the purpose and character of the use. Fair use protects the use of copyrighted material for comment and criticism. Thus, a journalist reviewing a play, CD, book, or movie may reprint excerpts to provide a context for the review. However, copying a substantial portion of the work may exceed fair use. In 1998, a federal district court dismissed a case involving ABC's broadcast of a television news report about marijuana. The story included a shot of the front cover and a photo from a recent *Newsweek* story on the subject. The court ruled that the use of the *Newsweek* images was a fair use (*Morgenstein v. ABC* [1998]).

When the press reviews works, fair use also demands that the nature of the copyrighted work be considered. For example, Harper and Row Publishers was preparing the release of President Gerald Ford's memoirs, *A Time to Heal. Time* magazine had paid for the exclusive right to print a prepublication excerpt. The *Nation* magazine acquired a copy of the manuscript and printed a lengthy article four weeks before the book came out—and before the *Time* magazine excerpt was scheduled to appear. The *Nation* article included excerpts from the book, although only some 300 words of the 2,250-word article contained copyrighted material. However, the publisher argued in court, it was the heart of the book. *Time* magazine subsequently canceled its publication agreement with Harper and Row. The case raised the question of whether the *Nation*'s use of the book excerpts fell under fair use. The Supreme Court ruled that it was not fair use, because the book was not yet published, which is a key consideration in determining the nature of the copyrighted work. The Copyright Act recognizes the right of first publication, and the Court concluded that the *Nation* had undermined that right (*Harper & Row Publishers v. Nation Enterprises* [1985]).

The press has to remain sensitized to the fact that the First Amendment right to a free press does not include unlimited and unrestricted use of copyrighted material. The courts provide wide latitude for fair use, for commentary and criticism and use of facts. A particular expression of the facts—a news story, for example—can be copyrighted. This is an age where the media increasingly borrow from each other. Michael Kinsley, founding editor of *Slate.com*, has remarked that "most American news reporting and commentary on national issues derives—uncredited—from the *New York Times*" (Kinsley 2003). Local broadcast stations and local newspapers are reviewing each other's stories to ensure that their own story coverage is comprehensive. Knowing the difference between using facts from another story and violating copyright is critical for the contemporary press.

SPECIAL TOPICS: THE STUDENT PRESS

Many journalists get their start working on their high school newspaper, perhaps as part of a journalism course or as an extracurricular activity. For many, it is their first introduction to the "inverted pyramid" story structure, writing on deadline, and learning the meaning and limits of freedom of the press. The Supreme Court made it clear in *Tinker v. Des Moines School District* that students in public schools do not leave their First Amendment rights "at the schoolhouse gate," provided the exercise of those rights does not interfere with the educational process, such as by being disruptive or obscene or infringing on the rights of other students (*Tinker v. Des Moines School District* [1969]). Since then, however, concessions to the primacy of the educational process created a judicial opening for chipping away at the forcefulness of the language in the *Tinker* decision. In decisions since *Tinker*, the courts have limited student expression generally (*Bethel v. Fraser* [1986]), and a case that reached the Supreme Court in 1988 dramatically limited freedom of the student press.

Hazelwood East High School's newspaper, *Spectrum*, planned to publish articles on teen pregnancy and birth control and on the impact of divorce on children. In both stories the articles used quotations from unidentified students. School officials became concerned that the identity of the students might be learned and that the stories were unbalanced, so the principal canceled the stories. In a case whose rulings flip-flopped all the way to the Supreme Court, it was ultimately decided that school censorship of high school newspapers does not violate the First Amendment (*Hazelwood School District v. Kuhlmeier* [1988]). It was key to the decision that the newspaper was published as part of the educational curriculum. Because of that, the Court believed that determining limits on content was up to those responsible for the curriculum. The Court also suggested that a high school newspaper that functioned as an extracurricular activity might not be subject to the same limitations. The *Hazelwood* decision has served as a guideline for high school censorship of many newsworthy stories. For example, the principal of Salem High School, in Massachusetts, held up publication of the student newspaper, *Witches Brew*, because she objected to a story about new school bans on wearing hats and eating in the classroom out of concern that the stories would cause disruptions at the school (Student Press Law Center 2003a). Several states, including Colorado, Arkansas, Iowa, Massachusetts, California, and Kansas, have enacted legislation to ensure a higher level of protection for the student press than is afforded by the *Hazelwood* decision. However, according to a survey conducted by Freedom Forum and the

American Journalism Review, Americans do not believe high school students should have the same First Amendment rights as older students or adults (Student Press Law Center 2003b).

All of these court decisions apply to public schools as an extension of the state. They do not apply to private schools, where constitutional protections have substantially less bite. Furthermore, matters are somewhat different at the public college level, where the press enjoys a higher degree of protection than in high schools (*Kincaid v. Gibson* [2001]). It still makes a difference whether the college paper is at a private or a public school, but its connection to an academic department or the appointment of an academic adviser does not carry the kinds of administrative control it does with the high school press. Although it is of little comfort from a public relations standpoint, the courts have also suggested that if members of the administration keep their hands off the student newspaper, they may not be liable for what it prints (*Lentz v. Clemson University* [1995]).

College press freedoms can be limited in less direct ways. For example, in 1983 the University of Minnesota student newspaper published its "Finals Edition." It was intentionally offensive, containing racist, sexist, and homophobic remarks. After a flood of complaints about the paper, the university regents decided to make the student fee allocation to the newspaper voluntary. The court case that resulted concluded that the fee reduction was intended to punish the paper for a specific issue of the paper and thus was a violation of the First Amendment. However, the court suggested that a college administration could reduce fee allocations to a campus newspaper for other reasons that are unrelated to a desire to censor the paper (*Stanley v. McGrath* [1983]).

In a recent case of student press censorship, the dean of student affairs at Governors State University, in Illinois, insisted on reviewing each issue of the student newspaper, the *Innovator,* before it went to print. The Seventh Circuit Court of Appeals ruled that school officials at public colleges and universities could not demand to review student publications prior to publication. On January 8, 2004, the decision was reviewed en banc by the Seventh Circuit (Student Press Law Center 2004); as of this writing, the court's decision had not yet been issued. Overturning the appellate court's commitment to a free student press would have enormous ramifications for college newspapers.

BROADCASTING AND PRESS FREEDOMS

All the topics presented thus far apply generally to the press, including broadcast journalists. However, some aspects of broadcasting make the practice of broadcast journalism differ slightly from print journalism. First, it is important to understand the difference between printed publications and broadcasting in the eyes of the government. There is a long-standing assumption that anyone can start a newspaper, but not everyone can operate a broadcast station—and on one level this is true. There is no technological limit to the number of newspapers that can be published, assuming enough trees can be harvested to make the paper. Realistically, however, it must be recognized that starting a newspaper, printing it, and distributing it any distance to a significant audience is enormously expensive and capital intensive. Broadcasting, by contrast, is constrained by the physical limitations of how many broadcast signals can be transmitted without interfering with one another. Although technological developments have increased the number of broadcast signals that can fit within a given bandwidth, not everyone who wants one can have a license to broadcast.

Because of the limited spectrum available—a resource that "belongs" to the public—broadcasters operate as a trustee of the frequency on which they broadcast. According to the Radio Act of 1927 (44 Stat. §18), precursor of the Communications Act of 1934 (47 U.S.C. 151), broadcasters must operate in the "public interest, convenience and necessity" (referred to as the PICAN requirement). Historically, to evaluate whether broadcasters were operating in the public interest, they were required to fulfill a variety of obligations over the course of the license period. These included ensuring program diversity, maintaining good reception, and upholding a good character. Starting in 1949, the public interest was interpreted to include an additional requirement: the Fairness Doctrine.

Fairness Doctrine

In the most general sense, the Fairness Doctrine required broadcasters to devote a reasonable amount of airtime to controversial issues of public importance. Their coverage of those issues, over time, needed to be balanced and fair. Broadcasters also were required to ascertain issues of importance to their community and provide relevant programming to address them. The Fairness Doctrine provided a government-imposed imperative for local broadcast journalism that was significantly different from any obligations under which print journalists operated. The Fairness Doctrine was challenged in 1969, and the Supreme Court upheld its constitutionality, stating:

> Because of the scarcity of radio frequencies, the Government is permitted to put restraints on licensees in favor of others whose views should be expressed on this unique medium. But the people as a whole retain their interest in free speech by radio and their collective right to have the medium function consistently with the ends and purposes of the First Amendment. It is the right of the viewers and listeners, not the right of the broadcasters, which is paramount. (*Red Lion v. FCC* [1969] 390)

Even with a clear affirmation of the Fairness Doctrine by the Supreme Court, parts of it were under constant attack from opponents who believed it was having the opposite of its intended effect. In other words, they believed that compelling broadcasters to cover the news in a balanced and fair way was creating a "chilling effect" on speech because broadcasters were overly concerned about whether they could prove their coverage was fair. As a result, they tended to cover the minimum to meet the ascertainment requirement.

In the end, it is not clear that the good intentions of the Fairness Doctrine were ever manifested. Perhaps attempting to compel broadcasters to cover issues is inherently flawed, or perhaps the Fairness Doctrine didn't have enough bite to it. By the mid-1980s, the Federal Communications Commission (FCC) and Congress, with plenty of pressure from broadcasting lobby groups, became convinced that the trusteeship model of broadcasting, which was based on a scarcity principle, was no longer relevant given the wide range of media technologies available to consumers. Calling for full First Amendment protection for broadcasting (to match that enjoyed by print media), Congress and the FCC facilitated a significant shift in the regulation of broadcasting, moving toward a marketplace model. With this model, the PICAN requirement is defined in the language of the market. Simply stated, the public interest is that in which the public is interested (Fowler and Brenner 1982). In broadcasting, then, the public interest is determined with the tools of the market: the television (Nielsen) and radio (Arbitron) ratings system. If the public watches certain programming in great numbers, a broadcaster can conclude that the public is interested in that programming. In the deregulation fervor of the 1980s, the Fairness Doctrine was eliminated. Afterward, efforts to have the Fairness Doctrine reinstated through legislation made it through Congress, but were vetoed by Presidents Ronald Reagan and George H.W. Bush.

During this period, broadcast news was increasingly a profitable enterprise for local stations. Local broadcast journalism incorporated new approaches to the news: happy talk (the chattering and bantering between on-air news staff during the local news), feel-good stories, high-tech gadgets (e.g., Doppler radar and helicopters), and a growing reliance on visually driven news ("If it bleeds it leads").

The marketplace model appears to have paid off, because it arguably contributed to local news becoming more popular, generating more revenue and thus intensifying market competition. Moreover, by the standards of a marketplace model, stations were satisfying the PICAN requirement, as reflected in strong local news program ratings. Even with the attrition of viewers from broadcast news to other media, including cable and the Internet, 57 percent of the public still uses local television as their primary source of information (Pew Research Center 2002). Evaluated under the marketplace model, this is an undeniable success story. Evaluated under the old trusteeship model of broadcasting, however, the programming on local news is arguably more problematic. Journalists working in the broadcast media function with an interesting blend of old-fashioned, journalistic drive and the realistic requirements of their particular medium—short, visually driven stories, insufficient time to flesh out details in a story, reporters with an attractive, credible on-air presence, and the ability to talk on the spot. Nothing about the marketplace model of broadcasting specifically restricts the First Amendment rights of the press, but the insatiable need for visually interesting material and the medium's inability to effectively deliver complex, detailed information limit broadcast journalists from presenting some information as effectively as other media can.

Section 315: The Equal Time Rules

Some parts of the Communications Act of 1934 that speak to the spirit of the Fairness Doctrine survived the doctrine's elimination in 1987. Section 315 of the Communications Act is an example. Section 315, known as the equal time rules, requires that if a broadcaster lets any legally qualified candidate for public office have time on the broadcast station, the broadcaster must provide the opportunity for equivalent time to all other legally qualified candidates for the same office. For example, if Jim Johnson is running for governor of Michigan and buys political ad time on the station, that station must make equivalent time available for all other qualified candidates for governor. Equivalent time is usually interpreted to mean a similar length of airtime reaching an audience similar in size and demographics. This time does not have to be provided free unless it was given to Johnson free; the broadcaster can charge the same rate charged to Johnson. A broadcaster can avoid the equal time rule by not making any time available to candidates, with one exception: candidates for federal office. The rules were amended in 1971 and now require that broadcasters make a reasonable amount of time available for purchase by federal candidates at their most favored advertising rate. The appearance on-air of any federal candidate will trigger the equal time rules for other qualified candidates for the same office. Given the frequency with which political candidates appear on broadcast stations—in interviews, talk shows, late night television, hosting *Saturday Night Live*, and so on—how can coverage of candidacies occur without triggering the equal time rules? In 1959, Congress stipulated that bona fide news events constitute an exception to the rules. These include regularly scheduled newscasts, news interview shows, news documentaries (as long as the candidate is not the focus), and on-the-spot news. Thus, a broadcast journalist covering a candidate as part of a regular news program will not trigger Section 315. Candidate appearances on other types of programs might, however. Section 315's news exception has been interpreted to include debates, press conferences, and morning shows such as the *Today Show*. The FCC has also included the *Phil Donahue Show, Sally Jessy Raphael, Jerry Springer,* and *Politically Incorrect,* so it is possible that any syndicated issue-based afternoon talk show might be included. Any appearance by a candidate that does not fall under the exception for bona fide news events triggers the rules. After Arnold Schwarzenegger announced his candidacy in the California

gubernatorial recall election, broadcast stations rescheduled
Schwarzenegger movies to avoid triggering the rules for the 134
candidates competing in the race. Exceptions to the rules are sometimes made. The FCC reclassified Howard Stern's radio program
as a news show so that Schwarzenegger could appear (Rodeffer
2003). During the 2004 presidential primary campaign, Democratic
primary candidate Reverend Al Sharpton appeared as a host for
Saturday Night Live. Because Sharpton was not a legally qualified
candidate in more than ten states, the equal time rule did not apply
at the national level. However, in states where Sharpton was on the
primary ballot, it was likely that stations carrying the program
would have to provide free airtime to other Democratic primary
candidates. As a result, thirty-two markets did not carry the program. Nevertheless, an NBC affiliate in Columbia, Missouri, still
ran the program because of its popularity. The station manager explained, "We felt the most appropriate thing to do is to show it and
be willing to accommodate those who might seek equal time"
(Sawyer and Morath 2003).

Finally, when political candidates do air political ads, can
broadcasters refuse the ad because of its content? A case arose out
of a political ad aired by Daniel Becker, a Georgia Republican
running for a House seat. It was not a typical ad but rather a
thirty-minute prolife infomercial that included images of aborted
fetuses. A television station wanted to refuse the ad or air it late at
night, when fewer children would be watching. The U.S. Court of
Appeals for the D.C. Circuit made it clear that broadcasters may
not control the content of political ads in any way (*Becker v. FCC*
[1996]). At the same time, broadcasters will not be held liable for
the content of political ads.

One extension of the equal time rule mandates equal time for
ads supporting a candidate in which the candidate does *not* appear.
The addition of the Zapple rule, named for Nicholas Zapple, former communications counsel for the Senate Committee on Commerce, who requested from the FCC clarification on the Fairness

Doctrine, sweeps under the Section 315 equal time provisions ads *about* qualified candidates. If such an ad created by the supporters of a qualified candidate appears, then supporters of other qualified candidates can request equal time.

Abolition of Personal Attack and Political Editorial Rules

These rules were manifestations of the Fairness Doctrine that survived the 1980s deregulation effort. Under the personal attack rules, if a station attacks the "honesty, character, integrity, or like personal qualities" of a specific person or groups, even while part of a discussion of a controversial issue, the station must do the following:

- Immediately notify the person attacked
- Provide that person with a tape or summary of what transpired
- Provide an opportunity for the person to respond

The political editorial rule stated that if a station aired an editorial taking a position on a legally qualified political candidate, the station must do the following:

- Provide the opposing candidate(s) with a tape of the editorial
- Provide the opposing candidate(s) with an opportunity to respond

However, the rules have been under attack since the early 1980s from broadcast lobby groups on First Amendment grounds. Similar challenges to the right of reply in newspapers were settled when the Supreme Court unanimously struck down a Florida statute permitting a right of reply to editorial attacks of political candidates in newspapers (*Miami Herald Publishing Co. v. Tornillo* [1974]). In 1983, the FCC issued a Notice of Proposed Rulemaking seeking feedback on a proposal to eliminate the two rules—but nothing happened. Lobby groups filed another petition with the FCC in 1987 asking for an expedited ruling. Again nothing happened. Another request came in 1990 saying the rules were obsolete. Finally, in 1998, the FCC admitted to being deadlocked on the issue. Lobby groups eventually appealed to the judicial system, and in 1999 a federal court ordered the FCC to provide a justification for keeping the rules (*Radio-Television News Directors Association v. FCC* [1999]). With insufficient progress from the FCC, the court ordered the rules immediately repealed on October 11, 2000, just twenty-seven days before the presidential election (*Radio-Television News Directors Association v. FCC* [2000]).

There are competing arguments over the impact of eliminating these rules. The decision to make this change in broadcast policy reflects a growing belief that the technical differences that once justified different regulatory frameworks for broadcasting and print no longer exist. There is no real scarcity (the argument goes), so there is no reason for the FCC to make policy on that basis. On the one hand, there are more full-time broadcast outlets in each market than there are daily newspapers. On the other hand, more broadcast stations within a single market are owned by the same company. These competing views of the constitutional status of broadcast journalism will drive much of the future debate over the regulation of broadcast news and information.

Indecency Standards

Because of the pervasive and intrusive nature of broadcasting technology, the courts and the FCC justify content restrictions in the case of sexual material that is indecent—a standard less protective of expression than the obscenity standard. This indecency standard emerged from a 1978 case involving George Carlin's *Filthy Words* monologue. The monologue was aired midafternoon as part of an on-air discussion on contemporary attitudes toward language. The host warned listeners beforehand about the language in Carlin's twelve-minute monologue. A man and his son tuned in to the station after the monologue began, so they did not hear the disclaimer. The father complained to the FCC. That complaint put in motion a series of rulings by the FCC reinforcing the law's prohibition on obscene, indecent, or profane language in broadcasting (18 U.S.C. §1464). Requests were made by media interests for reassurance that the indecency standard would not apply to news, and claims were made that the FCC was censoring broadcasting, something that exceeded its powers. Eventually the debate reached the Supreme Court. The Court recognized the FCC's ability to enforce content-based rules without running afoul of the First Amendment (*FCC v. Pacifica* [1978]).

However, the FCC does not have free rein to control content. It cannot censor by imposing a prior restraint. It cannot revoke a license for an indecency infraction. It may levy fines and use violations as a factor in considering license renewal applications. With the popularity of "shock jocks," the FCC has levied some significant fines. At the end of 2003, Infinity Broadcasting was fined $357,000 (spread across a number of their stations) for a 2002 St. Patrick's Cathedral sex stunt during the *Opie and Anthony* show (the two shock jocks were subsequently fired). In early 2004, the FCC proposed a $755,000 fine against Clear Channel Communications, the largest owner of radio stations in the country. The fine, the highest single fine ever levied by the FCC, was based on objectionable segments of the show *Bubba the Love Sponge,* which aired twenty-six times. At the same time, FCC chair Michael Powell, arguing that the current maximum per-incident fine is not enough of a deterrent, asked Congress for a tenfold increase, to $275,000 (Salant 2004).

Powell might be right, given the track record of the ultimate shock jock, Howard Stern. Indecency fines connected to his broadcasts through the 1990s totaled $1.7 million. Infinity Broadcasting, which has about 200 stations, and which has been the recipient of most of the fines related to Howard Stern's show, negotiated a settlement with the FCC whereby they did not pay a "fine" but instead made a $1.7 million "donation." Because the company did not pay for the specific violations, the FCC will not be able to consider the indecency "fines" as part of any Infinity license renewal requests.

At first glance, one would not expect indecency standards to be a concern for broadcast journalists. There is a suggestion that news would be exempt, but the FCC did not explicitly exempt news from indecency violations. What the FCC has said is that the context of the expression is central to determining indecency. For example, a news program about medical options for people with herpes might use sexually explicit language, but in a context that is unlikely to result in an indecency violation. However, if Howard Stern did a show on herpes, it is possible that the context might be more gratuitously sexual and subject to an indecency fine.

The lines are beginning to blur in an unusual way. As noted earlier, Howard Stern's radio show was reclassified as a news program to allow him to interview Arnold Schwarzenegger during the California gubernatorial recall election without triggering equal time rules for the other candidates (see the discussion on equal time rules).

In another example, a television news program was fined for content over which it had no control. In January 2004, a San Francisco television station was the first television station to be fined for indecent material. The FCC proposed fining the station $27,500 for broadcasting indecent material on its morning news show. During an interview of a member of a puppetry program titled "Puppetry of the Penis," the performer briefly exposed himself. The FCC claimed that the station should have anticipated the possibility. The fact that the broadcast in question was a news program did not appear to be a mitigating factor.

Although not involving the press per se, the 2004 CBS Superbowl halftime show, produced by MTV (both CBS and MTV are owned by Viacom) reinvigorated the FCC's efforts to clamp down on broadcast indecency after a "wardrobe malfunction" resulted in the singer Janet Jackson exposing one breast on national television.

OBSERVATIONS ABOUT
CABLE TELEVISION AND THE INTERNET

Most of the issues facing cable and the Internet are future oriented and will be addressed in the next chapter. But it is important to understand the impact that both media have had on the nature of news.

Cable television has been around for a long time. As far back as the mid-1950s, homes in rural mountainous areas have shared a tall community antenna with wires running to each house. Today, cable is a 100-plus channel universe with an insatiable hunger for content. The launch of 24-hour news channels has increased the demand for stories and visuals. These channels have reinvigorated international news coverage and provided audiences with a steady diet of news, if one takes a generous view of the definition of news. Evidence of cable news's success is the challenge to CNN's dominance by MSNBC, Fox News, and CNBC. Local news stations are jumping on board with the introduction of regional cable news channels.

Additionally, cable television is not bound to the same indecency rules governing broadcasting. Since it is not delivered through the airwaves and simple technology is available to block cable channels, the courts provide cable companies greater leeway on content. Most cable systems also provide "access" channels. Community members can produce and air their own programs for these channels. Talk and issue-based news shows are some of the most common programs on these channels, but numerous communities have had to deal with more controversial content such as neo-Nazi programming, Ku Klux Klan talk shows, and community news and issue programming delivered by naked hosts. The lack of editorial control over the content of access programming is a characteristic that cable shares with the Internet.

The Internet, while much younger, also provides an almost unlimited outlet for news. Unlike broadcast and print media, the Internet has no gatekeepers, either preventing good information from being disseminated or preventing poorly researched news or downright false information from being posted on the Web. The implications of these technological innovations, especially in terms of reinventing the ways audiences interpret the validity of news and information, cannot be underestimated. It is in the twenty-first century where those new ways of thinking about freedom of expression for a whole new kind of press will be played out.

REFERENCES AND FURTHER READING

American Civil Liberties Union of Michigan. 1999. "Battle Creek Mayor Stifles Free Speech" (16 April). Available at *http://www.aclumich.org/ modules.php?name=News&file=article&sid=32.*

Arce, Rose. 2003. "Jayson Blair Sells Tell-All Book." CNN.com (10 September). Available at *http://www.cnn.com/2003/SHOWBIZ/books/ 09/10/jayson.blair.book/.*

Carvajal, Doreen. 1991. "The Great Quote Question: How Much Tampering with Quotations Can Journalists Ethically Do?" *FineLine: The Newsletter on Journalism Ethics* 3:1, 8.

Coté, John. 2004. "Prosecutors: Peterson Fueled Publicity." *The Modesto Bee* (4 January). Available at *http://www.modbee.com/local/story/ 7962621p–8836040c.html.*

Dennis, Everette E., David Stebenne, John Pavlik, Mark Thalhimer, Craig LaMay, Dirk Smilli, Martha FitzSimon, Shirley Gazsi, and Seth Rachlin. 1991. *The Media at War: The Press and the Persian Gulf.* New York: Gannett Foundation Media Center.

Dias, Monica. 2002. "Leggett's Case Revives Talk about Shield Law." *News Media and the Law* 26:7.

Eaton, Sabrina. 2003. "Bernstein Blasts Professor, School's 'Throat' Probe." *Cleveland Plain Dealer* (25 April):A2.

Fowler, Mark, and Daniel Brenner. 1982. "A Marketplace Approach to Broadcast Regulation." *Texas Law Review* 60:207–257.

Gaines, Bill, et al. 2003. "Dean Unyielding on Fielding." Department of Journalism, University of Illinois, Urbana-Champaign. Available at *http://deepthroatuncovered.com/story/21.html.*

Gottschalk, Jack A. 1983. "'Consistent with Security' . . . A History of American Military Press Censorship." *Communications and the Law* 5:35–52.

Graefe, Jeffrey T. 1993. "Note: Communications Law: Differential Taxation of the Media: Leathers v. Medlock: Prejudicial or Profitable?" *Oklahoma Law Review* 46:713–728.

Hopkins, Wat W. ed. 2000. *Communications and the Law*. Northport, AL: Vision Press.

Kinsley, Michael. 2003. "Sympathy for the *New York Times*." *Slate.MSN.com* (21 May). Available at *http://slate.msn.com/id/2083377/.*

Knightley, Phillip. 1975. *The First Casualty: From the Crimea to Vietnam: The War Correspondent as Hero, Propagandist, and Myth Maker*. New York: Harcourt Brace Jovanovich.

Kurtz, Howard. 2003. "New York Times Story Gives Texas Paper a Sense of Déjà Vu." *Washington Post* (30 April):C01.

Middleton, Kent R., William E. Lee, and Bill F. Chamberlin. (2004). *The Law of Public Communication*, 6th ed. New York: Pearson.

New York City Department of Transportation. 2004. "Newsracks Introduction." Available at http://www.nyc.gov/html/dot/html/permits/newsracksintro.html

OMB Watch. 2002. "The Government in Sunshine Act." *OMB Watch* (1 February). Available at *http://www.ombwatch.org/article/articleview/193/1/67/.*

Overbeck, Wayne. 2004. *Major Principles of Media Law*. Belmont, CA: Thompson.

Packer, Cathy, and Karla K. Cower. 1997. "The Persistent Problem of Media Taxation: First Amendment Protection in the 1990s." *Journalism and Mass Communication Quarterly* 74:579–589.

Pember, Don R. 2003. *Mass Media Law*. New York: McGraw-Hill.

Penenberg, Adam L. 1998. "Lies, Damn Lies, and Fiction." *Forbes.com* (11 May). Available at *http://www.forbes.com/1998/05/11/otw3.html.*

Pew Research Center. 2002. "Public News Habits Little Changed by September 11th." Available at *http://people–press.org/reports/ display. php3?ReportID=156.*

Pressman, Steve. 2004. "An Unfettered Press: Libel Law in the United States." U.S. Department of State, International Information Programs. Available at *http://usinfo.state.gov/products/pubs/press/press08.htm.*

Reporters Committee on Freedom of the Press. 1996. "Two Federal Appellate Courts Vote to Allow Cameras" (8 April). Available at *http://www.rcfp.org/news/1996/0408m.html.*

———. 1998. "Paparazzi Bill Passes Legislature, Awaits Governor's Approval" (21 September). Available at *http://www.rcfp.org/news/1998/0921l.html.*

———. 2000. "The News Media Must Keep Fighting the 'Gag Instinct'." *The News Media and The Law* (Spring). Available at *http://www. rcfp.org/news/mag/24-2/edit-thenewsm.html.*

———. 2002. "Newspapers Battle Newsrack Ordinances." *The News Media and The Law* (Winter). Available at *http://www.rcfp.org/news/ mag/26-1/new-newsrack.html.*

———. 2004. "Paying the Price." Available at *http://www.rcfp.org/ jail.html.*

Rodeffer, Mark H. 2003. "NBC Affiliates May Not Show Sharpton on 'SNL'." CNN.com (4 December). Available at *http://www.cnn.com/ 2003/ALLPOLITICS/12/04/elec04.prez.sharpton.snl.*

Salant, Jonathan D. 2004. "Hearing on On-Air Indecency Focus on Fines, FCC Vigilance." *Philadelphia Inquirer* (29 January). Available at *http://www.philly.com/mld/inquirer/news/magazine/daily/7820545. htm.*

Sawyer, Jon, and Eric Morath. 2003. "Sharpton on 'SNL' Thrusts Equal Time into Spotlight." *St. Louis Post-Dispatch* (8 December). Available at *http://www.stltoday.com/stltoday/news/stories.nsf/News/Nation/.*

Shapiro, Martin. 1972. *The Pentagon Papers and the Courts.* San Francisco: Chandler Publishing Co.

Smolla, Rodney A. 1999. *Law of Defamation.* 2nd ed. St. Paul, MN: West.

Stephenson, Donald Grier. 1979. "Fair Trial–Free Press: Rights in Continuing Conflict." *Brooklyn Law Review* 46:39–66.

Stone, Geoffrey R. 2003. "Judge Learned Hand and the Espionage Act of 1917: A Mystery Unraveled." *University of Chicago Law Review* 70:335–358.

Student Press Law Center. 2003a. "Mass. Principal Prevents Paper from Publishing Articles Critical of Her Policies" (10 December). Available at *http://splc.org/newsflash.asp*.

Student Press Law Center. 2003b. "Few Support More First Amendment Rights for High School Students, Survey Finds" (8 August). Available at *http://splc.org/newsflash_archives.asp*.

Student Press Law Center. 2004. *"Hosty v. Carter:* The Latest Battle for College Press Freedom." Available at *http://www.splc.org/legalresearch.asp?id=49*.

Tedford, Thomas L. 2001. *Freedom of Speech in the United States,* 4th ed. State College, PA: Strata Publishing.

Warren, Samuel, and Louis Brandeis. 1890. "The Right to Privacy." *Harvard Law Review* 4:193–220.

Yank Magazine. 2002. "Yank Magazine Files Suit Against San Francisco for Violations of Freedom of the Press and Free Speech." News release, 5 April.

4

TWENTY-FIRST-CENTURY
ISSUES

When reviewing the progress and evolution of the First Amendment's protection of press freedoms, one has an impulse to suggest that the twenty-first century is an extraordinary time to be a journalist. There is some truth to such a statement. There are more ways to "be" a journalist than ever before. Technological options for news delivery systems continue to multiply. Technology has reshaped the face of news in exciting if also problematic ways.

Yet, as earlier chapters have shown, each of the past few centuries has been marked by its own extraordinary moments for journalism and press freedoms, some good and some troubling. Certainly not every moment was inspiring or representative of the best of journalistic ethics or practices. Not every press-related court decision reaffirmed the principal value this country places on the free flow of information. Yet each century contained instances of journalistic greatness, from the work of the abolitionist press to the courageous war coverage in Vietnam to the emblematic and iconic work of Bob Woodward and Carl Bernstein.

What does this new millennium have in store for freedom of the press? Certainly there are events, ideas, and challenges yet unanticipated. However, with only a few years of the twenty-first century having passed, already some fascinating trends in press freedoms are emerging. Technological advances continue to send surges through the practice of journalism, altering, for example, the power dynamic between the press and the military. New forms of information control are emerging on the heels of literally instantaneous transmission of front-line war news. No longer are obstacles such as geographical distance or remoteness a barrier to timely transmission of news.

Technological innovation is changing the very definition of journalist as the Internet provides the means for anyone to practice "the trade." There is no cyberspace editor scrutinizing content or ensuring that professional standards of journalism are maintained. Journalists themselves are using cyberspace to explore new forms of expression through the use of Web logs ("blogs"), a virtual space that allows journalists to break free of traditional notions of the journalistic writing structure (the inverted pyramid) and create something on the order of a journalist's "journal."

Technological convergence, in combination with two decades of deregulation, is reshaping the ownership and business structures of the media. Large corporations are swallowing smaller media outlets. Local new operations are consolidating, regionalizing, and networking. A single company may own more and more media within a single market. Cities fortunate enough to host two daily newspapers increasingly find the papers merging noneditorial operations under joint operating agreements.

These patterns suggest that two significant forces are driving twenty-first-century press freedoms: technological innovation and shifts in media regulation. Much of this chapter will integrate the two. For example, some technological innovations are promoting new regulatory frameworks, undermining the rationale for other regulatory structures and ultimately outpacing most regulatory efforts. Likewise, existing regulatory traditions are shaping the use of new technologies. To begin, however, let's look at the twenty-first-century extensions of the classic areas of press law: trends in the traditional areas of libel and privacy law.

The New Libels: Product Disparagement, Business Defamation, and SLAPP Lawsuits

With all the news stories about mad cow disease and safe food supplies, farmers and ranchers have a deepening sense of what bad publicity can do to the health of their industries. The media have a unique ability to inflate the level of public attention to and concern about issues that have a relatively minor impact through intensive coverage. Communication theorists refer to this as the agenda-setting effect of news coverage (McCombs and Shaw, 1972). Although the press is not necessarily effective at directly telling the public what to think, it seems particularly good at telling the public what to think *about*. In other words, intense coverage of a topic raises its relative importance in the public mind. Intensive coverage is the modus operandi of the highly competitive modern media industry, which has an insatiable appetite for content. This hunger is heightened by the presence of multiple 24-hour cable news networks, hours of daily local news broadcasts, primetime network news programs, and Internet versions of all of these media as well as most print news.

The surge of public concern about the risk of mad cow disease is a good example of agenda setting. In early 2004, there was one documented case of mad cow disease in the United States, traced to a cow imported from Canada. That single case prompted calls to test every cow for the disease (not realistically possible) and resulted in the destruction of hundreds of cattle out of concern that other cows from the Canadian herd (imported to the States but never clearly identified) might also be infected. The media fascination with the story may well lead to improvements in the handling of meat products, but that is an outcome unrelated to the importance the news attached to an isolated instance of mad cow disease. Similar effects arose from the severe acute respiratory syndrome (SARS) scare in late 2003. And there continues to be an excessive media-fed fear that a child will be abducted by a stranger, when in fact the overwhelming majority of abductions are committed by acquaintances or family members.

The economic fallout from these news-constructed crises can be significant. Toronto, for example, with numerous reported cases of SARS, lost substantial tourist revenue. So it may not seem surprising that some states have passed laws that make journalists increasingly vulnerable to product disparagement lawsuits. These trade libel or "veggie" libel laws exist in about thirteen states, mainly states with big investments in food production. One of the first notable lawsuits of this kind occurred in the mid-1990s, when CBS was sued for a *60 Minutes* segment on apple producers' use of a chemical called Alar (daminozide). The *60 Minutes* report suggested that consumption of Alar, typically sprayed on apples as a preservative, was linked with cancer. Not surprisingly, apple consumption declined, costing growers an estimated $130 million. Washington apple growers sued under Washington's food disparagement law, claiming the CBS report was false or greatly exaggerated. The appellate court dismissed the case because the apple growers faced the impossible task of proving that CBS's claim was false (*Auvil v. CBS 60 Minutes*, 67 F.3d 816 [1995]).

On the heels of the Alar case, product disparagement laws were modified to better protect the agricultural industry, allowing food producers to sue the media when false information (that is, information that is not based on reliable scientific data) was published suggesting the product was unsafe. In other words, any news report suggesting a food product was unsafe had better be supported by reliable scientific data. This requirement has increased the press's exposure to trade libel suits. Even if the media are likely to prevail in such a lawsuit, they have to expend money and resources on a defense.

Returning to the example of mad cow disease, it first appeared on the U.S. media's radar in 1996, when British researchers announced a connection between mad cow disease and a fatal human brain disorder. The researcher thought the most likely source of infection was consumption of infected beef. The sequence of the media events that followed is described in the opinion of a U.S. district court in Texas:

> The British Health Minister's announcement generated numerous reports in the United States. Print media reports included: A March 21, 1996, *New York Times* article announced "Britain Ties Deadly Brain Disease to Cow Ailment." On March 28, 1996, *The Wall Street Journal* ran an article entitled "Agriculture Officials Say Mad-Cow Risk Is Small in U.S. but Don't Rule It Out." An April 5, 1996, *New York Times* article that quoted an expert estimating that "a teaspoonful of highly infective cattle feed is enough to cause mad-cow disease." An April 8, 1996, *Newsweek* headline read, "Mad Cow Disease in the U.S.? Don't panic, but one version's already here." Television reports included: A March 14, 1996, *Dateline* report on Mad Cow Disease which included video of a CJD [Creutzfeldt-Jakob disease] victim hospitalized in New York. On March 22, 1996, CNBC's *America's Talking* aired a segment on Mad Cow Disease that featured a debate between Dr. Gary Weber and Howard Lyman. The CNBC program attracted the attention of staffers on *The Oprah Winfrey Show* to Weber and Lyman as prospective guests for the "Dangerous Foods" program. (*Texas Beef Group v. Winfrey*, 11 F. Supp. 2d 858 [N.D. Texas 1998] 861)

During the discussion of mad cow disease on the *Oprah* show, Winfrey commented, "It has just stopped me cold from eating another burger." As a testimony to the power of the *Oprah* show, cattle prices dropped. Texas ranchers sued Winfrey, putting to the test the state's False Disparagement of Perishable Food Products Act. Winfrey prevailed, but not because of her free press or free speech rights (although she may ultimately have prevailed on First Amendment grounds) but because the Texas judge determined that beef in the form of live cattle was not a perishable agricultural product.

As with traditional libel law, the constitutional protection provided to the press requires that the plaintiff bear the burden of proof. Thus, in the *Winfrey* case, ranchers faced the burden of proving that Winfrey intended to harm the industry by knowingly making false statements. Likewise, in October 2003, Sharper Image filed a product disparagement lawsuit against Consumers Union over a report criticizing the effectiveness of its Ionic Breeze Quadra air cleaner. Consumers Union brought a "special motion to strike" in order to force Sharper Image "to show that its claims have legal and factual merit, thus placing a heavy burden of proof on the plaintiff" (Consumers Union 2003).

Another defamation tort permits businesses to sue if false defamatory statements harm the company's reputation. The business defamation tort has been used more than once to target Consumers Union, which publishes *Consumer Reports,* a product testing and review magazine. In the mid-1980s, the Bose Corporation unsuccessfully sued Consumers Union over a critical review of the company's speakers (*Bose Corp. v. Consumers Union,* 466 U.S. 485 [1984]). A trade libel lawsuit with the Suzuki Motor Corporation over a poor safety rating for its Samurai SUV is pending. Suzuki is requesting $60 million in damages. The automobile company must show that Consumers Union acted with actual malice. The initial efforts on the part of Consumers Union to have the case dismissed were unsuccessful, and a jury trial is scheduled for late 2004. However, in a severely divided Ninth Circuit Court en banc hearing, Judge Alex Kozinski articulated the key concern about trade libel lawsuits:

> I find it incomprehensible that a review truthfully disclosing all this information could be deemed malicious under *New York Times Co. v.*

Sullivan, 376 U. S. 254 (1964). If CU can be forced to go to trial after this thorough and candid disclosure of its methods, this is the death of consumer ratings: It will be impossible to issue a meaningful consumer review that a band of determined lawyers can't pick apart in front of a jury. The ultimate losers will be American consumers denied access to independent information about the safety and usefulness of products they buy with their hard-earned dollars (*Suzuki Motor Corp. v. Consumers Union of United States, Inc.,* 330 F.3d [2003], 1110– 1113).

Kozinski's language is reminiscent of earlier court justifications for the protection of commercial speech. Although commercial speech does not enjoy the same level of vigorous protection that other forms of speech do, the courts recognize the importance of protecting a company's right to advertise because of the importance of providing customers with the information necessary to make informed choices. Consumers Union clearly enjoys the full protection provided to the press, but its legal problems represent the kind of risks the press runs into when criticizing the products and activities of major corporations.

Businesses have yet another means by which to sue critics of the company, products, policies, or practices. A company, especially a large one, has far more resources for the financial expense of a lawsuit than most individuals or small-scale media companies. Thus, a lawsuit or the threat of a lawsuit may provide sufficient pressure to squelch further criticism. These suits, known disparagingly as strategic lawsuits against public participation (SLAPP), are a relatively new legal strategy. The term SLAPP was coined by two University of Denver faculty members in a 1988 article outlining the implications such suits have for political participation (Canan and Pring 1988).

Some states have created anti-SLAPP statutes to serve as a deterrent to the use of SLAPP suits. In recent years, the California Supreme Court, for example, has broadly interpreted the reach of the state's anti-SLAPP statute. In three decisions, the court strengthened "the protection for expressive activities by confirming that the statute applies to any lawsuit arising from a defendant's exercise of First Amendment rights—even where the plaintiff did not subjectively intend to chill the defendant's expression, and even where the defendant's expression is alleged to be a breach of confidentiality or otherwise unlawful" (Sager and Wilcox 2003). Toward the end of 2003, the California legislature passed an amendment to the bill to address the growing number of businesses that were, ironically, using the anti-SLAPP statute against consumers (California Code of Civil Procedure, Sec. 425.17, 2004). The amendment focused on stopping what Governor Gray Davis called the "corporate abuse" of the statute and refocused its purpose of protecting the First Amendment rights of California citizens (Office of the Governor of California 2003).

In spite of the growing number of business and trade libel suits and product disparagement suits, determining when the press has acted with actual malice is extremely difficult, because it is a much higher standard than the simple making of a mistake. The plaintiff must show that the press knowingly published false information or was reckless in addressing its responsibility to verify the story's truthfulness before publishing. Additionally, the courts often recognize that the press must have the First Amendment "space" to make a mistake. The "single mistake rule" protects the press from lawsuits resulting from a single error by requiring that plaintiffs prove that the statements in question reflect a pattern of journalistic incompetence or recklessness.

As new areas of libel develop, some of them, such as product disparagement and business or trade libel, demand serious judicial scrutiny. The press has a well-established constitutional and common law protection against libel charges. Unless the plaintiff is a private individual and the defamation is an issue of private concern, the plaintiff generally bears the entire burden of proof. That protection, in combination with the requirement that the plaintiff bears the difficult challenge of proving that the defamatory statement was false, provides a wide mantle of protection for the press.

WHERE'S THE GATEKEEPER?
THE CHALLENGE OF THE INTERNET

Not too long ago, a delightful television advertisement for high-speed DSL Internet service aired that began with a man sitting off in a room surfing the Internet. He hears his computer say in a computer-like voice, "You have reached the end of the Internet. Please go back." He gets up and walks into the next room; his wife asks why he is not still surfing the 'Net, to which he responds that he is finished. In reality, of course, there is no end of the Internet, because there are no real boundaries. It is a seemingly endless collection of everything from high-quality research to news to junk to commerce to pornography. This expanse of virtual space poses all sorts of interesting challenges and opportunities for the press. It is also making a mess of the established, comparatively tidy categories of media law. The Internet does not face spectrum limitations, as broadcasting does, yet it delivers content to the user in a way that is visually similar to broadcasting. Children and youths use the Internet readily, and arguably young people are using the Internet more often than they do other informational media, such as newspapers. Today's youths, if they read news, are likely to read it online.

Users of the Internet—which consists of a vast array of linked networks—gain access to the World Wide Web—comprising innumerable documents, home pages, images, and so on—by subscribing to an Internet service provider (ISP), such as Earthlink, America Online, Juno, Net-Zero, and so on. The relationship between the Internet and users makes it different from other media. The current regulatory environment for the Internet, shaped by several court decisions, appears to mimic that of print media more than those of broadcasting and cable television. Still, concerns remain about the Internet because of the availability of inappropriate material to minors (such as sexually explicit images and unmonitored "chat rooms") as well as privacy, security, and fraud. The continuing problem facing any regulatory effort is, simply, the slow-moving machinery of government, which leaves regulators struggling to keep pace with a class of technology that is developing in rapid and unexpected ways.

Along with the explosion of information on the Internet, there is plenty of "journalism" in cyberspace, which makes freedom of the press an important consideration. Most newspapers have on-line editions, for example, and most broadcast news networks and stations have highly developed Web sites. Search portals, such as those of Yahoo, Google, Netscape, and so on, use news services in an effort to hold users at the portal site longer while ad banners appear. Most traditional news outlets, including the *New York Times*—"the newspaper of record"—offer customized news delivery, which one legal scholar, concerned about the civic repercussions of selective exposure to customized information, calls the "Daily Me" (Sunstein 2001). How, then, do traditional free press issues translate to the virtual world?

Appropriation and the Internet

One of the new forms of misappropriation involves the plethora of unauthorized images of celebrities appearing on the Web. Generally, this is not a pressing issue for journalists (unless they maintain private Web sites), because use of celebrity images on a Web site as part of a news story is not subject to appropriation lawsuits. But the line between news and non-news Web sites is hazy, and thus it is not completely clear when use of a "likeness" is newsworthy and when it may constitute unauthorized appropriation.

There are more visual cues associated with traditional forms of news—newspapers, news magazines, television news—that help in discerning when the news exemption applies. The Web can be less clear. The visual norms of the Web are still emerging and are not always distinct. A Web site for the NBC *Today* show and a fan site for the *Today* show may not look significantly different. One may have to look at other clues, such as the URL or copyright information to determine the nature and ownership of the site.

Also, although *appropriation* is not a concern with news, *copyright* is a different story. If a news organization publishes someone else's photograph of a celebrity on its Web site, the organization may be in violation of copyright.

Finally, a critical factor in regulation of the Web is that the Internet is not confined by the geopolitical boundaries of the nation-state. This means that the ability to sue for content on Web sites based outside the United States is dramatically limited. It also means that, because a Web site based in Oklahoma can be viewed anywhere, a celebrity seeking to sue for appropriation can go jurisdiction shopping to find a sympathetic court or favorable state laws.

Libel and the Internet

Who is liable when a defamatory statement is posted on the Internet? One of the new areas of libel law involves determining the extent of liability for ISPs and other Web sites hosting listservs, bulletin boards, or discussion groups. The Telecommunications Act of 1996 and the parts of the Communications Decency Act that survived constitutional challenge provide a protective shell for ISPs. Internet service providers may screen out obscene material and interact with content in other ways in an effort to manage services such as bulletin boards. In such cases, a federal appellate court has ruled that ISPs are not liable for content posted by a third party (*Zeran v. America Online*, 129 F.3d 327 [1997]). This protection does not apply to the producers of content. Journalists or media firms that maintain their own Web sites are liable for the content of their sites. E-mail messages are also subject to libel suits if they contain defamatory material and are widely disseminated and otherwise meet the standards of proof for libel.

The number of Internet libel cases is growing. One notable Internet defamation case involved the cyber-gossip of Matt Drudge on his Web site, the *Drudge Report*. The *Drudge Report* garnered public attention when it broke the story of the President Clinton–Monica Lewinsky affair. But it was Drudge's later story in which he suggested that President Clinton's aide, Sidney Blumenthal, had a history of spousal abuse that triggered the first high-profile libel case involving a "news" Web site. Drudge retracted his story the next day, but Blumenthal filed a $30 million lawsuit against Drudge and AOL, the ISP that carried some of Drudge's content. The suit against AOL was dropped because of the *Zeran* ruling (*Blumenthal v. Drudge*, 26 Media L. Rep. 1717 [1998]), but the case against Drudge proceeded. At one point, Drudge tried to get the case dismissed by arguing that it was a SLAPP suit. The court denied the petition (*Blumenthal v. Drudge*, 29 Media L. Rep. 1347 [2001]). Ultimately, Blumenthal dropped the suit and paid a small fee to Drudge's legal counsel, with the condition that Drudge not countersue (Kurtz 2001). One notable outcome of the case was that in one of the rulings the court determined that Drudge was *not* a journalist. If the case had proceeded to trial, that may have affected the level of fault that Blumenthal would have needed to prove.

Blogs: Random Acts of Journalism?

The practice of journalism has found a home in most forms of media, including the Internet. Moreover, what it takes to be called a journalist is relatively loosely defined. It is easy to conclude that the content reported in daily newspapers is journalism, even if it is not always good journalism. Most magazine writing falls under the umbrella of journalism, whether it is a lengthy *New Yorker* magazine piece or a brief description of European fashion trends in *Mademoiselle*. We might categorize the stories differently— hard news, soft news, features, and so on—but they are still recognized as journalism. The work of the New Journalists—defined by a kind of creative nonfiction and emblematized by Hunter S. Thompson, Tom Wolfe, and Truman Capote in the 1960s and 1970s—found legitimacy as a journalistic enterprise over time. In short, journalism encompasses many forms of writing that diverge markedly from the traditional inverted pyramid story structure and explore different narrative storytelling styles.

The Internet is yet another medium for practicing journalism. Although the colonization of the Web by the traditional media has largely been an extension of the local, regional, and national news outlets, a new form of Internet journalism that goes beyond news media Web sites is gaining momentum. Journalists themselves are creating and maintaining official and personal Web logs, or "blogs." Blogs are continuously updated Web-based postings. They tend to be more personal and opinionated, and, depending on their purpose, they may contain additional or breaking news that didn't fit into the confines of newspaper or news broadcast formats. This new phenomenon comes with its own vocabulary. People who post blogs are bloggers. The practice of posting blogs is called blogging.

In one form or another, blogs have been around as long as the World Wide Web has. The first Web log is generally attributed to Dave Winer, who remains an active voice in the debates surrounding the use of blogs in journalism (Lasica 2001a). It was the development of blogger-friendly software (the first being Pitas.com in July 1999) that dramatically expanded the growth of these "diaries" on the Web.

The first newspaper blog is credited to the Charlotte *Observer* in North Carolina, which provided ongoing Web postings during Hurricane Bonnie in 1998 (Scanlan 2003). It was an innovative way to provide up-to-the-minute coverage of a major regional event. The content was like that of traditional news; it was the way it was delivered that was new. But simply posting print versions of stories or providing breaking news updates is not the only way journalists use blogs. Technology journalist and blogger J.D. Lasica refers to Web logs as the "anti-newspaper," meaning that they have some characteristics that are distinctly different from traditional news media.

Where the editorial process can filter out errors and polish a piece of copy to a fine sheen, too often the machinery renders even fine prose limp, lifeless, sterile, and homogenized. A huge part of blogs' appeal lies in their unmediated quality. Blogs tend to be impressionistic, telegraphic, raw, honest, individualistic, highly opinionated, and passionate, often striking an emotional chord (Lasica 2001a).

Blog content may range from "daily minutiae to manifestoes to sophisticated political and cultural commentary and reporting" (Jensen 2003). Blogs often include a mechanism for readers to provide feedback, which creates a more interactive relationship between journalists and readers than exists with newspapers or broadcast news. Dan Gillmor, a *San Jose Mercury News* columnist and author of one of the longest continuously published blogs, finds that the most interesting quality of his blog is the interactive, participatory nature of his entries. Readers respond, comment, and correct postings in what amounts to an ongoing conversation (Lasica 2001a).

Breaking news lends itself well to the blog format. *Florida Today* posted continual updates on the *Columbia* shuttle explosion. KFOR-TV reporter Sarah Stewart blogged the developments of a high-profile murder trial using a laptop and an Internet connection through a cell phone. David Abrams, of the Virginia *Gazette,* blogged the trial of Washington, D.C., sniper John Allen Muhammad. Using wireless technology, he filed minute-by-minute updates that mimicked live reporting. It is a comparatively effective alternative to live continuous coverage when courtrooms do not allow the use of cameras (American Press Institute 2004a).

Blogs sometimes function as a supplement to a reporter's print or broadcast news story. A reporter might use a blog to provide additional news or background facts and Web links, or to develop personal reflections or opinions that would not be appropriate as part of an objective news story. This type of reflective, opinion-based blogging, however, raises a host of questions about the practice of journalism. For blogs associated with an existing media outlet, such as a newspaper, how opinionated may a reporter or columnist be in an online forum? What are the editorial obligations of a newspaper to ensure credibility and accuracy in a blog? Some newspapers require that blogs pass through an editor before posting. The *Sacramento Bee* instituted such a policy after readers complained about the postings of Daniel Weintraub during the California gubernatorial recall election. However, passing material through the editorial process may increase the media outlet's liability for its content.

Many new media outlets do not edit their blogs. Gregg Easterbrook, a senior editor at the *New Republic,* maintained an unedited blog on the magazine's Web site. In one posting he made ethnic slurs about the heads of Disney and Miramax studios as part of an entry about the Quentin Tarantino movie *Kill Bill Vol. 1.* His remarks prompted him to issue an apology, which was also posted on JewishFilm.com. The incident provides real insight into the pitfalls associated with the immediacy of blogs:

I'm ready to defend all the thoughts in that paragraph. But how could I have done such a poor job of expressing them? Maybe this is an object lesson in the new blog reality. I worked on this alone and posted the piece—what you see above comes at the end of a 1,017-word column that's otherwise about why movies should not glorify violence. Twenty minutes after I pressed "send," the entire world had read it. When I reread my own words and beheld how I'd written things that could be misunderstood, I felt awful. To anyone who was offended I offer my apology, because offense was not my intent. But it was 20 minutes later, and already the whole world had seen it. (Easterbrook 2003)

In this case, the recognition of the mistake seemed sufficient to end the matter. That has not always been the case. At least one journalist has been fired for content on his blog. Steve Olafson, a reporter for the *Houston Chronicle,* maintained a personal blog under the pseudonym Banjo Jones. In his blog, he criticized some of the public officials he covered as a reporter. He also criticized the *Chronicle.* When his identity was revealed, he was fired because his boss believed he had "compromised his ability to do his job" (Gallagher 2002).

Another type of blog is emerging in concert with the 2004 elections. "Watchblogs" are dedicated to tracking election coverage in various media. Typically they are maintained by regular citizens, not by journalists or media outlets. Watchblogs, an entirely new spin on the letter to the editor, reader feedback, and media criticism, are designed to monitor press coverage of the election. In short, it is a watchdog for the watchdog. Most watchblogs operate with a political or ideological agenda. Some do a comprehensive job of monitoring the record of reporting on candidates, and others remain anonymous and lack credibility.

The wide range of blogs illustrates the ongoing debate over the way blogs reinvent journalism on the Internet. As with much Web content, notions of objectivity and editorial gatekeeping are not presumed. Professional training and adherence to a set of professional norms are not a prerequisite to "doing" journalism.

The fluidity of blogging practices has generated plenty of skeptics about the role of blogs in newsgathering. Instead of exercising editorial oversight, some media outlets pressured their journalists to shut down their blogs. CNN asked correspondent Kevin Sites, who was covering the war in Iraq, to shut down the blog he started in early March 2003. After a six-month hiatus, Sites's blog is back, and he is a freelance journalist on assignment for NBC News. His Web site, *www.kevinsites.net,* carries a disclaimer that the space is a personal site and is not affiliated with NBC.

The *New York Times* started a blog called *"Times* on the Trail" to cover the 2004 political campaign. The *Times* exercises editorial control over the blog, but intends to use the site in a different way. According to Len Apcar, editor in chief of *NYTimes.com,*

> We thought there were a lot of blogs out there, but we didn't neces-
> sarily think that the quality was very good. We thought that there was
> a lot of rumor out there, a lot of wild opinion being bandied about,
> but we also thought there was a vehicle here for short-form informa-
> tion, continuous updating, some development observations, insights,
> that might not rise to a full article but are worthy of reporting. (Dube
> 2004)

Apcar called the debates over editing and over whether a news-paper should blog a "red herring." He refers to the *New York Times* experiment not as a blog but as an updated news service. The *Times* may be breaking new ground in its particular approach to managing blog content, but it is by no means at the forefront of media blogs. There are at least 100 different official, ongoing news media blogs. They tend to be less controversial journalistically than the 100-plus independent journalists' Web logs (American Press Institute 2004b). These blogs, like that of Kevin Sites, men-tioned above, contain the personal reflections of journalists and remain formally distinct from the media outlet for which the jour-nalists work, or they are the blogs of journalists unaffiliated with any other media outlet.

An interesting emerging phenomenon seen with independent journalists is "blograising." Several journalists have placed appeals for financial contributions on their blogs. Most requests are for funding to cover costs associated with a specific story. For example, Christopher Allbritton, a former AP reporter, posted a request for funds to allow him to travel to Iraq as an independent reporter. His appeal brought in about $13,000 (Cox 2003). Independent journalists and blograising are presenting interesting questions about the practice of journalism, the editorial function, the notion of interested readers paying for a specific story, and, ultimately, whether blogging is a legitimate form of journalism.

Some online journalists believe blogging is the best form of journalism, free of constraints on expression and outside a system that is "inherently compromised by the business interests and skewed editorial policies of their publications" (Lasica 2001a). As one freelance journalist and blogger suggests, "blogging [is] neither superior or inferior to traditional journalism—just infinitely fascinating" (Lasica 2001b). Blogging may be the "purest form of journalism" (Heyboer and Rosen 2004, 10). The jury is still out on blogging as a form of journalism, but in the wake of the war in Iraq and in the heat of the 2004 presidential campaign, blogs are increasingly common on the Web and continue to have an impact on traditional forms and structures of news delivery.

In the end, more questions than answers about blogging remain. Are bloggers journalists? Mickey Kaus, who operates the Web log, *kausfiles.com,* believes they are journalists, but a different kind of journalist operating in an environment with different standards (Rutenberg 2004). Yet the issue remains unsettled. The judge in Blumenthal's libel suit against Matt Drudge, for example, concluded that Drudge was not a journalist.

If we are to assume that bloggers are journalists, should they enjoy the same press protections that traditional media journalists enjoy? Will the traditional rules of libel and invasion of privacy apply to bloggers? Will plaintiffs filing lawsuits against bloggers have to show actual malice? Will various codes of professional practice emerge in order to mitigate the kinds of journalism that generate lawsuits? Would such codes stifle the freewheeling form of blogs?

Should professional norms and structures be established for blogs so that it is easier to distinguish objective news coverage from opinion? Should blogs be considered valid or reliable news sources? Should media outlets edit blogs and risk liability? Would it violate reporters' First Amendment rights for a media employer to require its journalists not to file Web logs?

Is the growth of Web logs a reaction to the diminishing credibility of mainstream media? Is blogging a possible solution to the growing concentration of ownership in the media and the potential narrowing of ideas that accompanies it? Will blogging democratize the Web, opening new venues for diverse expression, or go mainstream as more media start their own blogs? Is the incorporation of blogs into traditional media outlets a way to create a more interactive interface with the audience and perhaps reverse the exodus of viewers and readers to other media?

Blogging is not going away, and it presents itself in forms that are clearly etched by journalistic norms. There are a host of unresolved professional, ethical, and legal questions associated with blogging that will be carried well into the twenty-first century.

THE BUSINESS OF THE MEDIA: TWENTIETH-CENTURY OWNERSHIP ISSUES

The exodus of television viewers mentioned above and broadcast audience fragmentation are growing concerns among broadcast news media, which historically have counted on large audience numbers to generate revenue for their advertiser-supported industry. Much of the attrition is due to the growth of cable and satellite television, but there is some evidence that news consumers are migrating to alternative news sources for information, including those available through the Internet (Project for Excellence in Journalism 2004). The attrition to the Internet is still minimal compared with the impact of major media news sources, and it has not reached a point where it is replacing current sources of news.

For example, in a 2003 study of news coverage of the war in Iraq, respondents were asked to choose the source(s) they used most often for news. Eighty-seven percent of Americans with Internet access still turn to the television for their news. Even more reassuring for mainstream news organizations is evidence that their own Web sites are a main source of information even for Internet users. For example, of those who went online for news:

- 32 percent used television network news Web sites
- 29 percent used newspaper Web sites
- 15 percent used government sponsored sites
- 10 percent used foreign news sites
- 8 percent used alternative news sites
- 4 percent used blogs (Smith 2003)

Still, the Internet is a player in the media environment, as evidenced by the almost universal presence of Internet sites for commercial media and news outlets. That presence adds additional punch to the deregulatory argument that there are sufficient media choices to reconsider whether limits on media ownership remain justified. Not surprisingly, the FCC continues to loosen ownership limitations that have been in place since the mid–twentieth century. The deregulatory trend gained momentum in the 1980s, but it is a key twenty-first century issue for the press. Although ownership patterns are not an express limit on freedom of the press in the classic sense of direct government restrictions, there is an argument that *nonregulatory* structural changes to the media industry, like a growing concentration of ownership, have an impact on the philosophical justifications used for protecting the press, namely, the importance of preserving the "marketplace of ideas."

Thus, it is not surprising that the changing ownership patterns of the mass media have become a source of increasing concern among media critics, analysts, and scholars specifically because of a belief that it exacerbates economic pressure on the news-gathering operations of the media and further limits the range of ideas. The trend in ownership concentration is remarkable. Media companies were, at one time, limited to owning seven television stations, seven AM radio stations, and seven FM radio stations (with no more than one television station in the same market). Today, a media company may own as many radio stations as it can afford (as exemplified by Clear Channel's inventory of over 1,200 radio stations—an average of 5.7 stations per market). Additionally, the number of television stations is structured on the audience "reach" of a single company. Under the original 7/7/7 rule, in addition to limiting the number of stations a single company could own, the total reach of one company could not exceed 25 percent of the national audience. This effectively meant that the big media companies of the late 1970s (primarily ABC, NBC, and CBS) owned and operated stations in the largest urban markets. Other network-affiliated stations were owned by numerous companies and simply contracted to carry a particular network's programming during certain parts of the day. However, the ownership "cap" increased to 35 percent as part of the late-twentieth-century deregulatory trend.

In June 2003, the FCC proposed raising the cap to 45 percent. While the proposal for the new cap was under consideration, Viacom and Fox purchased stations that pushed their companies' reach to 39 percent each. At the culmination of contentious public debate over what would happen to the Fox and Viacom stations if the cap did not expand to 45 percent—a debate that reached its peak during the parallel criticism of Viacom's CBS network's refusal to air a political ad during the 2004 Superbowl (discussed below)—Congress attached a rider to an appropriations bill reducing the cap to 39 percent, backing off the FCC's proposed 45 percent cap. This congressional move saved Viacom and Fox from having to divest some media holdings, but it is still opposed by media watch groups as well as by small broadcasters who are afraid of being swallowed up by larger companies.

Ownership caps are not the only ownership issue shaping the early twenty-first century. In June 2003, the FCC eliminated the newspaper/broadcast cross-ownership ban. Before this ruling, a media company could not own a newspaper and a broadcast outlet in the same market. The Third Circuit Court of Appeals ordered a stay of the new rule pending judicial review. Civic groups argue that the conglomeration of ownership reduces the diversity of views in broadcasting and reduces localism in news and public affairs. Small broadcasters also joined the request to restrict ownership of newspapers and broadcast outlets in the same market. Newspaper companies are complaining about being singled out, noting that the FCC already allows a company to own both a cable system and a broadcast outlet within a given market.

On a larger scale, conglomeration of the media continues. For example, below is a listing of the top nine television companies, based on 2002 revenue (note that some of these companies have other media holdings, such as radio stations, cable television, and newspapers):

- News Corporation (Fox TV) owns 35 stations in 26 markets ($2.3 billion)
- Viacom owns 35 stations in 28 markets ($1.8 billion)
- General Electric (NBC-TV) owns 14 station in 14 markets ($1.7 billion)
- Tribune Co. owns 26 stations in 22 markets ($1.2 billion)
- Disney (ABC-TV) owns 10 stations in 10 markets ($1.2 billion)
- Gannett owns 21 stations in 19 markets ($880 million)
- Hearst-Argyle owns 27 stations in 24 markets ($780 million)
- Sinclair owns 62 stations in 39 markets ($756 million)
- Belo owns 19 stations in 15 markets ($700 million) (Broadcasting and Cable 2004a)

The mom-and-pop cable businesses, common until the early 1980s, have largely disappeared. In their place are several large companies, such as Comcast, Time Warner, and Cox. The major broadcast networks are owned by larger parent corporations. General Electric has owned the NBC network for decades. CBS, once owned by Westinghouse, is now part of Viacom (also one of the largest television station groups). ABC was purchased by Capital Cities, which was purchased by the Walt Disney Corporation. In February 2004, Comcast, the largest cable company, announced a $54.1 billion bid for Disney. Although the offer was rejected by Disney CEO Michael Eisner, a hostile takeover by Comcast is still possible.

There was a time when media companies were not permitted to be vertically integrated and own the means of producing, distributing, and transmitting media content. Those restrictions dissipated with the deregulatory fervor of the 1980s and 1990s. Now media corporations commonly own production studios, distribution companies, and the broadcast or cable outlets to air their products. The Comcast bid for Disney is a reflection of its need for high-quality programming to complement its extensive cable delivery system as the largest cable provider in the country. The purchase of Disney would position Comcast to remain competitive with other vertically integrated media corporations, such as the News Corporation (owner of Fox News Channel, Fox Sports Network, FX, Fox Broadcasting Network, television stations, DIRECTV, and 20th Century Fox production studios as well as significant newspaper and publishing holdings).

The Jessica Lynch story illustrates the way in which vertical integration may affect news content. As part of the intense bidding for an interview with Lynch, who had been a prisoner of war in Iraq, CBS made her an offer that outlined a multifaceted package of possible media products involving MTV, Simon and Schuster Publishers, CBS entertainment, and CBS News (CBS News 2003). Critics have raised questions about whether these kinds of offers indicate that news operations are not distinctly separate from other entertainment and publication divisions of large media corporations.

Content-based regulations have always been most restrictive for broadcasters and the broadcast medium. For example, the broadcasting editorial rule prevented broadcasters from taking editorial positions on the air. The rule was rationalized on the spectrum scarcity principle: Not everyone could have a license to broadcast, so broadcasters could not use their unique and special position to editorialize. In the fall of 2000, shortly before the national elections, the FCC eliminated the broadcast editorial rule. Now broadcasters have the same First Amendment freedom to editorialize that newspapers have long enjoyed. Given the wide-ranging media options available to the public, the scarcity principle no longer seemed persuasive as a justification for restricting the First Amendment freedoms of broadcasters.

This change, combined with the increasing concentration of media ownership, set in motion another trend in media news. Note that among the top nine station group owners listed above, most have more stations listed than markets listed. In other words, many group owners own or operate more than one station in a market, either through duopoly or local marketing agreements. This ownership structure allows the consolidation of news services. In some markets television group owners are cutting costs by combining news operations and providing a regional news service from a central location. As pointed out by NewsLab, a nonprofit training and research resource for television newsrooms, the Seattle market provides a good example of television news consolidations. "Viacom-owned KSTW airs a 10 P.M. newscast produced by Cox-owned KIRO across town, using KIRO reporters and anchors. It's easy enough to see what KSTW gets out of the arrangement—a local newscast where it had none. But what does the audience get? Basically, the same homogenized news, at a different time on a different channel" (Potter 2003). At the very least, studies suggest that the quality and quantity of local news have declined in recent years (USCLaw 2003).

The pattern is already entrenched in radio news. There are more radio stations on the air than ever, but hardly any provide local news outside of drive time weather and traffic reports. Concern about news coverage seems to be supported by the comments of Lowry Mays, founder and CEO of Clear Channel: "If anyone said we were in the radio business, it wouldn't be someone from our company. . . . We're not in the business of providing news and information. We're not in the business of providing well-researched music. We're simply in the business of selling our customers products" (Chen 2003).

Newspapers are not immune to the trends apparent in broadcasting, although the trends are manifested quite differently. Newspapers have not had to face the regulatory hand of the FCC, in part because they face no physical scarcity, nor do they use the public airwaves. Ironically, though, the majority of cities in the United States have only one daily newspaper, but many have four or more television stations and ten or more radio stations. Such figures raise interesting questions about where the *real* scarcity lies. In fact, newspaper scarcity is driven by economic factors, not physical limitations or regulatory oversight. Over the past decade or so, cities have seen competing daily newspapers suffer severe economic losses. In many of the cities that long had two competing daily newspapers, one has been driven out of business. To avoid the growing trend toward single-newspaper towns, the federal government permits two newspapers to join noneditorial functions if one of the papers is clearly on the brink of financial failure. Joint operating agreements (JOAs) under the Newspaper Preservation Act provide a limited antitrust exemption and are intended to maintain the diversity of editorial content that would be lost if one of the newspapers went out of business.

A relatively recent example of a JOA occurred in Denver, Colorado. Until January 5, 2001, the *Denver Post,* owned by MediaNews Corp., and the *Denver Rocky Mountain News,* owned by the E.W. Scripps Howard Company, competed vigorously in the Denver market. Both papers suffered economically, in part because the competition suppressed advertising rates. U.S. Attorney General Janet Reno agreed with the Department of Justice's Antitrust Division that the *Denver Rocky Mountain News* was in danger of financial failure. A third entity was jointly created to handle printing and commercial operations for both papers. The news and editorial departments remained separate (DenverPost. com 2001). The papers continue to publish separate issues during the week. The *Denver Rocky Mountain News* publishes the Saturday paper, and the *Denver Post* publishes the Sunday paper (Vuong 2001).

There is some concern that JOAs are entered into too quickly. In the Denver case, questions were raised about whether the *Denver Post* was sufficiently open with its financial data, and some criticism was leveled at the *Denver Rocky Mountain News* because it apparently still had the advertising base to survive. With any JOA, a larger concern is whether the editorial positions of the papers will soften or whether the news staff may be less competitive. One interesting aside in the Denver case is that while the two newspapers competed, advertising rates were kept artificially low for the Denver market—so low, in fact, that the nearby city of Aurora was unable to launch an economically viable daily newspaper. As a result, Aurora was one of the largest cities in the country without a daily newspaper.

In the end, JOAs are likely to remain a twenty-first-century solution for the few remaining cities that have struggling competing daily newspapers.

WAR AND THE NEW JOURNALIST

Through much of this book, the history of press censorship has been presented as a struggle between the press and the government over the question of prior restraint. Many aspects of this press/government relationship were clarified during the twentieth century. It remains extremely difficult for the government to justifiably censor the press, but national security has remained a well-established exception since it was first articulated by the Supreme Court in the 1931 *Near* decision. The press/government dance around national security concerns continues into the twenty-first century with new challenges driven in part by technological innovation. As discussed in Chapter 3, the court never addressed the constitutionality of the press pool system because the Gulf War ended and the court concluded the issue was moot, in spite of plaintiff pleadings that resolution was necessary for future military/press relations. Still, the government recognized the shortcomings of the press pool system during the Gulf War. From a military public relations or propaganda perspective, the front-line successes were never effectively covered by the press under the pool system.

Thus, with both sides dissatisfied with aspects of the pool system, an alternative system of using "embedded" reporters was tested during the war in Iraq. The embed system had enormous public relations appeal because it provided independent documentation of the military front-line effort with the credibility that accompanies such coverage. As a subtle form of control, the embed system placed reporters in close contact with individual soldiers and successfully played on the power of the personal relationships between reporters and soldiers that inevitably developed over time. Reporters had ample opportunity to tell the human stories of individual military personnel—the same people who were protecting them from injury during military action.

The enormous impact of live video imagery of intense combat pulled audiences into the emotion and power of the fighting. Without question, this new arrangement served the interests of both the military and the media well. Never did the military look so good, and never did the media come away with such rich visual material and compelling personal stories.

At the same time, the embed system raises serious questions about journalists' objectivity. Might it have been difficult for journalists to be objective about the troops who actively protected their lives? Sharing hardships, dangers, exhaustion, and loss of life put journalists in a complicated relationship with the people they were covering. Journalists are still reflecting, with hindsight, on whether the embed system might have at times jeopardized journalistic objectivity.

The embed system was not without challenges from the media. Larry Flynt, publisher of *Hustler* magazine, questioned the constitutionality of placing *any* limits on the number of journalists traveling with the troops after his reporter was barred from accompanying the first wave of troops entering Afghanistan in late 2001. All press coverage was dramatically limited initially and limited to covering maneuvers such as food drops and air strikes. By May 2002, *Hustler* had an embedded journalist in Afghanistan. Still, Flynt pursued the constitutional question in court. The U.S. Court of Appeals for the D.C. Circuit ruled in early 2004 that reporters do not have a constitutional right to be embedded with troops, although they are free to cover the war on their own (*Flynt v. Rumsfeld*, 2004 U.S. App. LEXIS 1561). This is not a surprising ruling given that the courts have supported military decisions to deny press access to military bases where the remains of soldiers were delivered.

In addition to the public relations advantages of the embed system, the new arrangement was also prompted by another technologically driven shift in military/press relations. Communication technology innovations over time have generally served to limit the military's ability to control the dissemination of information simply by controlling journalists' mobility. During the invasion of Afghanistan, improved technology allowed journalists to be remarkably mobile while still providing live reports from the field. Dispatches that formerly required a mobile van full of transmission equipment and a satellite link now can be made with equipment that fits in a small suitcase. The refinement of videophone technology makes it possible to transmit low-quality video images from anywhere a journalist can make the satellite link. This development makes live remote reporting highly portable. Journalists moved into Afghanistan on their own to gather stories from small bands of Afghan fighters and local villagers. Similar video technology drove much of the visual coverage during the war in Iraq. The cover image on the jacket of this book, showing the late David Bloom embedded in Iraq, is illustrative of the kind of coverage possible with videophone and satellite technology. Bloom made regular live reports from his specially outfitted M-88 tank recovery vehicle, tagged the "Bloommobile." The vehicle was equipped with a gyrostabilized camera (the kind used on helicopters to produce smooth video while moving). Bloom's signal was microwaved to a support vehicle several miles behind and then transmitted to a satellite relay to NBC.

The rules governing the press under the embed system allowed for live broadcasts (when troops were not engaged in combat), and the material was not censored, but the guidelines prohibited the transmission of any information on military planning or the location of military units. Geraldo Rivera, reporting for Fox News, lost his embed slot when, during one of his live reports, he drew a map in the sand describing the general location of his unit. Eight days after his expulsion from Iraq, Rivera reappeared on Fox News reporting from Kuwait as an independent journalist. Peter Arnett was fired from MSNBC/NBC for giving an interview to Iraqi television in which he stated, "It is clear that within the United States there is growing challenge to President Bush about the conduct of the war and also opposition to the war." Five days later his stories started appearing in the *London Daily Mirror.*

What are the concerns about the embed process for the audience? One prevailing criticism of the embed system is that no one embedded journalist had much insight into the larger patterns, issues, and context of the war (Smith 2003; LaFleur 2003). Like ethnographers, journalists were looking deep, talking about the minute details, telling personal stories of soldiers, and bringing to the audience a narrow slice of the picture. The big picture was harder to see. Sketches were provided by nonembedded or "unilateral" journalists, although they struggled to gain access to the heart of military action.

The long-term impact of the new reporter embed system will play out over the next few years. One thing is clear already: The implications of the embed system for press freedoms are critical. Any restriction on the press comes at a cost to First Amendment rights. The issues raised by the pool system, the embed system, and any other effort to use national security as a justification for restricting the press chips away at the ideal of a free and unencumbered press. The ability to report independently on the activities of the government goes to the heart of the First Amendment.

CLIMATE OF SECRECY

The heightened security resulting from the terrorist attacks of September 11, 2001, and the invasion of Afghanistan and Iraq have changed the degree of press access to governmental activities related to terrorism. The USA PATRIOT Act, for example, weakens privacy protections for electronic communications, allowing the government to monitor communications more easily. Immigration and Naturalization Service (INS) hearings, previously open to the public, have become closed for security reasons, and INS records have been sealed. The Courts of Appeals in the Third and Sixth Circuits have split on whether closing deportation hearings to the press violates the First Amendment. The Sixth Circuit held the rules unconstitutional. Judge Damon Keith quoted Justice Hugo Black's dissent in the Pentagon Papers case, saying, "The word 'security' is a broad, vague generality whose contours should not be invoked to abrogate the fundamental law embodied in the First Amendment. The guarding of military and diplomatic secrets at the expense of informed representative government provides no real security for our Republic" (*Detroit Free Press v. Ashcroft,* 303 F.3d 681 [2002], 693). The judge added that the executive branch, empowered by the USA PATRIOT Act,

> seeks to uproot people's lives, outside the public eye, and behind a closed door. Democracies die behind closed doors. The First Amendment, through a free press, protects the people's right to know that their government acts fairly, lawfully, and accurately in deportation proceedings. When government begins closing doors, it selectively controls information rightfully belonging to the people. Selective information is misinformation. The Framers of the First Amendment "did not trust any government to separate the true from the false for us." They protected the people against secret government. (*Detroit Free Press v. Ashcroft,* 303 F.3d 681 [2002], 683; footnotes omitted)

A couple of months later, the Third Circuit Court of Appeals ruled that INS proceedings were not the same as criminal and civil trials and therefore did not require the same degree of openness to the press. The security concerns at stake thus overrode the right of a free press (*New Jersey Media Group v. Ashcroft,* 308 F. 3d 198 [2002]). The U.S. Supreme Court declined to review the Third Circuit decision. The Department of Justice has not appealed the Sixth Circuit decision. With the split in these two circuit decisions, the issue remains largely unresolved.

There are other areas where the press is facing diminished access to government information. The Justice Department, under the direction of Attorney General John Ashcroft, and empowered by the 2002 Homeland Security Act has taken "a more conservative approach toward interpreting the federal Freedom of Infor-

mation Act" (Dalglish 2003, 3). As a result, the government is releasing less information to the press. The act also removes some
government advisory committees from open meeting laws (Chaddock 2002). Possibly the most damaging part of the Homeland Security Act for journalists is the provision that "criminalizes disclosure of information" that is not (and should not be) classified
(Daugherty 2003, 9). The risk of criminal prosecution may have a
chilling effect on journalists' coverage of the government's activities with regard to domestic and international terrorism.

As part of the USA PATRIOT Act, the government has begun
to identify foreign terrorist organizations (FTOs). An organization
labeled as such may have its assets frozen; no one in the United
States may provide any material support to the organization; and
noncitizens associated with the organization can be prevented
from entering the United States. By late 2003, the list included
thirty-six organizations. One of the questions raised under the
laws guiding designated FTOs is whether official or unofficial Web
sites may be censored, sanctioned, or regulated in some manner.
Many of the targeted Web sites, such as "The Road to Jihad" and
the official sites of Hizbollah and the Islamic Resistance Movement (HAMAS), regularly change URLs to thwart hackers, so it is
difficult to locate them even if there are legitimate means of imposing sanctions on them. Furthermore, many are hosted outside the
United States and thus outside the reach of U.S. law. Nevertheless,
given the traditionally high level of protection for publishers under
the First Amendment's free press rights, questions arise about the
protection available to those publishing on the Web, information
that is not legally obscene, is not a violation of national security,
and does not advocate likely and imminent lawless action. Highly
provocative publications, such as *The Anarchist Cookbook* (a
recipe book for building explosives), or *Hit Man: A Technical
Manual for Independent Contractors* (a how-to manual on killing
people) have not been censored by the government, although the
Fourth Circuit Court of Appeals did suggest that the publisher of

Hit Man could be liable for the death of three people (*Rice v. Paladin Enterprises,* 128 F. 3d 233 [1997]). Ironically, although the publisher agreed to stop publishing *Hit Man,* he forfeited his copyright and the text of the book is now available in its entirety on the Web. So far, no one has sued the Web site owner. The courts ruled that an antiabortion Web site called "The Nuremberg Files," which posted publicly available personal information (home address, phone number, license plate information, etc.) about doctors who perform abortions, could be censored. Initially, the Ninth Circuit Court of Appeals recognized that the information on the site might increase the likelihood of harm to these doctors, but it was not clear that the information would produce imminent lawless action. Later, in an en banc rehearing, the court concluded that elements of the site posed a threat to the named doctors and had to be removed (*Planned Parenthood at Columbia/Willamette, Inc. v. American Coalition of Life Activists,* 290 F.3d 1058, [9th Cir. 2002]). The antiabortion site is occasionally available via the Internet without the offending content of the original Nuremberg Files site. However, the original site is "mirrored" at times, on a Web server in the Netherlands—beyond the reach of U.S. law. Clearly, the twenty-first century will remain a battleground over where to draw the line, with Web site publishers posting highly offensive or provocative content that stretches the limits of a free press.

THE OLDEST PROFESSION MEETS THE NEWEST TECHNOLOGY

The Internet, as discussed in Chapter 3, presents a hornet's nest of First Amendment issues, from copyright to incitement to illegal activity. Nowhere have the courts struggled more than with publication of sexually explicit material on the Internet. This twenty-first-century issue brings to a crossroads historically protected sexual material in a medium that is arguably more accessible and even more intrusive than other pornographic media. The most heated debate related to Internet pornography is generated when the question of children enters the mix. The courts have determined that sexually explicit material cannot all be banned solely on the grounds that it may be inappropriate for children. Adults have a constitutionally protected right to view pornographic material, as long as it is not legally obscene and does not involve children. The press also has a constitutional right to publish sexually explicit material that is not legally obscene.

Thus, the question becomes that of how to protect an adult's constitutional right to pornography and a publisher's right to a free press while protecting the welfare of minors. With print, video, or film pornography, the answer has been not to censor but to control access to the material by minors. The problem became more complicated with the advent of the Internet for a variety of reasons. First, young users of the Internet are often more adept at navigating, searching, and circumventing barriers to Web site access than adults, who did not grow up with Internet technology. Stories abound of kids beating filtering software such as Net Nanny and CyberPatrol. Second, Web sites have an ability to get around filters with deceptive meta-tags, shifting URLs, and other techniques similar to those used to baffle search engines and to undermine spam filters. Some adult Web sites provide warnings about the material they contain beyond their home page and require visitors to check a box stating that they are at least eighteen years old. This tactic may provide some liability protection for the content providers but is not likely to be an effective deterrent to a motivated minor. Some Web sites attempt to screen out minors by requiring that a credit card number be provided before a user can enter the site, under the assumption that minors do not have access to credit cards. Some sites have misleading URLs and home pages (see *www.whitehouse.com*, for example—bearing in mind that the official White House site ends with ".gov," not ".com") with relatively explicit images readily available without entering the site itself. Penthouse.com's home page contains a variety of women in sexually explicit poses, often bare breasted. Thus, although sexually explicit Web sites may include "barriers" to entry, they do not provide the same level of protection as the requirement of proof of age before a person can buy *Hustler* magazine or enter an adult store or movie theater.

In grappling with this issue, Congress has passed several laws designed to control access to sexually explicit material on the Internet. However, initial attempts to control pornography did not withstand First Amendment scrutiny. In 1997, the Communications Decency Act of 1996 was struck down by the Supreme Court (*Reno v. ACLU*, 521 U.S. 844 [1997]). The Court unanimously ruled that the law was overbroad because it encompassed speech that was constitutionally protected for adults.

Subsequent legislative efforts to narrow the language of bills restricting pornography focused on protecting children. The first result was the Children's Online Protection Act of 1998 (COPA). However, COPA was challenged and ruled overbroad in federal district court, and then at the appellate level it was ruled too reliant on "community standards" to determine what is harmful to minors. In 2002, the Supreme Court heard the appeal and remanded the case to the lower court, reversing the appellate decision and asking the lower court to further consider the law as a whole (*Ashcroft v. ACLU*, 535 U.S. 564 [2002]). The case then worked its way back to the Supreme Court after being ruled unconstitutional at the appellate court level for a second time. Oral arguments before the Court occurred in March 2004 and a narrowly divided Court decided four months later that the Child Online Protection Act violated the First Amendment because there were less restrictive means to limit minors' access to pornography (*Ashcroft v. American Civil Liberties Union* [2004]).

Some free press and free speech advocates argue that the least restrictive means of controlling children's access to Internet pornography is the use of filtering software or the creation of a controlled domain that is safe for children. Requiring use of a credit card—a component of the COPA—goes too far in the minds of civil libertarians, because for privacy reasons, adults may not want to provide credit card information in order to view material that otherwise would be freely accessible. According to the American Civil Liberties Union (ACLU), which challenged the law before the Supreme Court, the law criminalizes expression involving "sexual advice and education, Web-based chat rooms and discussion boards involving sexual topics, and Web sites for bookstores, art galleries, and the news media" (ACLU 2004).

In 2002 the Supreme Court struck down the Child Pornography Protection Act of 1996 (CPPA), which criminalized computer-generated images of child pornography. In an affirmation of the free expression rights of Internet publishers, the Court ruled that digital imagery of "virtual" minors engaged in sexual activity is not the same as pornography using actual minors (which is not protected expression). The banning of child pornography has long been based on the harm it causes children. Such harm is difficult to demonstrate in the case of virtual, computer-generated images. Justice Kennedy noted that the law, if upheld, might have banned artistic or literary expression that portrayed minors engaging in sexual activity. Movies such as *American Beauty* (which won an Academy Award) and *Traffic* would have been at risk of falling within the reach of the CPPA (*Ashcroft v. Free Speech Coalition*, 535 U.S. 234 [2002]).

Other Internet protection laws have been more successful, in part because they have not infringed on publishers' right to a free press. Instead they focus on providing mechanisms to prevent access to sexually explicit material by children. The Children's Internet Protection Act requires that all libraries receiving federal funding for Internet access must provide filtering software on their Internet computers. The Supreme Court upheld the law when it was challenged by the American Library Association (*United States v. ALA*, 539 U.S. 194 [2003]). However, there was no majority opinion; instead the decision was made up of numerous concurring opinions. Thus, the specific law was upheld and is now in effect, but the precedental power of the Court's opinion is less clear.

The Children's Online Privacy Protection Act of 1998 (COPPA) requires that Web site operators targeting children under thirteen years old seek verifiable consent from a parent before collecting personal information about a child Web user (including Web activity tracked with "cookies"). Furthermore, the law provides measures for the protection of children's privacy and safety online. One element of COPPA that raises First Amendment concerns is that without being able to collect certain information about children, Internet services have a more difficult time determining the age of users for some free Web services such as chat or e-mail.

The intersection of children's welfare and key Internet issues such as privacy and control of pornography remains unsettled at the beginning of the twenty-first century. Navigating the government's special interest in the welfare of children and the competing right of a free press will make the Internet a contentious arena for articulating future press freedoms in the virtual world.

MEDIA, POLITICS, AND CULTURAL NORMS

The Radio Act of 1927 introduced the requirement that broadcasters operate in the "public interest, convenience, and necessity." Over the years, the media and the press seem to have degraded in the eyes of the public. Newton Minow, an FCC chair appointed by President Kennedy, set the stage for public dialogue about television in a 1961 address to the National Association of Broadcasters in which he famously referred to television as a "vast wasteland" (Minow 1991). His statement was in response to the failure of broadcasters to meet their obligation to serve the public as well as their private interests.

Minow's words fell hard on an industry recently rocked by the quiz show and payola scandals. During his two-year service on the FCC, Minow became a household name and brought to a larger audience the idea that television could be something more than it was. In subsequent years the debate about the state and quality of broadcasting ebbed in and out of public discussion. Sometimes public pressure produced change, if only temporarily. In the 1970s, public pressure pushed the networks to introduce after-school programming such as *Schoolhouse Rock* and ABC's *Afterschool Specials*. In the 1980s, the deregulation of broadcasting, which included a shift in the very meaning of the public interest, seemed to go unchallenged, possibly overshadowed by the growth in cable television.

Peggy Charren, a homemaker disillusioned with the quality of television programming for children, started Action for Children's Television in 1968. Her efforts reintroduced a strong public interest obligation to children's programming with the passage of the Children's Television Act of 1990 (CTA). The law established multifaceted limits on advertising during children's programming, set minimum numbers of hours of educational programming, and required broadcasters to report their educational programming as part of their license obligation. In principle, failure to meet the requirements of the CTA could result in a challenge to the broadcaster's license renewal. However, leaving it up to broadcasters to define what programming is educational resulted in a show such as *Mighty Morphin' Power Rangers* being reported as educational programming because it taught the triumph of good over evil.

Although much of this history reflects a struggle over regulation of content and does not have a direct impact on freedom of the press, these kinds of concerns speak to the underlying justifications of why we as a country are committed to protecting the press. At this point in the early twenty-first century, we see juries increasingly willing to punish reporters who use provocative or even outrageous methods to gather information (thus the growth of news-gathering torts and intentional infliction of emotional distress lawsuits). The public appears to be responding to the increasing propensity of broadcast television, in its competition with cable television and other media, to push the edge of cultural norms or abandon any obligation to higher-quality programming or issues of public concern.

Nowhere is this more evident than in the recent events involving CBS. On January 25, 2004, a significant percentage of Americans turned on their televisions to watch the broadcast event of the year: Superbowl XXXVIII. Although most remember the controversy generated by the football game's half-time show featuring singers Janet Jackson and Justin Timberlake, many were unaware of a controversy associated with the Superbowl broadcast in the weeks preceding the game. CBS, a subsidiary of Viacom, refused to air a political ad submitted by the nonprofit advocacy organization MoveOn.org. The organization had spent months building a grassroots campaign to challenge the policies of the Bush administration, and its ad was the winning entry in a contest in which over 1,100 such ads were created and submitted by the general public. Fund-raising efforts collected the $2.25 million needed to air the thirty-second ad once during the Superbowl. However, CBS held firm on its network policy of not airing advocacy ads. Controversy erupted when it was discovered that CBS nevertheless intended to air an advocacy ad paid for by the White House Drug Policy Office—among the barrage of Superbowl ads about beer, flatulent horses, and erectile dysfunction. CBS's justification was that the MoveOn.org ad was an advocacy ad, whereas the White House ad was a public service announcement. Nevertheless, the network was accused quite openly of truckling to the current administration, which was poised to affirm new ownership limits highly favorable to CBS (and Fox Broadcasting).

Then, during the Superbowl's halftime show (produced by MTV, which is also owned by Viacom), Justin Timberlake, in a choreographed dance sequence, ripped off part of Janet Jackson's bustier, exposing her breast. CBS already had a brief delay on the signal and was able to cut away to a wide camera shot almost immediately. The fallout from the event has taken on a life of its own.

For example, the producers of the NBC network show *E.R.* were compelled by network executives to remove a brief shot of an elderly woman receiving emergency care, because the shot involved ripping opening her shirt, briefly exposing her breast. The network-level decision was prompted by NBC affiliate stations' nervousness over carrying the scene on the heels of the Superbowl flurry. The NBC affiliates were afraid it could expose them to FCC indecency fines. Never mind that on a previous episode of *E.R.* there had been a similar emergency room shot in which a patient's breast was briefly exposed. Katie Couric, during a February 5, 2004, *Today* show interview with Noah Wyle, one of the actors on *E.R.*, made an offhand, half-joking, but revealing comment about being careful to not overly criticize NBC for the decision to edit *E.R.* because she didn't want to get fired.

The 2004 Grammy Awards program, airing two weeks after the Superbowl, prompted an apology from CBS, when the hip-hop group Outkast's performance of *Hey Ya*, in stereotypical Native American costume, elicited from the Native American Cultural Center a public condemnation, a formal complaint with the FCC, and a call for a boycott of CBS, Arista Records (Outkast's label), and the National Academy of Recording Arts and Sciences (a Grammy sponsor).

But it didn't end there. As mentioned in Chapter 3, the FCC began to reevaluate its indecency fine structure, hoping to increase the fine tenfold, from $27,500 per incident to $275,000. Congress beat the FCC to the punch when the House voted to raise fines for broadcasters and entertainers from $27,500 and $11,000, respectively, to *$500,000* each (Hulse 2004). The House also introduced the Clean Airwaves Act (H.R. 3687). Although historically the FCC has defined indecent material as patently offensive sexual content *and* has considered the context in which the language or imagery was used, this bill specifically identifies eight words that, regardless of context, would be subject to FCC fines.

Three television networks and Clear Channel Communications have agreed with the proposed new law on indecency. In the midst of this, Clear Channel (which has over 1,200 radio stations) and Infinity Broadcasting (owned by Viacom) adopted zero-tolerance policies for indecency. Thus, Clear Channel canceled *The Howard Stern Show* (the most common target for FCC fines) and the controversial *Bubba the Love Sponge* (WXTB-FM, Atlanta) and developed a policy of making radio disc jockeys pay a portion of any future indecency fines (Eggerton 2004). Additionally, both radio and television outlets are implementing a several-minute delay in broadcasting live events and programs.

The industry trade publication, *Broadcasting and Cable* magazine, lambasted the willingness of broadcasters to capitulate to the groundswell of interest in reregulating media content: "From expunging Bubba to stifling Stern, broadcasters are sacrificing control over content on the altar of political expedience. . . . [T]his universal knee-jerk reaction—emphasis on the jerk—is a shameful chapter in broadcasting history. At a time electronic media should be fighting for their rights, they are happily giving them away" (Broadcasting and Cable 2004b).

These shifts raise the question of whether the press remains insulated from content pressures facing the media in general. In a time of reactive concern about offending people and in a time with increased concentration of ownership of media interests, can the press act autonomously? One example that raises concern about press autonomy is MSNBC's decision to cancel *Donahue*, Phil Donahue's talk show. Donahue's show, like several other talk shows, was considered news programming for regulatory purposes. From early on there had been some complaints from viewers that Donahue's opinions were too liberal. There was pressure from NBC and its parent company, General Electric, to change the tone of Donahue's delivery after focus groups indicated that Donahue seemed "unpatriotic."

Rick Ellis, co-owner of a Web site dedicated to daytime television, noted:

> While it's unclear just when the decision was made to cancel Donahue, nearly everyone interviewed for this piece believe that the reasons are more complex than just liberal vs. conservative. "This is a ratings-driven business, and it's important not to lose track of that in this discussion," one CNN executive told me on Monday. "But I won't lie and tell you that your public beliefs and persona don't matter to viewers. . . . There are a lot of people out there who believe that the press is inherently liberal. And I would be an idiot if I did anything to encourage that conversation." One journalist who works at a competing network says that in the end, the most important lesson to come out of this story is the increasing use of focus groups and polling to determine news programming. "While Donahue isn't claiming to be Edward R. Murrow—he is a talk show host—he's talking about the news, with newsmakers. It's a distinction that escapes most viewers anyway. And if we're moving towards a future where network wonks are testing everything before they let us report it . . . Well, frankly, that scares the hell out of me." (Ellis 2003)

This book goes to press on the heels of the backlash against the cultural excesses of broadcast programming. Cable and satellite programming have managed to slip under the radar of an angry Congress and FCC. Only those members of Congress who opposed the vote to increase indecency fines have articulated a concern over the First Amendment issues raised by punishing the content of media. With the dilution of any public interest burden on broadcasters, all that is left is reactive regulation. Many issues regarding the current trend in indecency laws remain a concern. Small broadcasters, including community radio stations and college stations, would be unable to pay the new fines. And yet it is the small, volunteer-run or student-run stations—typically with minimal professionally trained staff—that have the greatest chance of running afoul of FCC guidelines (Kosseff 2004).

CONCLUSION

The twenty-first century will host more complex challenges to freedom of the press than have been faced in previous centuries. Many of the traditional concerns about press freedoms have been hashed out over the past 100 years to a certain level of clarity. The continuing struggles related to libel, invasion of privacy, and prior restraint are in the details. For example, it is just plain hard for the government to levy a prior restraint on the press. The government faces an enormous burden in attempting to justify such an action. However, technological innovations have opened new areas of legal exploration for libel, invasion of privacy, and prior restraint. Determining how traditional legal protections translate to the new media environment is a twenty-first-century challenge.

Nonlegal constraints on freedom of the press will play a major role in the twenty-first century. Increasing concentration of media ownership and new forms of journalism adapting to new technologies are just two examples of what the press will navigate in the future. The Project for Excellence in Journalism's *State of the News Media 2004*, released in March 2004, is designed to be an annual assessment of the news media in print, broadcasting, cable television, and on the Internet. It intends to evaluate content, audience composition and attitudes, economic shifts, ownership patterns, and journalistic norms. The 2004 report lists eight trends in journalism that succinctly set the stage for future concerns and raise important questions about the future of press freedoms outside the legal arena:

1. A growing number of news outlets are chasing relatively static or even shrinking audiences for news.

2. Much of the new investment in journalism today—much of the information revolution generally—is disseminating the news, not collecting it.
3. In many parts of the news media, we are increasingly getting the raw elements of the news as the end product.
4. Journalistic standards now vary even inside a single news organization.
5. Without investing in building news audiences, the long-term outlook for many traditional news outlets seems problematic.
6. Convergence seems more inevitable and potentially less threatening to journalists than it may have seemed a few years ago.
7. The biggest question [concern for the future of quality journalism] may not be technological but economic.
8. Those who would manipulate the press and public appear to be gaining leverage over the journalists who cover them (Project for Excellence in Journalism 2004).

Throughout this text these concerns have been raised in one form or another. These trends will contribute to the shape of journalism in the coming years. Although they do not raise explicit concerns about *government* control of the press, the shifts in ownership, technological innovation, economic priorities and pressures, and professional norms of the profession will be some of the indicators of the future health of a free and unfettered press in the United States.

REFERENCES AND FURTHER READING

ACLU. 2004. "ACLU Returns to Supreme Court in Renewed Challenge to Internet Censorship Law" (2 March). Available at *http://www.aclu.org/Privacy/Privacy.cfm?ID=15143&c=252*.

American Press Institute. 2004a. "Top CyberJournalist Stories of 2003." *Cyberjournalist.net,* available at *http://www.cyberjournalist.net/news/ 000854.php.*

American Press Institute. 2004b. "The Cyber Journalist List." *Cyberjournalist.net,* available at *http://www.cyberjournalist.net/cyberjournalists. php.*

Broadcasting and Cable. 2004a. "Cable Systems: Top 100" (23 February):2A.

Broadcasting and Cable. 2004b. "Get Some Guts" (1 March):34.

Canan, Penelope, and George W. Pring. 1988. "Strategic Lawsuits against Public Participation." *Social Problems* 35(5):506–519.

CBS News. 2003. "CBS Deal for Jessica Lynch?" *CBSNews.com* (16 June). Available at http://www.cbsnews.com/stories/2003/06/16/entertainment/main558929.shtml.

Chaddock, Gail Russell. 2002. "Security Act to Pervade Daily Lives." *CSMonitor.com* (21 November). Available at http://www.csmonitor. com/2002/1121/p01s03-usju.html.

Chen, Christine. 2003. "Clear Channel: Not the Bad Boys of Radio." *Fortune.com* (18 February). Available at *http://www.fortune.com/fortune/ ceo/articles/0,15114,423802,00.html.*

Consumers Union. 2003. "Consumers Union Files Motion to Strike Sharper Image Lawsuit under California Anti-SLAPP Statute." *Consumers Union* (3 November). Available at *http://www.consumersrightto-know.org/.*

Cox, Liz. 2003. "'Blograising' Begins." *Columbia Journalism Review* 42(2):9.

Dalglish, Lucy. 2003. "The Ups and Downs of Homeland Security." *News Media and the Law* 27(1):3.

Daugherty, Rebecca. 2003. "Homeland Security Act Blocks Unclassified Information from Public, Protects Companies That Provide It." *News Media and the Law* 27(1):9.

DenverPost.com. 2001. "Department of Justice News Release." *DenverPost.com* (5 January). Available at *http://63.147.65.175/business/ joa0105b.htm.*

Dube, Jonathan. 2004. "Q&A with NYTimes.com Editor on Blogs." *Cyberjournalist* (12 February). Available at *http://www.cyberjouranlist.net/ new/000935.php.*

Easterbrook, Greg. 2003. "An Apology from Greg Easterbrook Re: New Republic, Jews, Kill Bill Film Violence." *JewishFilm.com* (17 October). Available at *http://members3.boardhost.com/jewishfilm/msg/624.html.*

Eggerton, John. 2004. "Assume the Position." *Broadcasting and Cable* (1 March):2–3.

Ellis, Rick. 2003. "Battling for the Soul of *Donahue*." *AllYourTV.com* (5 March). Available at *http://allyourtv.com/0203season/news/03042003buyersregret.html.*

Gallagher, David. 2002. "Reporters Find New Outlet, and Concerns, in Web Logs." *New York Times* (23 September):C9.

Heyboer, Kelly, and Jill Rosen. 2004. "Bloggin' in the Newsroom." *American Journalism Review* 25(8):10–11.

Hulse, Carl. 2004. "House Votes, 391–22, to Raise Broadcasters' Fines for Indecency." *NYTimes.com* (12 March). Available at *http://www.nytimes.com/2004/03/12/politics/12INDE.html.*

Jensen, Mallory. 2003. A Brief History of Weblogs." *Columbia Journalism Review* 42(3):22.

Kosseff, Jeff. 2004. "Small Broadcasters Fear Vote May Spell Disproportionate Fines Over Content." *Oregonian* (11 March):B1, B4.

Kurtz, Howard. 2001. "Clinton Aide Settles Libel Suit against Matt Drudge—at a Cost." *Washington Post* (2 May):C01.

LaFleur, Jennifer. 2003. "Embed Program Worked, Broader War Coverage Lagged." *News Media and the Law* 27(2):4.

Lasica, J.D. 2001a. "Weblogs: A New Source of News." (31 May). Available at *http://www.ojr.org/ojr/workplace/1017958782.php.*

Lasica, J.D. 2001b. "Blogging as a Form of Journalism." *Online Journalism Review* (24 May). Available at *http://www.ojr.org/ojr/workplace/1017958873.php.*

McCombs, Maxwell, and Donald Shaw. (1972). "The Agenda Setting Function of Mass Media." *Public Opinion Quarterly* 36(2):176–187.

McEvoy, Sharlene A. 1990. "'The Big Chill': Business Use of the Tort of Defamation to Discourage the Exercise of First Amendment Rights." *Hastings Constitutional Law Quarterly* 17:503–532.

Minow, Newton. 1991. *How Vast the Wasteland Now?* New York: Gannett Foundation Media Center.

Office of the Governor of California. 2003. "Governor Davis Signs Legislation Protecting First Amendment Rights/Ending Frivolous Lawsuits." *Office of the Governor* (10 September). Available at *http://www.cjac.org/hotissues/sb515/L03105.pdf.*

Potter, Deborah. 2003. "The Big Get Bigger." *NewsLab* (6 March). Available at *http://www.newslab.org/articles/fccrule.htm.*

Project for Excellence in Journalism. 2004. "State of the News Media 2004." *Journalism.org* (15 March). Available at *http://www.stateofthenewsmedia.org/index.asp.*

Rutenberg, Jim. 2004. "In Politics, the Web Is a Parallel World with Its Own Rules." *NYTimes.com* (22 February). Available at *http://www. nytimes.com/2004/02/22/weekinreview/22rute.html?th.*

Sager, Kelli, and Rochelle Wilcox. 2003. "California Supreme Court Affirms Expansive Reading of Anti-SLAPP Statute." *FindLaw,* available at *http://library.lp.findlaw.com/articles/file/00010/008701/title/Subject/ topic/Constitutional%20Law_First%20Amendment%20-%20Freedom%20of%20Speech/filename/constitutionallaw_1_86.*

Scanlan, Chip. 2003. "Blogging Bonnie." *Poynter Online* (18 September). Available at *http://www.poynter.org/content/content_View.asp?id= 48413.*

Smith, Terence. 2003. "The Real-Time War." *Columbia Journalism Review* (May/June):26–28.

Sunstein, Cass. 2001. *Republic.com.* Princeton, NJ: Princeton University Press.

Tannenbaum, Wendy. (2003). "'Actual Malice' and Product Disparagement." *News Media and the Law* 27(3):11.

USCLaw. 2003. "Who Owns Your News." *USCLaw* (Spring). Available at *http://lawweb.usc.edu/lawmag/archive/spring03/features/news.*

Vuong, Andy. 2001. "New Script for Weekend Readers." *DenverPost.com* (31 March). Available at *http://63.147.65.175/business/joa0331a.htm.*

5

KEY PEOPLE, CASES, AND EVENTS

Abrams v. United States (1919)

Abrams and four other Russian citizens living in the United States were convicted under the 1918 Amendment to the Espionage Act of distributing two antiwar leaflets containing seditious messages. The Supreme Court used the bad tendency test to uphold the conviction of all five defendants. Justices Holmes and Brandeis, advocating for greater protection of speech, used their new clear and present danger test from the *Schenck* decision as the basis to dissent from the majority decision to uphold the convictions. It is in this case that Justice Holmes first introduced the "marketplace" metaphor (see Marketplace of Ideas).

Absolute Privilege

A libel and slander defense that immunizes a speaker from a defamation lawsuit, no matter how defamatory the speech might be, and even if the words were spoken with a bad intent. This privilege is granted to public officials speaking in their official capacity (e.g., a senator speaking on the floor of Congress) and to certain public documents (e.g., court documents).

Actual Malice

In a defamation or invasion of privacy suit, a plaintiff bears the burden of demonstrating fault. For lawsuits against the press, public officials and public figures must, and private individuals may have to, show that the defendant acted with actual malice—that is, that the defendant knowingly lied or acted with a reckless disregard for the truth.

Ad Hoc Balancing

When conflict occurs between speech or press freedoms and other values such as the right to a fair trial, the court must balance each value against the others. With ad hoc balancing, the courts consider the competing rights on a case-by-case basis, without giving one value preference over another. Critics of ad hoc balancing claim that this strategy relies too heavily on the personal biases of judges or justices. This balancing approach is not commonly used in First Amendment claims because of the courts' tendency to weigh the importance of free expression values more heavily than other values (see Preferred Position Balancing).

American Civil Liberties Union (ACLU)

The ACLU was founded in 1920 by a group of people, including Roger Baldwin and Crystal Eastman, who were concerned about the erosion of liberties embodied in the Constitution, the Bill of Rights, and subsequent constitutional amendments. Today the ACLU is the largest civil rights advocacy group in the country. Even though the ACLU is perceived as a "liberal" organization, it is nonpartisan and works to protect individuals whose civil rights are violated, without regard to their political orientation. The ACLU has defended Americans in some of the most provocative free expression cases, often fighting for the free speech rights of controversial and unpopular groups, such as the Ku Klux Klan. In recent years, the ACLU has challenged efforts to blur the line separating church and state, the law enforcement practice of racial profiling, and the government's curtailment of due process and privacy rights with the passage of the Patriot Act after the September 11, 2001, terrorist attacks.

Anti-Federalists

The Anti-Federalists, in direct opposition to the Federalists, opposed the ratification of the 1787 Constitution because 1) it centralized too much power in the federal government to create a structure reminiscent of British rule, and 2) it failed to explicitly protect fundamental individual rights. The Anti-Federalists, led by the political platform of Thomas Jefferson, believed in a laissez-faire government, or a federation of relatively autonomous states with responsive local governments. With enough votes at the Constitutional Convention to hold up the ratification of the Constitution, the Anti-Federalists successfully negotiated the promise of a Bill of Rights to secure individual liberties. The Bill of Rights was ratified four years later.

Appellate Courts

Appellate courts are part of the judicial structure at both the state and federal levels. Appellate courts generally hear appeals from courts at lower levels. Appellate courts consider errors in law and in legal procedure, but they do not review facts introduced at the original trial court level.

Appropriation

One of the four invasion of privacy torts. Appropriation is the taking of a person's likeness for commercial gain without the person's permission. When celebrities sue for appropriation, they base the lawsuit on their right to publicity, or the right to control the exploitation of their likeness. Persons whose likeness does not have a clear commercial value can sue for appropriation, but in this case they base the lawsuit on their right to privacy—to control their image in order to protect themselves from shame, embarrassment, or humiliation.

Bad Tendency Test

This was the prevailing judicial test in the United States for free speech until the early twentieth century. It enabled the government to restrict speech that possessed a tendency to create an evil that the government had a right to prevent. In the early twentieth century, the test came under challenge by Justice Holmes's clear and present danger test (see *Schenck v. United States* [1919] and *Abrams v. United States* [1919]), but it remained the de facto standard until the late 1960s, when it was replaced with the incitement standard of protection for free expression.

Blackstone, William (1723–1780)

Eighteenth-century British jurist and legal scholar whose work *Commentaries on the Laws of England* was used for more than a century as the foundation of all legal education in Great Britain and the United States. The *Commentaries* provided an introduction to English law in a clear style that was easily understandable to the public. Although the authority of his sources, the accuracy of his statements, and the relevancy of his point of view have been subjected to severe criticism, the *Commentaries* are still significant as a comprehensive history of English law.

Blogs

Blogs, or Web logs, are a new form of journalistic practice colonizing the World Wide Web. Created by journalists, blogs may be personal and opinionated, and may or may not be controlled editorially by a journalist media outlet. Blogs often contain ongoing postings or up-to-the-minute updates of material previously published in traditional media.

Brandeis, Louis D. (1856–1941)

Brandeis, the son of Jewish immigrants, was appointed to the Supreme Court in 1916, serving for almost twenty-three years. With no prior judicial experience, Brandeis joined Holmes in developing the clear and present danger test in the *Schenck v. United States* (1919) and *Abrams v. United States* (1919) decisions. Brandeis also contributed to the *Gitlow v. New York* (1925) and *Near v. Minnesota* (1931) opinions as well as other First Amendment cases. He retired from the Court in 1939.

Brandenburg v. Ohio (1969)

When a Ku Klux Klan leader in Ohio was recorded on film threatening the president, Congress, and the Supreme Court, he was convicted under Ohio's Criminal Syndicalism Act, which made it a crime to advocate violence and terrorism for political reform. The Supreme Court overruled the conviction and established the incitement standard, a much higher level of protection for expression (see Incitement Standard).

Cato's Letters

Cato's Letters is a collection of essays on political liberty, including freedom of speech and press, written by John Trenchard and Thomas Gordon in the eighteenth century. Printed in colonial newspapers under the pseudonym Cato, the essays were widely read in the American Colonies and played a major role in laying the philosophical foundation for the American Revolution.

Change of Venue

A change of venue is a change in the location of a trial. It is one of the options available to a trial judge concerned that excessive pretrial publicity will undermine a defendant's Fourth Amendment right to a fair trial.

Clear and Present Danger Test

The clear and present danger test was introduced by Justice Holmes in his majority opinion in *Schenck v. United States* (1919). In contrast to the traditional bad tendency test, Holmes argued that speech deserved greater protection and should be prevented only if the words created a "clear and present danger that they will bring about the substantive evils Congress has a right to prevent." It took decades for the courts to fully embrace the standard, although Justices Holmes and Brandeis continued to develop a compelling argument for adopting this higher standard of protection for expression.

Cohen v. Cowles Media Co. (1991)

During a gubernatorial race, a petitioner from one party gave court records concerning the other party's candidates to local newspapers. He did so after receiving a promise of confidentiality from the reporters. When the reporters identified him as the source of their information, the petitioner sued for breach of contract. In this landmark case, the Supreme Court ruled that breaking an agreement of confidentiality, such as revealing the identity of an anonymous news source, is essentially acquiring information unlawfully and is not protected by a First Amendment right to publish truthful information about newsworthy events without fear of being sued.

Common Law

Developed in England, common law is an inductive system of law in which a legal rule is developed over a series of court decisions and becomes historical understanding and customary practice. Fundamental to common law is the concept that judges should look to the past and follow court precedents, a principle known as stare decisis. Press law in the United States is rooted in both common law and constitutional law.

Comstock Act

The Comstock Act or Law, named for its key advocate, Anthony Comstock, was passed by Congress in 1873. This statute tightened rules against mailing "obscene, lewd, or lascivious" books or pictures as well as "any article or thing designed for the prevention of conception or procuring of abortions."

Comstock, Anthony (1844–1915)

American reformer who helped organize the New York Society for the Suppression of Vice in 1873. Comstock crusaded against books, papers, pictures, and establishments he considered injurious to public morals. As a result of his efforts, some 2,500 persons were convicted on morals charges. Comstock is most notably remembered for being responsible for Congress's passage in 1873 of the so-called Comstock Act or Comstock Law, which prevented the distribution of obscene material through the U.S. postal system.

Concurring Opinion

A concurring opinion is written by a judge or justice to go along with either a majority or a dissenting opinion. In a concurring opinion the author typically explains additional or different reasons why he or she agrees with the ruling.

Constitutional Law

Constitutional law is the body of law deriving from the U.S. Constitution and dealing primarily with governmental powers, civil rights, and civil liberties.

Contempt of Court

When a party to a court proceeding violates the proceeding in some manner, he or she may be held in contempt of court. A contempt charge can lead to a fine or imprisonment. For example, journalists who refuse to divulge sources may be charged with contempt and imprisoned until they reveal their sources or the court decides to release them.

Criminal Libel

In common law, a malicious attempt to expose the state or a person to hatred, contempt, or ridicule that may subject the author to criminal sanctions. Criminal libel is prosecuted by the state and not adjudicated as a civil tort. Because of constitutional protections of free speech, criminal libel is rarely prosecuted.

Damages

Damages are the monetary award given to a winning plaintiff in a lawsuit. There are several types of damages. Actual damages are awarded on proof of actual harm, such as loss of reputation. Special damages are awarded on the basis of evidence of demonstrated monetary loss. Nominal damages are a symbolic award, such as the award of one dollar, when the intended goal of the lawsuit is simply a judgment against the defendant. Presumed damages may be awarded to a plaintiff without proof of harm. Finally, punitive damages are a monetary award to the plaintiff intended not so much to compensate for harm but to punish the defendant. Because "punies," as these damages are sometimes called, can be extremely large, they have sparked calls for tort reform.

Defamation

The umbrella term for a tort involving any false communication that injures a person's reputation. If the communication is spoken, it is called slander; if published or broadcast, it is called libel.

Defendant

In a civil lawsuit, a defendant is the party against whom a lawsuit, such as a libel suit, is filed. In a criminal proceeding, the defendant is the party against whom the state files charges.

Dissenting Opinion

A dissenting opinion is written by judges or justices who disagree with the court majority opinion. The dissenting opinion is not considered legal precedent and is not generally influential on future decisions. However, there are notable examples of how a dissenting opinion ultimately swayed the court in future rulings. For example,

Justices Holmes and Brandeis's argument for the clear and present danger standard was launched in the majority opinion in *Schenck* and moved to the dissenting opinion in *Abrams*. It continued to be articulated as part of dissenting opinions until both justices retired. Ultimately the courts adopted a standard of protection very similar to the one Justices Holmes and Brandeis advocated.

Douglas, William O. (1898–1980)

Appointed to the Supreme Court in 1939 with no prior judicial experience, Justice Douglas served for thirty-six and a half continuous years (a record), and retired in 1975, five years before his death. He was known as a staunch defender of individual rights and was closely involved in many of the Jehovah's Witnesses free speech cases in the 1940s and other key free expression cases in the 1960s, such as *Brandenburg v. Ohio* (1969). He was active in creating a large sphere of protection for the press, arguing in *New York Times v. United States* (1971) that there may never be a permissible prior restraint on the press. As such, Justice Douglas was often referred to as an "absolutist" when it came to the protection of free expression.

Eldred v. Ashcroft (2003)

After the Sonny Bono Copyright Term Extension Act of 1998 lengthened copyright protection an additional twenty years, Eldred filed a court challenge of the act's constitutionality. Eldred, who operated a Web site that made available the complete text of books after they entered into the public domain, found his efforts severely hampered by the new copyright extension act. The Supreme Court ruled against Eldred, arguing that the act was not unconstitutional, the extension was not intended to extend copyright indefinitely, and that the "fair use" exception under the Copyright Act of 1976 allowed for limited creative use.

Electronic Communications Privacy Act of 1986

The act sets federal guidelines for access, use, disclosure, interception, and privacy protection of electronic communications.

Embedded Journalist

An embedded journalist is assigned to report from within a military unit during a military action. This type of war coverage was first attempted in the 2001 invasion of Afghanistan and more fully deployed for the 2003 invasion of Iraq. It was designed to allow journalists front-line access to military action while providing the military with a venue to show successes from the front lines, something the military was not successful in doing with the press pool system of a decade earlier. Critics of the embed system are concerned that context and perspective are lost when a journalist reports a very narrow spectrum of information and is literally living with and protected by the very troops he or she is covering. Supporters of the system cite the improved access journalists enjoy, especially with the ability to transmit live visual reports via videophone and satellite link. In the war in Iraq, official censorship of embedded journalists was limited to national security concerns, such as troop locations and military plans. At least one embed, Geraldo Rivera, was removed from the front line for reporting tactical information when he sketched a map showing the 101st Airborne Division's approximate location in Iraq during a Fox News report.

En Banc Hearing

French for "on the bench"; a hearing by the full court of all the appeals judges in a jurisdiction that has more than one three- or four-judge panel. The larger number sits in judgment when the court feels that there is an important issue at hand or when requested by both parties.

English Bill of Rights (1689)

One of the basic documents in English law, outlining the earliest civil and political liberties afforded to Englishmen during the late seventeenth century.

English Licensing System

The English licensing system, in existence until 1694, prohibited any publication without a government-granted license. This enabled the Crown to exert control over criticism of the English government and reap the economic benefits of monopolizing the English book trade through its charter of the Stationers' Company. In partial response to concerns about similar government control of the press in the nascent United States, the First Amendment, guaranteeing the freedom of press among other individual liberties, was created to abolish such prior restraints on publication.

Equal Time Rule

Incorporated as Section 315 of the 1934 Communications Act, the equal time rule states that if one legally qualified candidate for public office receives airtime, either free or by purchase, the broadcast station or cable operator must provide equal airtime at an equal price to all other legally qualified candidates for the same public office. Exemptions to the equal time rule include bona fide news events, such as press conferences, debates, spot news, and, more recently, appearances on talk shows.

Espionage Act of 1917, Sedition Act of 1918

Laws passed by Congress two months after the United States entered World War I. After the laws were amended the following year, they contained key provisions that permitted the punishment of speech that conveyed false statements, interfered with the military, promoted the success of the country's enemies, obstructed recruitment, or criticized the U.S. system of government, including its symbols. Aggressive prosecutions were conducted against socialist protestors under the Espionage Act, and many, including Eugene V. Debs, a candidate for the presidency, were sentenced to a decade in prison.

Fair Comment and Criticism

Fair comment and criticism is a common law libel defense that protects a journalist who publishes a defamatory opinion, with a basis in fact, about a matter of public concern.

Fair Use

Fair use is a reasonable and limited use of a copyrighted work without the author's permission. Fair use is a defense to infringement claims, depending on the purpose or character of the use, the nature of the copyrighted work, the amount of the work used, and the economic impact of the use. Fair use permits limited copying of an original creation that has been properly copyrighted but has not yet fallen into the public domain.

Fairness Doctrine

A 1949 Federal Communications Commission ruling that required broadcasters, as a condition of their license, to identify, seek out, and cover in a balanced and comprehensive way, issues of community importance. Broadcasters had to document their efforts to fulfill the requirements of the Fairness Doctrine at license renewal time. The Fairness Doctrine's constitutionality was unsuccessfully challenged in the 1969 Supreme Court case *Red Lion Broadcasting v. FCC*. However, as part of the 1980s deregulatory momentum in which the FCC was swept up, the Fairness Doctrine was repealed in 1987.

False Light

False light is one of the invasion of privacy torts. Not widely recognized as a valid invasion of privacy claim, false light occurs when substantially false material about a person is published and when publication of such material would be offensive to a reasonable person. Additionally, the publisher of the material must be at fault in the same way fault is determined in libel (negligence or actual malice, if the topic is of public concern). Fictionalization and distortion are two possible ways to put someone in a false light.

Federal Communications Commission (FCC)

The federal administrative agency charged with regulating communications by radio, television, wire, satellite, and cable. The FCC, established by the 1934 Communications Act, governs over all fifty states, the District of Columbia, and U.S. territories. It is responsible for administering the spectrum licensing process and all federal communication laws. The FCC consists of five members appointed by the president. No more than three of the members can be from the same political party.

Federalists

The Federalists were one of the first two political parties in the United States. Influential members of the Federalist party included John Adams and Alexander Hamilton, who both fought for ratification of the federal Constitution of 1787. The Federalists believed in a central and nationalized government. The Federalist party dominated the government until its defeat in the election of 1800. Although the Federalist party disappeared by 1828, its principles had given form to a new government and its leaders had established a national economy, created a national judicial system, and laid the foundations for principles of foreign policy still in effect today.

Freedom of Information Act (FOIA)

The FOIA is a federal law that established guidelines for public disclosure of documents and materials created and held by federal agencies, unless the information falls into one of nine categories of exempted material. This law enables journalists to uncover documents previously closed to public inspection. Since it was approved by Congress in 1966, the law has been amended several times.

Gag Order

A court order requiring either trial participants, including attorneys, or, less often, the media to desist from reporting on one or more aspects of a case. Gag orders against trial participants are an increasingly common strategy to minimize pretrial publicity and help ensure that defendants have a fair trial. It is more problematic, and thus less common, to "gag" the press.

Gertz v. Welch (1974)

Attorney Elmer Gertz was falsely accused in the magazine *American Opinion* of having a criminal record and of being a Communist supporter. Gertz sued for libel. The Supreme Court used the opportunity to redefine the law of defamation. In its opinion, the Court balanced the interests of protecting private citizens from libel and preventing the media from suffering excessive monetary awards. In the process, the Court ruled that private persons do not have to meet the stringent actual-malice standard as set forth in *New York Times v. Sullivan* (1964) even if the subject matter was of public interest.

Government in Sunshine Act (1976)

The Act requires that most federal agencies conduct their business meetings in public unless the meeting topics fit into one of ten exemptions detailed in the statute. The act defines meetings as any gathering, formal or informal, of agency members. The law also requires that notice of public meetings be given one week in advance, and agencies are required to record minutes at the meeting. Historically, the courts have interpreted the law as applicable only to federal agencies whose members are appointed by the president. Several states have created and adopted similar open-meetings laws. Also known as the Federal Open-Meetings Law.

Grand Jury

A grand jury's function is to determine whether there is sufficient evidence to indict a party on criminal charges. It comprises ordinary citizens selected in a manner that mirrors the selection of trial juries. Grand juries do not determine guilt or innocence: they determine only whether there is sufficient evidence for a trial. A grand jury may gather evidence in a variety of ways, one of which is by subpoena. Journalists have been subpoenaed to testify about confidential information before grand juries. Unless they can quash the subpoena on First Amendment grounds of privilege, they may be held in civil contempt and imprisoned indefinitely.

Hazelwood School District v. Kuhlmeier (1988)

In this landmark case, the Supreme Court ruled that school officials are legally entitled to exercise control (including prior restraint) over the content of school-sponsored expressive activities, such as student newspapers. The Court's decision dramatically narrowed the First Amendment rights of students in public schools. Although controversial, the *Hazelwood* decision did not overrule the *Tinker* standard (*Tinker v. Des Moines School District* [1969]) as applied to individual student expression, which is not part of school-sponsored activities or curriculum.

Hicklin Rule

A definition of obscenity derived from the British Court in the 1820s. The rule defined anything obscene that "tends to deprave and corrupt those whose minds are open to such immoral influences and into whose hand it may happen to fall." The Hicklin rule, often described as using the standard of what is appropriate for a child when determining obscenity, further explained that if any part of a work is considered obscene under this definition, then the entire work is obscene. The 1957 decision in *Roth v. United States* supplanted the Hicklin rule and offered a dramatically wider protection under the First Amendment for sexually explicit material. In 1973, the Supreme Court weakened the protection of sexually explicit expression in *Miller v. California*.

Holmes, Oliver Wendell, Jr. (1841–1935)

After serving as chief justice of the Massachusetts Supreme Court, Oliver Wendell Holmes Jr. joined the U.S. Supreme Court in 1902 and spent the next thirty years shaping American jurisprudence. During that time, Holmes significantly contributed to modern

First Amendment jurisprudence through several landmark cases concerning the protection of speech and press freedoms. With Justice Brandeis, Holmes was the key architect of the clear and present danger test first articulated in the *Schenck v. United States* (1919) decision and afterward argued in *Abrams v. United States* (1919) and subsequent First Amendment cases until its progeny, the incitement standard, was formally adopted by the Court in 1969, more than thirty years after Holmes's death. In addition to his advocacy for the clear and present danger standard, Holmes's eloquent dissent introduced the marketplace of ideas metaphor in the *Abrams* decision and his concurring opinion with Brandeis in *Whitney v. California* (1927), where they stated that the best remedy for unpopular speech is more speech, not censorship. Although he left the Court more than half a century ago, in 1932, Holmes's landmark opinions and dissents continue to influence and shape constitutional law and freedoms.

Incitement Standard

Established by the Supreme Court in the 1969 *Brandenburg v. Ohio* decision, the incitement standard protects expression unless the expression is aimed at "inciting or producing an imminent lawless action and is likely to incite or produce such action." This is the contemporary standard for preventing government prosecution for expression.

Indecency

Indecency, the standard used in broadcasting for patently offensive sexual material, is far less tolerant of sexually explicit expression than the obscenity standard. Broadcasting faces this limit on expression because of the pervasive nature of the medium. The indecency standard was first articulated in the *FCC v. Pacifica* (1973) decision, when the Court upheld the FCC's right to levy fines on radio and television stations if they broadcast indecent material. In order to preserve the constitutionally protected right of adults to view or listen to sexually explicit material that is not obscene, the FCC created safe harbor hours—a late-night window during which broadcasters may air indecent material without risk of sanctions.

Injunction

An injunction is a court order that compels a person or organization to stop certain actions pending consideration of the issue at a later hearing. The court usually issues an injunction to prevent an irreparable harm. Judges may issue temporary injunctions, pending a court's later decision, or they may issue a permanent injunction at the end of a hearing that indefinitely prohibits a party from engaging in certain actions. The injunction imposed on the *New York Times* over publishing the Pentagon Papers (*New York Times v. United States* [1971]) is an example of a temporary injunction. The permanent restriction against Frank Snepp from publishing anything associated with his work at the CIA without prepublication review by the agency (*Snepp v. United States* [1980]) is an example of a permanent injunction.

Intrusion

One of the four invasion of privacy torts that provide legal recourse when one person intrudes on the solitude of another person. This is a unique tort for the press, because it turns on the press's information gathering method rather than the information itself. Thus, a journalist using inappropriate news-gathering methods can be sued for intrusion even if the information obtained is newsworthy and true (defenses in other torts against the press), and even if it is never published.

Invasion of Privacy

The publicizing of private information about a person when such publicizing would be considered offensive to a reasonable person and the information is not newsworthy or of legitimate public concern or interest. Invasion of privacy lawsuits against the press are growing in number and often are combined with a defamation lawsuit.

Joint Operating Agreement

During this era of intense newspaper competition, it is increasingly difficult for two newspapers competing in the same market to survive financially. The Antitrust Division of the U.S. Department of Justice has been permitting joint operating agreements (JOAs) under which two competing newspapers enter into a legal agreement to share all resources—business, advertising, production, and so on—except editorial staff. Supporters of JOAs claim that the agreements help preserve editorial competition and prevent a market from being served by only one newspaper. Critics remain concerned that JOAs are granted too quickly and that they will undermine the diversity of ideas as well as competitive advertising rates.

Libel

Part of the defamation tort, libel is a false published (printed or broadcast) statement that injures an individual's reputation.

Majority Opinion

Also known simply as an opinion, written after a court hears oral arguments and reflects the position of the majority of the justices. One of the justices is assigned to write the majority opinion explaining why the majority of justices ruled the way they did in the court's decision. The majority opinion establishes precedent for future court decisions unless it is overruled in a future court decision. Concurring and dissenting opinions may accompany the majority opinion.

Marketplace of Ideas

The marketplace of ideas is a metaphor for an "expressive" environment where all ideas are available for citizens to access. The marketplace of ideas metaphor was hinted at by John Milton in *Areopagitica* (1644) and further conceptualized by John Stuart Mill, an English philosopher and free speech advocate, in *On Liberty* (1859). Both philosophers believed that truth will be revealed only when it is free to circulate within the marketplace of ideas. In American law, Justices Holmes and Brandeis were the first justices to actually use the term "marketplace," in their landmark dissent in *Abrams v. United States* (1919). The concept of the marketplace of ideas continues to influence modern First Amendment jurisprudence in spite of a growing concern about the nonjudicial economic factors that dilute the metaphor's validity.

Mill, John Stuart (1806–1873)

Nineteenth-century British philosopher who had a great impact on struggles for personal freedoms in England. In his most famous essay, *On Liberty* (1859), Mill argued that free expression was essential for three reasons: (1) the censored opinion may be true and the accepted opinion may be erroneous; (2) even truth needs to be challenged and tested; and (3) there exists some degree of truth in all opinions. Because of his advocacy of civil liberties, Mill was considered a radical by members of Parliament. Today he is thought to be one of the forefathers of the personal freedoms that are now protected in American law under the First Amendment.

Miller v. California (1973)

In this case the Supreme Court established the current legal test for obscenity, taking a step back from the great protection offered under the 1959 Roth test. Now sexually explicit material may be declared obscene under existing state law if the average person applying contemporary community standards of the local community would find that the work as a whole appeals to the prurient interest. Additionally, the work must lack any serious scientific, literary, artistic, or political value (known as the SLAPS test).

Milton, John (1608–1674)

Seventeenth-century English philosopher and poet best known for his epic poem *Paradise Lost*. Milton also penned one of the early calls to abolish the English licensing system. In his essay *Areopagitica*, he argued that licensing was unnecessary because truth would always triumph in a free and open encounter with falsehood. Although Milton did not believe in extending speech or press freedoms to everyone, he is still considered one of the earliest champions of expressive freedoms now protected under the First Amendment.

Neutral Reportage

In some jurisdictions, neutral reportage is a press defense against a libel lawsuit. The defense rests on the journalist's balanced, neutral reporting of a defamatory statement made by a responsible person or organization about a public official or public figure involved in a newsworthy public controversy.

New York Times v. United States (1971)

When the *New York Times* published three articles in a series of investigative reports based on secret Pentagon documents (known as the "Pentagon Papers") leaked by former U.S. Department of Defense analyst Daniel Ellsberg, the government requested an injunction against future publication. Although the federal district court refused to grant the injunction, the U.S. appeals court reversed this decision and issued a restraining order. After the appeals court refused to grant an injunction against the *Washington Post* for publishing the same documents, the Supreme Court reviewed both cases simultaneously. The Court ruled against the government, arguing that granting an injunction would be an act of prior restraint. Although an injunction imposing prior restraint would be permissible in some cases, this was not such a case, because the government did not convincingly show that publication of the information would cause irreparable harm to national security. This decision represented a high point for press protection against prior restraint.

Obscenity

Obscenity is a legal definition for sexually explicit material that is not protected by the First Amendment. Historically, obscenity was defined under the Hicklin rule (borrowed from the English courts in the early nineteenth century) as sexual material inappropriate for a child. A progressive Supreme Court dramatically expanded protection of sexual material in 1959, requiring, among other standards, that the material in question be utterly without redeeming social value. The Court refused to protect expressions that meet this standard because, as Justice Brennan put it, they are "no essential part of any exposition of ideas, and are of such slight social value as a step to truth that any benefit that may be derived from them is clearly outweighed by the social interest in order and morality." A conservative turn in the Court opened the door to a new standard for obscenity, rooted in local community standards and requiring only that the work in question lack any serious scientific, literary, artistic, or political value. Since 1973, in order to be declared obscene, expression must meet the Miller test for obscenity (see *Miller v. California*).

Pentagon Papers

In 1971, top-secret documents from the U.S. Department of Defense detailing the country's growing military involvement in Vietnam, despite the administration's public claims to the contrary, were leaked to the *New York Times,* which published some of them. The government quickly sought a court injunction to prevent the *Times* from any further publication of the documents. This case led to the landmark Supreme Court decision in *New York Times v. United States* (1971), in which the Court required clear evidence that the information in question would do irreparable harm to national security before a prior restraint can be imposed.

Preferred Position Balancing

With the courts' effort to balance competing rights, typically freedom of expression holds a "preferred position." In other words, the assumption is that free expression rights should prevail unless there are compelling reasons to favor another right. Preferred position balancing is the most common approach to adjudicating competing rights when free expression rights are at stake.

Press Pool System

The press pool system, originally the brainchild of British Prime Minister Margaret Thatcher, emerged out of the sting of negative press coverage toward the end of the Vietnam War, coupled with the outrage of the press after it was shut out of the invasion of Grenada. The pool system had a rough start during the invasion of Panama, but it was fully implemented during the 1991 Gulf

War. Journalists selected by the U.S. military would be placed with military troops. Their movements would be controlled and troop interviews sometimes "chaperoned" by a public affairs officer. Pool reporters were required to share their information with the rest of the media. Press pools enabled the military to control media coverage of the conflict. However, both the press and the military were dissatisfied with the system. The press felt too constrained, and the military realized that many of the positive accomplishments of the war were not covered. Beginning with the 2001 invasion of Afghanistan, the government tried "embedding" journalists with the troops (see Embedded Journalists).

Prior Restraint

A government action restricting speech or publication before its actual expression. Prior restraint is a violation of the First Amendment unless the speech is deemed obscene or defamatory, threatens national security, or creates a clear and present danger to society.

Public Figure

One of the possible classifications of a plaintiff in a defamation or invasion of privacy lawsuit. It may apply to a plaintiff who is well known or who voluntarily thrusts him- or herself into a public controversy in an effort to affect its outcome. A plaintiff who is classified as a public figure must demonstrate a high level of fault, known as actual malice, in order to win a libel judgment against the press (see Actual Malice).

Qualified Privilege

In libel law, qualified privilege protects a journalist from a libel suit if he or she publishes privileged yet defamatory information (such as court documents or comments of public officials in their official capacity), as long it is presented in a fair and balanced manner (see Absolute Privilege).

Red Lion Broadcasting Co. v. FCC (1969)

In 1969, the Red Lion Broadcasting Company officially challenged the constitutionality of the FCC's Fairness Doctrine (1949), which required broadcasters to seek out and provide balanced airtime coverage to controversial public issues, including a "right of reply" for those who were subjected to a personal attack. The Fairness Doctrine imposed obligations on local broadcast journalism that were significantly different from any obligations imposed upon print media. The Supreme Court unanimously upheld the constitutionality of the Fairness Doctrine, ruling that the doctrine promoted freedom of speech and helped "preserve an uninhibited marketplace of ideas." Nevertheless, the Fairness Doctrine was eliminated during the 1990s deregulatory fervor.

Retraction

A retraction is the correction or withdrawal of an incorrect or defamatory statement by a publisher. Typically it includes a correction of facts and an apology. Under typical retraction laws, a plaintiff must give a publisher an opportunity to retract the statement before a libel or defamation suit may be started. If the publisher honors the request for a retraction of the statement, the retraction will reduce and sometimes cancel any damage judgment the plaintiff might later seek in a lawsuit.

Schenck v. United States (1919)

Charles Schenck, the general secretary of the Socialist party, was charged with and convicted of violating the 1917 Espionage Act by mailing out antidraft literature in protest of the government. The Supreme Court upheld his conviction, ruling that the mailing of antidraft literature was not protected expression under the First Amendment. It was in this decision that Justice Holmes first announced the clear and present danger test, arguing that speech should be protected unless it presents a clear and present danger to society. Unfortunately for Schenck, Holmes concluded that the distribution of the leaflets posed and clear and present danger.

Sedition Act of 1798

The Sedition Act made it a criminal offense to print or publish false, malicious, or scandalous statements directed against the U.S. government, the president, or Congress; to foster opposition to the lawful acts of Congress; and to aid a foreign power in plotting against the United States. Any individual violating the act faced a fine, imprisonment, or both. Although it raised numerous First Amendment questions, the law was never formally challenged before the Supreme Court, because at that point in U.S. history the Court's power to declare acts of the other branches of government unconstitutional was not yet established (this power, known as judicial review, came with *Marbury v. Madison* in 1803). The Sedition Act became a focal point of the 1800 presidential campaign, ending the Federalists' control of the presidency with the election of Thomas Jefferson. Jefferson allowed the act to expire in 1801.

Slander

Slander is the act of making an oral false defamatory statement that injures a person's reputation. Because broadcasting is considered a form of publication, defamation lawsuits resulting from broadcast media are heard as libel cases, not slander cases.

Star Chamber

The English Star Chamber, so named because of the stars painted on the chamber's ceiling, was established by King Henry VII in 1487. The Star Chamber, much hated by the English people, exercised wide civil and criminal jurisdiction. The court had the power to order defendants tortured into confession, to impose fines and prison sentences, and even to mutilate guilty parties. In 1586, a Star Chamber decree effectively strengthened the practice of prior restraint against publishing. In the seventeenth century, the Star Chamber actively suppressed any opposition to the Stuart monarchies, including verbal opposition and the publication of subversive materials. The controls sparked an outcry against the Star Chamber and inspired early arguments for the freedom of speech and press. In 1641 the Star Chamber was abolished by Parliament.

Stationers' Company

The Stationers' Company is deemed one of the most effective censorship bodies of the English licensing system of the late sixteenth and early seventeenth centuries. Under the authority of Queen Elizabeth, all printers had to register their presses with the Stationers' Company, which meant that the Stationers' Company acted as the warden of England's publishing and enhanced the control of information under the English licensing system. Eventually the Stationers' Company and the strict licensing laws and printing acts that haunted printers were eliminated, and the Stationers' Company was officially outlawed in 1710 by England's first parliamentary copyright law, the Statute of Anne.

Subsequent Punishment

Subsequent punishment refers to the government's ability to impose punishment for the publication of information after the fact.

Arguments have been made that aggressive subsequent punishment of publication is effectively a prior restraint on publishing. In other words, journalists will be less inclined to publish if they are concerned about the risk of being punished for the action.

Supreme Court

The Supreme Court is the highest court in the U.S. judicial system. Since the 1803 *Marbury v. Madison* decision, the Court has been able to exercise the power of judicial review and rule laws unconstitutional. Rulings of the Supreme Court are binding on all lower courts in the country. The state court system also has the equivalent of a supreme court, which functions in a similar manner at the state level and has the power of judicial review for the state constitutions.

Tabloid Journalism

The term "tabloid" originally referred to newspapers whose pages were about half the size of regular newspapers. The term has since become associated with a style of journalism that is prone to sensationalism and provocative coverage of celebrities, sex, heinous crimes, human disasters, and anything that would qualify as bizarre. Because of the nature of their coverage, tabloids have frequently been targeted by those captured in its pages on charges of libel and invasion of privacy.

Time, Place, or Manner Restrictions

Although the Supreme Court has held that public speech should be granted some constitutional protection, that protection is not unconditional. Time, place, or manner restrictions enable the government to regulate when, where, or how a public speech or assembly may occur, as long as the government can demonstrate a compelling interest in the regulation and the regulation is unrelated to the content of the regulated message. For some time the law required the government to show that the regulation had the least restrictive impact on speech, but with a later shift in the Supreme Court's view, such regulation was allowed to stand if the government demonstrated that it was the most efficient content-neutral way to meet its goal.

Tinker v. Des Moines School District (1969)

Three high school students in Des Moines were suspended for wearing black armbands to school in protest of U.S. involvement in the Vietnam War, and their case made its way to the Supreme Court. The Court ruled that students' First Amendment rights were not left at the schoolhouse gate. Unless the expression disrupted the education process, students retained their First Amendment rights in public school. Future cases involving students' freedom of speech expanded school powers to control speech (*Bethel v. Fraser,* 478 U.S. 675 [1986]) and the student press (*Hazelwood School District v. Kuhlmeier,* 484 U.S. 260 [1988]).

Writ of Certiorari

An order from a higher court to a lower court to send all documents in a case so that the higher court can review the lower court's decision. The U.S. Supreme Court uses a writ of certiorari in determining what cases it will hear.

Zenger, John Peter (1697–1746)

John Zenger was a German-American newspaper publisher and printer who became famous in 1734 when he was arrested and imprisoned on seditious libel charges after printing articles in his newspaper, the *New York Weekly Journal,* criticizing the colonial governor of New York. Zenger's lawyer, Andrew Hamilton, argued that truth should be a defense for libel. This was a novel argument, because at that time juries did not determine facts of the case, such as whether the statement in question was defamatory—this was the purview of the judge. However, after Hamilton's impassioned plea, the jury refused to punish Zenger. After this case, juries determined the facts in defamation cases, and truth became a defense against libel.

Zapple Rule

The Zapple rule—established in response to a letter to the FCC by Nicholas Zapple, former communications counsel for the Senate Committee on Commerce asking for clarification of the Fairness Doctrine—is an extension of the equal time rule to supporters of candidates. For example, if a supporter of a legally qualified candidate receives airtime, then supporters of all other legally qualified candidates for the same office are permitted to get equivalent airtime at equivalent rates.

6

Documents

John Milton, *Areopagitica* (1644)

John Milton's famous essay, Areopagitica, *served as inspiration for many of the early advocates for the freedom of speech and press. The essay challenged the English licensing system, but it is the brief language below—placing enormous faith in the power of truth to emerge triumphant under a system in which all ideas are available—that goes to the heart of freedom of the press.*

And though all the winds of doctrine were let loose to play upon the earth, so Truth be in the field, we do injuriously by licensing and prohibiting to misdoubt her strength. Let her and Falsehood grapple; who ever knew Truth put to the worse, in a free and open encounter?

Cato's Letters

John Trenchard and Thomas Gordon were English Whigs who harshly criticized King William III and various aspects of monarchical authority in a series of letters written under the pseudonym Cato and published between 1720 and 1723. Published in the London Journal *and the* British Journal, *these letters called for the defense of personal liberties—including the freedom of speech and of the press—both in England and the United States. The author of each letter is identified by the initial appearing at the end of each letter—"T" for Trenchard, "G" for Gordon. Their most famous and highly quoted letters, Nos. 15, 32, 100, and 101, appear here in their original syntax. No. 15 broadly defends the importance of free expression, connecting it to the central principle of liberty and freedom from a despotic government. The remaining three letters address libel. The second and third letters were written by Trenchard about eighteen months after the initial letter by Gordon. Note the way the authors navigate the distinction between criminal and civil libel and connect their argument to the importance of criticizing corrupt government. These three essays are presented in their entirety so the reader can develop a sense of the writing and syntax of the time.*

Of Freedom of Speech: That the Same is Inseparable from Publick Liberty,
Number 15 (February 4, 1720)
SIR,
Without freedom of thought, there can be no such thing as wisdom; and no such thing as publick liberty without freedom of speech: Which is the right of every man, as far as by it he does not hurt and controul the right of another; and this is the only check which it ought to suffer, the only bounds which it ought to know.

This sacred privilege is so essential to free government, that the security of property; and the freedom of speech, always go together; and in those wretched countries where a man cannot call his tongue his own, he can scarce call any thing else his own. Whoever would overthrow the liberty of the nation, must begin by subduing the freedom of speech; a thing terrible to publick traytors.

This secret was so well known to the court of King Charles I that his wicked ministry procured a proclamation to forbid the people to talk of Parliaments, which those traytors had laid aside. To assert the undoubted right of the subject, and defend his majesty's legal prerogative, was called disaffection, and punished as sedition. Nay, people were forbid to talk of religion in their families: For the priests had combined with the ministers to cook up tyranny, and suppress truth and the law. While the late King James, when Duke of York, went avowedly to mass; men were fined, imprisoned, and undone, for saying that he was a papist: And, that King Charles II might live more securely a papist, there was an act of Parliament made, declaring it treason to say that he was one.

That men ought to speak well of the governors, is true, while the governors deserve to be well spoken of; but to do publick mischief, without hearing of it, is only the prerogative and felicity of tyranny: A free people will be shewing that they are so, by their freedom of speech.

The administration of government is nothing else, but that attendance of the trustees of the people upon the interest and affairs of the people. And as it is the part and business of the people, for whose sake alone all publick matters are, or ought to be, transacted, to see whether they be well or ill transacted; so it is the interest, and ought to be the ambition, of all honest magistrates, to have their deeds openly examined, and publickly scanned: Only the wicked governors of men dread what is said of them; *Audivit Tiberius proba queis lacerabitur, atque perculsus est.* The publick censure was true, else he had not felt it bitter.

Freedom of speech is ever the symptom, as well as the effect, of good government. In old Rome, all was left to the judgment and pleasure of the people; who examined the public proceedings with such discretion, and censured those who administered them with such equity and mildness, that in the space of three hundred years, not five publick ministers suffered unjustly. Indeed, whenever the commons proceeded to violence, the great ones had been the aggressors.

Guilt only dreads liberty of speech, which drags it out of its lurking holes, and exposes its deformity and horror to day-light. Horatius, Valerius, Cincinnatus, and other virtuous and undesigning magistrates of the Roman commonwealth, had nothing to fear from liberty of speech. Their virtuous administration, the more it was examined, the more it brightened and gained by enquiry. When Valerius, in particular, was accused upon some slight grounds of affecting the diadem; he, who was the first minister of Rome, did not accuse the people for examining his conduct, but approved his innocence in a speech to them; he gave such satisfaction to them, and gained such popularity to himself, that they gave him a new name; *inde cognomen factum Publicolae est;* to denote that he was their favourite and their friend. *Latae deinde leges. Ante omnes de provocatione adversus magistratus ad populum,* Livii, lib. ii. cap. 8.

But things afterwards took another turn; Rome, with the loss of its liberty, lost also its freedom of speech; then men's words began to be feared and watched; then first began the poisonous race of informers, banished indeed under the righteous administration of Titus, Nerva, Trajan, Aurelius, &c. but encouraged and enriched under the vile ministry of Sejanus, Tigellinus, Palas, and Cleander: *Querilibet, quod in secreta nostra non inquirant principes, nisi quos odimus,* says Pliny to Trajan.

The best princes have ever encouraged and promoted freedom of speech; they knew that upright measures would defend themselves, and that all upright men would defend them. Tacitus, speaking of the reign of some of the princes above-mention'd, says with ecstasy, *Rara temporum felicitate, ubi sentire quae velis, & quae sentias dicere liceat:* A blessed time, when you might think what you would, and speak what you thought!

The same was the opinion and practice of the wife and virtuous Timoleon, the deliverer of the great city of Syracuse from slavery. He being accused by Demoenetus, a popular orator, in a full assembly of the people, of several misdemeanors committed by him while he was general, gave no other answer, than that he was highly obliged to the gods for granting him a request that he had often made to them; namely, that he might live to see the Syracusians enjoy that liberty of speech which they now seems to be masters of.

And that great commander M. Marcellus, who won more battles than any Roman captain of his age, being accused by the Syracusians, while he was now a fourth time consul, of having done them Indignities and hostile wrongs, contrary to the League, rose from this seat in the Senate, as soon as the charge against him was opened, and passing (as a private man) into the place where the accused were wont to make their defense, gave free liberty to the Syracusians to impeach him: Which when they had done, he and they went out of the court together to attend the issue of the cause: Nor did he express the least ill-will or resentment towards these his accusers; but being acquitted, received their city into his protection. Had he been guilty, he would neither have shewn such temper or courage.

I doubt not but old Spencer and his son, who were the chief ministers and betrayers of Edward II would have been very glad to have stopped the mouths of all the honest men in England. They dreaded to be called traytors, because they were traytors. And I dare say, Queen Elizabeth's Walsingham, who deserved no reproaches, feared none. Misrepresentation of publick measures is easily overthrown, by representing publick measures truly: When they are honest, they ought to be publickly known, that they may be publickly commended; but if they be knavish or pernicious, they ought to be publickly exposed, in order to be publickly detested.

To assert, that King James was a papist and a tyrant, was only so far hurtful to him, as it was true of him; and if the Earl of Stafford had not deserved to be impeached, he need not have feared a bill of attainder. If our directors and their confederates be not such knaves as the world thinks then, let them prove to all the world, that the world thinks wrong, and that they are guilty of none of those villainies which all the world lays to their charge. Others too, who would be thought to have no part of their guilt, must, before they are thought innocent, shew that they did all that was in their power to prevent that guilt, and to check their proceedings.

Freedom of speech is the great Bulwark of Liberty; they prosper and die together: And it is the terror of traytors and oppressors, and a barrier against them. It produces excellent writers, and encourages men of fine genius. Tacitus tells us, that the Roman commonwealth bred great and numerous authors, who writ with equal boldness and eloquence: But when it was enslaved, those great wits were no more. *Postquam bellatum apud Actium; atque omnem potestatem ad unum conferri pacis interfuit, magna illa ingenia cessere.* Tyranny had usurped the place of equality, which is the soul of liberty, and destroyed publick courage. The minds of men, terrified by unjust power, degenerated into all the vileness and methods of servitude: Abject sycophancy and blind submission grew the only means of preferment, and indeed of safety; men durst not open their mouths, but to flatter.

Pliny the younger observes, that this dread of tyranny had such effect, that the Senate, the great Roman Senate, became at last stupid and dumb: *Mutam ac sedentariam assentiendi necessitatem.* Hence, says he, our spirit and genius are stupified, broken, and sunk for ever. And in one of his epistles, speaking of the works of his uncle, he makes an apology for

eight of them, as not written in the reign of Nero, which the spirit of
writing was cramped by fear; *Dubii sermonis octo scripsit fub Nerone—*
cum omne studiorum genus paulo liberius & erectius periculosum servitus
fecisset.

All ministers, therefore, who were oppressors, or intended to be oppressors, have been loud in their complaints against freedom of speech,
and the licence of the press; and always restrained, or endeavoured to restrain, both. In consequence of this, they have brow-beaten writers,
punished them violently, and against law, and burnt their works. By all
which they shewed how much truth alarmed them, and how much they
were at enmity with truth.

There is a famous instance of this in Tacitus: He tells us, that Cremu-
tius Cordus, having in his *Annals* praised Brutus and Cassius, gave offence to Sejanus, first minister, and to some inferior sycophants in the
court of Tiberius; who, conscious of their own characters, took praise
bestowed on every worthy Roman, to be so many reproaches pointed at
themselves: They therefore complain of the book to the Senate; which,
being now only the machine of tyranny, condemned it to be burnt. But
this did not prevent its spreading. *Libros cremandos censuere patres; sed*
manserunt occultati & editi: Being censured, it was the more sought after. "From hence," says Tacitus, "we may wonder at the stupidity of
those statesmen, who hope to extinguish, by the terror of their power,
the memory of their actions; for quite otherwise, the punishment of
good writers gains credit to their writings:" *Nam contra punitis ingeniis,*
gliscit auctoritas. Nor did ever any government, who practiced impoli-
tick severity, get any thing by it, but infamy to themselves, and renown
to those who suffered under it. This also is an observation of Tacitus:
Neque aliud reges, qui ea saevitiae usi sunt, nisi dedecus sibi, atque glo-
riam illis peperere.

Freedom of speech, therefore, being of such infinite importance to the
preservation of liberty, every one who loves liberty ought to encourage
freedom of speech. Hence it is that I, living in a country of liberty, and
under the best prince upon earth, shall take this very favourable opportunity of serving mankind, by warning them of the hideous mischiefs
that they will suffer, if ever corrupt and wicked men shall hereafter get
possession of any state, and the power of betraying their master: And, in
order to do this, I will shew them by what steps they will probably pro-

ceed to accomplish their traitorous ends. This may be the subject of my next.

Valerieus Maximus tells us, that Lentulus Marcellinus, the Roman consul, having complained, in a popular assembly, of the overgrown power of Pompey; the whole people answered him with a shout of approbation: Upon which the consul told them, "Shout on, gentlemen, shout on, and use those bold signs of liberty while you may; for I do not know [how] long they will be allowed you."

God be thanked, we Englishmen have neither lost our liberties, nor are in danger of losing them. Let us always cherish this matchless blessing, almost peculiar to ourselves; that our posterity may, many ages hence, ascribe their freedom to our zeal. The defence of liberty is a noble, a heavenly office; which can only be performed where liberty is: For, as the same Valerius Maximus observes, *Quid ergo libertas sine Cantone? non magnis quam Cato sine libertate.*

GI am, &c.

Reflections upon Libelling
No. 32 (June 10, 1721)

I design in this letter to lay before the town some thoughts upon libeling; a sort of writing that hurts particular persons, without doing good to the publick; and a sort of writing much complained of amongst us at this time, with great ground, but not more than is pretended.

A libel is not the less a libel for being true. This may seem a contradiction; but it is neither one in the law, or in common sense: There are some truths not fit to be told; where for example, the discovery of a small fault may do great mischief; or where the discovery of a great fault can do no good, there ought to be no discovery at all: And to make faults where there are none, is still worse.

But this doctrine only holds true as to private and personal failings; and it is quite otherwise when the crimes of men come to affect the publick. Nothing ought to be so dear to us as our country, and nothing ought to come in competition with its interests. Every crime against the publick is a great crime, though there be some greater than others. Ignorance and folly may be pleaded in alleviation of private offences: but when they come to be publick offences, they lost all benefit of such a plea: We are then no longer to consider only to what causes they are owing, but what evils they may produce: and here we shall readily find, that folly has over-turned states, and private ignorance been the parent of publick confusion.

The exposing therefore of publick wickedness, as it is a duty which every man owes to truth and his country, can never be a libel in the nature of things; and they who call it so, make themselves no compliment. He who is affronted at the reading of the ten commandments, would make the decalogue a libel, if he durst; but he tempts us at the same time to form a judgment of his life and morals not at all to his advantage: Whoever calls publick and necessary truths, libels, does but apprize us of his own character, and arm us with caution against his designs. I doubt not but if the late directors had been above the Parliament, as they once thought themselves, they would have called the votes of the House of Commons against them, false and scandalous libels.

Machiavel says, Calumny is Pernicious, but accusation beneficial, to a state; and he shews instances where states have suffered or perished for not having, or for neglecting, the power to accuse great men who were criminals, or thought to be so; and hence grew the temptation and custom of slandering and reviling, which was the only remedy that the people had left them: So that the evil of calumny was owing to the want of justice, and the people were more blameless than those whom they reviled; who, having forced them upon a licentiousness of speech, did very unkindly chide and punish them for using it. Slander is certainly a very base and mean thing: But surely it cannot be more pernicious to calumniate even good men, than not to be able to accuse ill ones.

I have long thought, that the world are very much mistaken in their idea and distinction of libels. It has been hitherto generally understood that there were no other libels but those against magistrates, and those against private men: Now, to me there seems to be a third sort of libels, full as destructive as nay of the former can possibly be; I mean, libels against the people. It was otherwise at Athens and Rome; where, though particular men, and even great men, were often treated with much freedom and severity, when they deserved it; yet the people, the body of the people, were spoken of with the utmost regard and reverence: "The sacred privileges of the people," "The inviolable majesty of the people," "The awful authority of the people," and "The unappealable judgment of the people," were phrases common in these wise, great, and free cities. Other modes of speech are since grown fashionable, and popular madness is now almost proverbial: But this madness of theirs, whenever it happens, is derived from external causes. Oppression, they say, will make a wise man mad; and delusion has not less force: But where there are neither oppressors nor impostors, the judgment of the people in the business of property, the preservation of which is the principal business of government, does rarely err. Perhaps they are destitute of grimace, mystery, refinements, shrugs, dissimulation, and reserve, and the other accomplishments of courtiers: But as these are only masks to conceal the absence of honesty and sense, the people, who possess as they do the substance, have reason to despise such insipid and contemptible shadows.

Machiavel, in the chapter where he proves that a multitude is wiser and more constant than a prince, complains, that the credit which the people should be in declines daily; for, says he, every man has liberty to speak what he pleases against them; but against a prince no man can talk without a thousand apprehensions and dangers. I have indeed often wondered, that the inveighing against the interest of the people, and calling their liberties in question, as has been and is commonly done among us by old knaves and young fools, has never been made an express crime.

I must own, I know not what treason is, if sapping and betraying the liberties of a people be not treason, in the eternal and original nature of things. Let it be remembered for whose sake government is, or could be, appointed; then let it be considered, who are more to be regarded, the governors or the governed. They indeed owe one another mutual duties; but if there be any transgressions committed, the side that is most obliged ought doubtless to bear the most: And yet is so far otherwise, that almost all over the earth, the people, for one injury that they do their governors, receive ten thousand from them: Nay, in some countries, it is made death and damnation, not to bear all the oppressions and cruelties, which men made wanton by power inflict upon those that gave it them.

The truth is; if the people are suffered to keep their own, it is the most that they desire: But even this is a happiness which in few places falls to their lot; they are frequently robbed by those whom they pay to protect them. I know that it is a general charge against the people, that they are turbulent, restless, fickle, and unruly: Than which there can be nothing more untrue; for they are only so where they are made so. As to either being fickle, it is so false, that, on the contrary, they have almost ever a strong bent to received customs, and as strong a partiality to names and families that they have been used to: And as to their being turbulent, it is as false; since there is scarce an example in an hundred years of any people's giving governors any uneasiness, till their governors had made them uneasy: Nay, for the most part, they bear many evils without returning one, and seldom throw off their burdens so long as they can stand under them.

But intending to handle this subject more at large in another letter, I return more directly to the business of libels.

As to libels against government, like all others, they are always base and unlawful, and often mischievous; especially when governments are impudently charged with actions and designs of which they are not guilty. It is certain, that we ought not to enter into the private vices or weaknesses of governors, any further than their private vices enter into their publick administration; and when they do, it will be impossible to stop people's mouths: They will be provoked, and shew that they are so, in spite of art and threats, if they suffer hardships and woe from the private gratification of their superiors, from whom they have a right to expect ease and happiness; and if they be disappointed, they will be apt to deal very freely with their characters.

In truth, most libels are purely personal; they fly at men rather than things; which proceeding is as injudicious as it is unmanly. It is mean to be quarrelling with faces, names, and private pleasures; things perfectly indifferent to the world, or things out of a man's own power; and 'tis silly, as it shews those whom we attack, that we attack them not for what they do, but for what they are: And this is to provoke them without mending them. All this therefore is libelling; an offense against which the laws of almost every country, and particularly of our own, have furnished a remedy in proportion to the consequence and quality of the person offended. And it is as just that reputation should be defended by law, as that property should.

The praise of well-doing is the highest reward that worthy and disinterested men aim at, and it is villainous and ungrateful to rob them of it; and those that do it, are libellers and slanderers. On the other hand, while censure and infamy attend evil-doers, it will be some restraint, if not upon them, yet upon others, from following their example: But if men be ever suffered to do what they please without hearing of it, or being accountable for it; liberty and law will be lost, though their names may remain. And whether acting wickedly with impunity, or speaking falsely with impunity, be likely to do most hurt to human society and the peace of the world, I leave all the world to judge: common equity says, that they both ought to be punished, though not both alike.

All libels, the higher they aim, the more malignity they acquire; and therefore when they strike at the person of the prince, the measure of their guilt is complete. The office of a prince is to defend his people and their properties; an excellent and painful office; which, where it is executed with honesty and diligence, deserves the highest applause and reward; and whoever vilifies and traduces him, is an enemy to society and to mankind, and will be punished with the consent of all who love either. And yet it is scarce possible, in a free country, to punish by a general law any libel so much as it deserves; since such a law, consisting of so many branches, and being of such vast latitude, would make all writing whatsoever, how innocent soever, and even all speaking, unsafe. Hence it is, that in Turkey, though printing were permitted, it would be of no use, because no body would dare to make any use of it.

As long as there are such things as printing and writing, there will be libels: It is an evil arising out of a much greater good. And as to those who are for locking up the press, because it produces monsters, they ought to consider that so do the sun and the Nile; and that it is something better for the world to bear some particular inconveniencies arising from general blessing, than to be wholly deprived of fire and water.

Of all sorts of libels, scurrilous ones are certainly the most harmless and contemptible: Even truth suffers by ill-manners; and ill-manners prevent the effect of lies. The letter in the *Saturday's Post* of the 27th past does, I think, exceed all the scurrilities which I have either heard, or seen, from the press or the pulpit. The author of it must surely be mad: he talks as if distraction were in his head, and a firebrand in his hand; and nothing can be more false, than the insinuations which he makes, and the ugly resemblances which he would draw. The paper is a heap of falsehood and treason, delivered in the style and spirit of billingsgate; and indeed most of the enemies to his Majesty's person, title, and government, have got the faculty of writing and talking, as if they had their education in that quarter.

However, as bad as that letter is (and I think there cannot be a worse), occasion will never be taken from scurrilous and traitorous writing, to destroy the end of writing. We know that in all times there have been men lying upon the watch to stifle liberty, under a pretence of suppressing libels; like the late King James, who, having occasion for an army to suppress Monmouth's Rebellion, would needs keep it up afterwards; because, forsooth, other rebellions might happen, for which he was resolved to give cause.

I must own, that I would rather many libels should escape, than the liberty of the press should be infringed; yet no man in England thinks worse of libels than I do; especially of such as bid open defiance to the present Protestant establishment.

Corrupt men, who have given occasion for reproach, by their base and dark practices with the late directors, being afraid of truths that affect them from the press, may be desirous of shutting it up: But honest men, with clear reputations, which they know foul mouths cannot hurt will always be for preserving it open, as a sure sign of liberty, and a cause of it.

The best way to escape the virulence of libels, is not to deserve them; but as innocence itself is not secure against the malignity of evil tongues, it is also necessary to punish them. However, it does not follow that the press is to be sunk, for the errors of the press. No body was ever yet so ridiculous to propose a law for restraining people from traveling upon the highway, because some who used the highway committed robberies.

It is commonly said, that no nation in the world would allow such papers to come abroad as England suffers; which is only saying, that no nation in the world enjoys the *liberty* which England enjoys. In countries where there is no liberty, there can be no ill effects of it. No body is punished at Constantinople for libelling: Nor is there any distinction there between the liberty of the press, and the licentiousness of the press; a distinction ever to be observed by honest men and freemen.

GI am, &c

Discourse Upon Libels
No. 100 (October 27, 1722)
SIR,
I intend in this, and my next letter, to write a dissertation upon libels, which are liberties assumed by private men, to judge of and censure the actions of their superiors, or such as have possession of power and dignities. When persons, formerly of no superior merit to the rest of their fellow-subjects, came to be possessed of advantages, by means which, for the most part, they condemned in another situation of fortune, they often have grown, on a sudden, to think themselves a different species of

mankind; they took it into their heads to call themselves the government, and though that others had nothing to do but to sit still, to act as they bade them, and to follow their motions; were unwilling to be interrupted in the progress of their ambition, and of making their private fortunes by such ways as they could best and soonest make them; and consequently have called every opposition to their wild and ravenous schemes, and every attempt to preserve the people's right, by the odious names of sedition and faction, and charged them with principles and practices inconsistent with the safety of all government.

This liberty has been approved or condemned by all men, and all parties, in proportion as they were advantaged or annoyed by it. When they were in power, they were unwilling to have their actions scanned and censured, and cried out, that such licence ought not to be borne and tolerated in any well-constituted commonwealth; and when they suffered under the weight of power, they thought it very hard not to be allowed the liberty to utter their groans, and to alleviate their pain, by venting some part of it in complaints; and it is certain, that there are benefits and mischiefs on both sides the question.

What are usually called libels, undoubtedly keep great men in awe, and are some check upon their behaviour, by shewing them the deformity of their actions, as well as warning other people to be upon their guard against oppression; and if there were no further harm in them, than in personally attacking those who too often deserve it, I think the advantages which such persons receive will fully atone for the mischiefs which they suffer. But I confess, that libels may sometimes, though very rarely, foment popular and perhaps causeless discontents, blast and obstruct the best measures, and now and then promote insurrections and rebellions; but these latter mischiefs are much seldomer produced than the former benefits; for power has so many advantages, so many gifts and allurements to bribe those who bow to it, and so many terrors to frighten those who oppose it; besides the constant reverence and superstition ever paid to greatness, splendor, equipage, and the shew of wisdom, as well as the natural desire which all or most men have to live in quiet, and the dread which they have of publick disturbances, that I think I may safely affirm, that much more is to be feared from flattering great men, than detracting from them.

However, it is to be wished, that both could be prevented; but since that is not in the nature of things, whilst men have desires or resentments, we are next to consider how to prevent the great abuse of it, and, as far as human prudence can direct, preserve the advantages of liberty of speech, and liberty of writing (which secures all other liberties) without giving more indulgence to detraction than is necessary to secure the other: For it is certainly of much less consequence to mankind, that an innocent man should be now and then aspersed, than that all men should be enslaved.

Many methods have been tried to remedy this evil: In Turkey, and in the eastern monarchies, all printing is forbidden; which does it with a witness: for if there can be no printing at all, there can be no libels printed; and by the same reason there ought to be no talking, lest people should talk treason, blasphemy, or nonsense; and, for a stronger reason yet, no preaching ought to be allowed, because the orator has an opportunity of haranguing often to a larger auditory than he can persuade to read his lucubrations: but I desire it may be remembered, that there is neither liberty, property, true religion, art, sciences, learning, or knowledge, in these countries.

But another method has been thought on, in these western parts of the world, much less effectual, yet more mischievous, than the former; namely, to put the press under the direction of the prevailing party; to authorize libels to one side only, and to deny the other side the opportunity of defending themselves. Whilst all opinions are equally indulged, and all parties equally allowed to speak their minds, the truth will come out; even, if they be all restrained, common sense will often get the better: but to give one side liberty to say what they will, and not suffer the other to say any thing, even in their own defence, is comprehensive of all the evils that any nation can groan under, and must soon extinguish every seed of religion, liberty, virtue, or knowledge.

It is ridiculous to argue from the abuse of a thing to the destruction of it. Great mischiefs have happened to nations from their kings and their magistrates; ought therefore all kings and magistrates to be extinguished? A thousand enthusiastick sects have pretended to deduce themselves from scripture; ought therefore the holy writings to be destroyed? Are men's hands to be cut off, because they may and sometimes do steal and murder with them? Or their tongues to be pulled out, because they may tell lies, swear, or talk sedition?

There is scarce a virtue but borders upon a vice, and, carried beyond a certain degree, becomes one. Corruption is the next state to perfection:

Courage soon grows into rashness; generosity into extravagancy; Frugality into avarice; justice into severity; religion into superstition; zeal into bigotry and censoriousness; and the desire of esteem into vainglory. Nor is there a convenience or advantage to be proposed in human affairs, but what has some inconvenience attending it. The most flaming state of health is nearest to a plethory: There can be no protection, without hazarding oppression; no going to sea, without some danger of being drowned; no engaging in the most necessary battle, without venturing the loss of it, or being killed; nor purchasing an estate, going to law, or taking physick, without hazarding ill titles, spending your money, and perhaps losing your suit, or being poisoned. Since therefore every good is, for the most part, if not always, accompanied by some evil, and cannot be separated from it, we are to consider which does predominate; and accordingly determine our choice by taking both, or leaving both.

To apply this to libels: If men be suffered to preach or reason publickly and freely upon certain subjects, as for instance, upon philosophy, religion, or government, they may reason wrongly, irreligiously, or seditiously, and sometimes will do so; and by such means may possibly now and then pervert and mislead an ignorant and unwary person; and if they be suffered to write their thoughts, the mischief may be still more diffusive; but if they be not permitted, by any or all of these ways, to communicate their opinions or improvements to one another, the world must soon be over-run with barbarism, superstition, injustice, tyranny, and the most stupid ignorance. They will know nothing of the nature of government beyond a servile submission to power; nor of religion, more than a blind adherence to unintelligible speculations, and a furious and implacable animosity to all whose mouths are not formed to the same sounds; nor will they have the liberty or means to search nature, and investigate her works; which employment may break in upon received and gainful opinions, and discover hidden and darling secrets. Particular societies shall be established and endowed to teach them backwards, and to share in their plunder; which societies, by degrees, from the want of opposition, shall grow as ignorant as themselves: Armed bands shall rivet their chains, and their haughty governors assume to be gods, and be treated as such in proportion as they cease to have human compassion, knowledge, and virtue. In short, their capacities will not be beyond the beasts in the field, and their condition worse; which is universally true in those governments where they lie under those restraints.

On the other side, what mischief is done by libels to balance all these evils? They seldom or never annoy an innocent man, or promote any considerable error. Wise and honest men laugh at them and despise them, and such arrows always fly over their heads, or fall at their feet. If King James had acted according to his coronation oath, and kept to the law, Lilly-Bulero might have been tuned long enough before he had been sung out of his kingdoms. And if there had been no South-Sea scheme, or if it had been justly executed, there had been no libels upon that head, or very harmless ones. Most of the world take part with a virtuous man, and punish calumny by the detestation of it. The best way to prevent libels, is not to deserve them, and to despise them, and then they always lose their force; for certain experience shews us, that the more notice is taken of them, the more they are published. Guilty men alone fear them, or are hurt by them, whose actions will not bear examination, and therefore must not be examined. It is fact alone which annoys them; for if you will tell no truth, I dare say you may have their leave to tell as many lies as you please.

The same is true in speculative opinions. You may write nonsense and folly as long as you think fit, and no one complains of it but the bookseller: But if a bold, honest, and wise book sallies forth, and attacks those who think themselves secure in their trenches, then their camp is in danger, they call out all hands to arms, and their enemy is to be destroyed by fire, sword, or fraud. But it is senseless to think that any truth can suffer by being thoroughly searched, or examined into; or that the discovery of it can prejudice true religion, equal government, or the happiness of society, in any respect: Truth has so many advantages above error, that she wants only to be shewn, to gain administration and esteem; and we see every day that she breaks the bonds of tyranny and fraud, and shines through the mists of superstition and ignorance: and what then would she do, if these barriers were removed, and her fetters taken off?

Notwithstanding all this, I would not be understood, by what I have said, to argue, that men should have an uncontrolled liberty to calumniate their superiors, or one another; decency, good manners, and the peace of society, forbid it: But I would not destroy this liberty by methods which will inevitably destroy all liberty. We have very good laws to punish any abuses of this kind already, and I well approve them, whilst they are prudently and honestly executed, which I really believe they have for the most part been since the Revolution: But as it cannot be denied, that they have been formerly made the stales of ambition and tyranny, to oppress any man who durst assert the laws of his country, or the true Christian religion; so I hope that the gentlemen skilled in the profession of the law will forgive me, if I entrench a little upon their province, and endeavour to fix stated bounds for the interpretation and execution of them; which shall be the subject of my next letter.

T*I am, &c.*

Second Discourse Upon Libels
No. 101 (November 3, 1722)

SIR,

I have been told that in some former reigns, when the attorney-general took it in his head to make innocent or doubtful expressions criminal by the help of forced innuendo's, the method of proceeding was as follows: If the counsel for the prisoner insisted, that the words carried no seditious meaning, but might and ought to be understood in a reasonable sense; he was answered, that this exception would be saved to him upon arrest of judgment; in the mean time the information was tried, and the malign intention of the words was aggravated and left to a willing jury; and then, upon a motion in behalf of the prisoner, to arrest judgment, because the words were not criminal in law, he was told, that the jury were judges of the intention; and having found it an ill one, it was too late to take the exception. Whether this was ever the truth, I have not lived long enough to affirm from my own knowledge; or, whether this method of proceeding be law now, I have not skill enough in that science to determine: But I think I may justly say, that if it be the law, it is worth the consideration of our legislature whether it ought to continue so.

It is certain, that there is no middle in nature, between judging by fixed and steady rules, and judging according to discretion, which is another word for fancy, avarice, resentment, or ambition, when supported by power, or freed from fear. And I have said in my former letter, that as there can be no convenience but has an inconvenience attending it, so both these methods of judging are liable to objections. There is a constant war between the legislature and the pleader; and no law was ever enacted with so much circumspection, but flaws were found out afterwards in it, and it did not answer all the purposes intended by the lawmakers; nor can any positive law be framed with so much contrivance, but artful men will slip out of it, and particularly in relation to libels.

There are so many equivoques in language, so many sneers in expression, which naturally carry one meaning, and yet may intend another, that it is impossible by any fixed and stated rules to determine the intention, and punish all who deserve to be punished. But to get rid of this inconvenience at the expence of giving any man or number of men a discretionary power to judge another's intentions to be criminal, when his words do not plainly denote them to be so, is subverting all liberty, and subjecting all men to the caprices, to the arbitrary and wild will, of those in power. A text in scripture cannot be quoted, without being said to reflect upon those who break it; nor the ten commandments read, without abusing all princes and great men, who often act against them all.

I must therefore beg leave to think, that it is a strange assertion, which, as I have heard, has been advanced by lawyers in Westminster-Hall; *viz.* That it is an absurdity to affirm that a judge and jury are the only people in England who are not to understand an author's meaning; which, I think, may be true in many instances, when they act judicially, and the words which he uses, candidly construed, do not import that meaning. Tiberius put many Senators to death for looking melancholy and dissatisfied, or enviously at his power; and Nero many others, for not laughing at his play, or laughing in the wrong place, or sneering instead of laughing; and very probably both judged right in their intentions; but sure no body will think amongst us, that such examples ought to be copied. A man by not pulling off his hat, or not low enough, by a turn upon his heel, by a frowning countenance, or an over-pleasant one, may induce his spectators to believe that he intends a disrespect to one to whom it is criminal to own it; yet it would be a strange act of power to punish him for this unobservance. So words may be certainly chosen with such art, or want of it, that they may naturally carry a compliment, and perhaps may mean it; and yet other people, by knowing that the person intended does not deserve one, may think him abused. And if this way of judging may be indulged in Westminster-Hall, the Lord have mercy upon poets, and the writers of dedications, and of the epitaphs too upon great men. Surely it is of less consequence to mankind, that a witty author should now and then escape unpunished, than that all men should hold their tongues, or not learn to write, or cease writing.

I do agree, when the natural and genuine meaning and purport of words and expressions in libelous writings carry a criminal intention, that the writer ought not to escape punishment by subterfuge or evasion, or by a sly interpretation hid in a corner, and intended only for a court of justice, nor by annexing new names to known things, or by using circumlocutions instead of single sounds and expressions; for words are only arbitrary signs of ideas; and if any man will coin new words to old ideas, or annex new ideas to old words, and let this meaning be fully understood, without doubt he is answerable for it. But when words used in their true and proper sense, and understood in their literal and natural meaning, import nothing that is criminal; then to strain their genuine signification to make them intend sedition (which possibly the author might intend too) is such a stretch of discretionary power, as must subvert all the principles of free government, and overturn every species of liberty. I own, that without such a power some men may escape censure who deserve censure, but with it no man can be safe; and it is certain, that few men or states will be aggrieved by this indulgence, but such as deserve much worse usage.

It is a maxim of politicks in despotick governments, that twenty innocent persons ought to be punished, rather than one guilty man escape; but the reverse of this is true in free states, in the ordinary course of justice: For since no law can be invented which can give power enough to their magistrates to reach every criminal, without giving them, by the abuse of the same law, a power to punish innocence and virtue, the greater evil ought to be avoided: And therefore when an innocent or criminal sense can be put upon words or actions, the meaning of which is not fully determined by other words or actions, the most beneficent construction ought to be made in favour of the person accused. The cause of liberty, and the good of the whole, ought to prevail, and to get the better of the just resentment otherwise due to the impertinence of a factious scribbler, or the impotent malice of a turbulent babbler.

This truth every man acknowledges, when it becomes his own case, or the case of his friends or party; and almost every man complains of it when he suffers by it: So great is this difference of men's having power in their hands or upon their shoulders. But at present, I think that no party amongst us can find their account either in the suppression, or in the restraint of the press, or in being very severe in their animadversion upon the liberties taken by it. The independent Whigs think all liberty to depend upon freedom of speech, and freedom of writing, within the bounds of manners and discretion, as conceiving that there is often no other way left to be heard by their superiors, nor to apprize their countrymen of designs and conspiracies against their safety; which they think ought to be done boldly, though in respect to authority, as modestly as can be consistent with the making themselves understood; and such amongst them as have lately quitted their independence, think themselves obliged to handle a subject tenderly, upon which they have exerted themselves very strenuously in another circumstance of fortune.

Very many of the Tories, who may be at present ranked amongst the former sort of men, and who every day see more and more the advantages of liberty, and forget their former prejudices, will not be contented hereafter to receive their religion and politicks from an ignorant licenser, under the direction of those who have often neither religion nor politicks. And even the Jacobites themselves are so charmed with their doughty performances, that they would not lose the pleasure of scolding at or abusing those whom they cannot hurt. Many of our spiritual guides will not be deprived of doing honour to themselves, and advantage to their flocks, from informing the world what they ought to believe by their particular systems; and the dissenting preachers are willing to keep their own flocks, and would not have the reasonableness of their separation judged of alone by those who differ from them, and have an interest in suppressing them. And I believe that all our world would be willing to have some other news besides what they find in the Gazette; and I hope that I may venture to say, that there is no number of men amongst us so very popular, as by their single credit and authority to get the better of all these interests.

But besides the reasons that I have already given, there is another left behind, which is worth them all; namely, that all the methods hitherto taken to prevent real libels have proved ineffectual; and probably any method which can be taken, will only prevent the world from being informed of what they ought to know, and will increase the others. The subjecting the press to the regulation and inspection of any man whatsoever, can only hinder the publication of such books as authors are willing to own, and are ready to defend; but can never restrain such as they apprehend to be criminal, which always come out by stealth. There is no hindering printers from having presses, unless all printing be forbidden, and scarce then: And dangerous and forbidden libels are more effectually dispersed, enquired after, and do more mischief, than libel openly published; which generally raise indignation against the author and his party. It is certain, that there were more published in King Charles II's and King James's times, when they were severely punished, and the press was restrained, than have ever been since. The beginning of Augustus's reign swarmed with libels, and continued to do so, whilst informers were encouraged; but when that prince despised them, they lost their force, and soon after died. And I dare say, when the governors of any country give no occasion to just reflections upon their ill conduct, they have nothing to fear from calumny and falsehood.

Whilst Tiberius, in the beginning of his reign, would preserve the appearance of governing the Romans worthily, he answered a parasite, who informed him in the Senate, of libels published against his person and authority, in these words, *Si quidem locutus aliter fuerit, dabo operam ut rationem factorum meorum dictorumque reddam; si persever-averit, invicem eum odero:* "If any man reflect upon my words or actions, I will let him know my motives and reasons for them; but if he still go on to asperse and hate me, I will hate him again." But afterwards, when that emperor became a bloody tyrant, words, silence, and even looks were capital.

T*I am, &c.*

WILLIAM BLACKSTONE, *COMMENTARIES ON THE LAWS OF ENGLAND,* BOOK 4 (1769)

Sir William Blackstone (1723–1780), a famous judge in the English court, published the four-volume Commentaries on the Laws of England, *which served as a compendium of English common law for that time. In volume 4, Blackstone summarizes the current state of freedom of the press in England. Specifically, he interprets the end of the licensing system as a commitment to a press free from a prior restraint on publishing. However, he continued to explain that "no prior restraint" did not translate into a blanket protection for the press if it published material that was "improper, mischievous, or illegal." Thus, Blackstone recognized the potential for the press to be subject to "subsequent punishment" after publication.*

[L]ibels . . . are malicious defamations of any person, and especially a magistrate, made public by either printing, writing, signs, or pictures, in order to provoke him to wrath, or expose him to public hatred, contempt, and ridicule. The direct tendency of these libels is the breath of the public peace, by stirring up the object of them to revenge, and perhaps to bloodshed.

The communication of a libel to any one person is a publication in the eye of the law: and therefore the sending of an abusive private letter to a man is as much a libel as if it were openly printed, for it equally tends to a breach of the peace. For the same reason it is immaterial with respect to the essence of a libel, whether the matter of it be true or false, since the provocation, and not the falsity, is the thing to be punished criminally: though, doubtless, the falsehood of it may aggravate its guilt, and enhance its punishment.

In a civil action . . . a libel must appear to be false, as well as scandalous; for, if the charge be true, the plaintiff has received no private injury, and has no ground to demand compensation for himself, whatever offence it may be against the public peace: and therefore, upon a civil action, the truth of the accusation may be pleaded in the bar of the suit. But, in a criminal prosecution, the tendency which all libels have to create animosities, and to disturb the public peace, is the sole consideration of the law.

In this . . . the liberty of the press, properly understood, is by no means infringed or violated. The liberty of the press is indeed essential to the nature of a free state: but this consists in laying no previous restraints upon publication, and not in the freedom from censure for criminal matter when published. Every freeman has an undoubted right to lay what sentiments he pleases before the public: to forbid this, is to destroy the freedom of the press: but if he published what is improper, mischievous, or illegal, he must take the consequences of his own temerity.

FIRST AMENDMENT TO THE U.S. CONSTITUTION

Ratified December 15, 1791

Congress shall make no law respecting an establishment of religion, or prohibiting the free exercise thereof; or abridging the freedom of speech, or of the press; or the right of the people peaceably to assemble, and to petition the Government for a redress of grievances.

Sedition Act (July 14, 1798)

The Sedition Act was part of a four-law package sponsored by the Federalist party and passed by Congress on the cusp of a war with France. Highly political in nature, the Sedition Act in particular was used to thwart political criticism leveled at the federal government by the Republican party under the leadership of Thomas Jefferson. The Sedition Act made it a criminal offense to print or publish false, malicious, or scandalous statements directed against the U.S. government or Congress. Controversy over the act played a notable role in Jefferson's successful bid for the presidency. When he took office, Jefferson pardoned those convicted under the act (including Benjamin Franklin's grandson), and the act was allowed to expire in 1801. The following excerpt includes the portion of the act that dramatically limited political expression in the United States.

[I]f any person shall write, print, utter or publish, or shall cause or procure to be written, printed, uttered or published, or shall knowingly and willingly assist or aid in writing, printing, uttering or publishing any false, scandalous and malicious writing or writings against the government of the United States, or either house of the Congress of the United States, or the President of the United States with intent to defame the said government, or either house of the said Congress, or the said President, or to bring them, or either of them, into contempt or disrepute; or to excite against them, or either or any of them, the hatred of the good people of the United States, or to stir up sedition within the United States, or to excite any unlawful combinations therein, for opposing or resisting any law of the United States, or any act of the President of the United States, done in pursuance of any such law, or of the powers in him vested by the constitution of the United States, or to resist, oppose, or defeat any such law or act, or to aid, encourage or abet any hostile designs of any foreign nation against the United States, their people or government, then such person, being thereof convicted before any court of the United States having jurisdiction thereof, shall be punished by a fine not exceeding two thousand dollars, and by imprisonment not exceeding two years.

John Stuart Mill, On Liberty (1859)

In this essay, John Stuart Mill advocates for the freedom of speech with three key arguments against the censorship of ideas: (1) the censored opinion may be true and the accepted opinion may be erroneous; (2) even truth needs to be challenged and tested; and (3) there exists some degree of truth in all opinions. With this essay, Mill also introduced the concept of the "marketplace of ideas," a metaphor that reappeared in Justice Holmes's 1919 opinion in Abrams v. United States.

If all mankind minus one, were of one opinion, mankind would be no more justified in silencing that one person, than he, if he had the power, would be justified in silencing mankind. Were an opinion a personal possession of no value except to the owner; if to be obstructed in the enjoyment of it were simply a private injury, it would make some difference whether the injury was inflicted only on a few persons or on many. But the peculiar evil of silencing the expression of an opinion is, that it is robbing the human race; posterity as well as the existing generation; those who dissent from the opinion, still more than those who hold it. If the opinion is right, they are deprived of the opportunity of exchanging error for truth: if wrong, they lose, what is almost as great a benefit, the clearer perception and livelier impression of truth, produced by its collision with error.

Schenck v. United States (1919)

Charles Schenck, general secretary of the Socialist party, oversaw the printing and distribution of about 15,000 leaflets in Philadelphia in August 1917. The leaflets passionately argued that conscription (military draft) was a crime against humanity and was intended only to serve the interests of the wealthy. It called on the reader not to "submit to intimidation." Schenck was charged with and convicted of violating the 1917 Espionage Act. In this landmark case, both the U.S. Court of Appeals and the U.S. Supreme

Court ruled that mailing of this antidraft literature posed a "clear and present danger" to society, enough to warrant the limiting of a person's freedom of speech rights. Although Schenck lost his appeal and went to prison, the case remains significant because in the opinion Justice Holmes announced a new standard for protecting speech: the "clear and present danger" test. Although it was decades before the test carried the full weight of the Court, the stage was set in the Schenck decision for an ongoing argument by Holmes and Brandeis that speech deserved far greater protection than provided by previous judicial precedent.

First, the text of the pamphlet is presented. It will allow the reader to understand the nature of the leaflet's language. It is important to consider the words in their historical context. After the leaflet, there follows the excerpt of Justice Holmes's opinion in which he announces a new standard for protecting expression.

Schenck's Pamphlet
ASSERT YOUR RIGHTS!
Article 6, Section 2 of the Constitution of the United States says: "This Constitution shall be the supreme law of the Land."

Article 1 (Amendment) says: "Congress shall make no law respecting an establishment of religion, or *prohibiting the free exercise thereof.*"

Article 9 (Amendment) says: "The enumeration in the Constitution of certain rights, shall not be construed to deny or disparage others retained by the people."

The Socialist Party says that any individual or officers of the law entrusted with the administration of conscription regulations, violate the provisions of the United States Constitution, the Supreme Law of the Land, when they refuse to recognize your right to assert your opposition to the draft.

If you are conscientiously opposed to war, if you believe in the commandment "thou shalt not kill," then that is your religion, and, you shall not be prohibited from the free exercise thereof.

In exempting clergymen and members of the Society of Friends (popularly called Quakers) from active military service, the examination boards have discriminated against you.

If you do not assert and support your rights, you are helping to "deny or disparage rights" which it is the solemn duty of all citizens and residents of the United States to retain.

Here in this city of Philadelphia was signed the immortal Declaration of Independence. As a citizen of "the cradle of American Liberty" you are doubly charged with the duty of upholding the rights, of the people.

Will you let cunning politicians and a mercenary capitalist press wrongly and untruthfully mould your thoughts? Do not forget your right to elect officials who are opposed to conscription.

In lending tacit or silent consent to the conscription law, in neglecting to assert your rights, you are (whether unknowingly or not) helping to condone and support a most infamous and insidious conspiracy to abridge and destroy the sacred and cherished rights of a free people. You are a citizen, not a subject! You delegate your power to the officers of the law to be used for your good and welfare, not against you.

They are your servants. Not your masters. Their wages come from the expenses of government which you pay. Will you allow them to unjustly rule you? The fathers who fought and bled to establish a free and independent nation here in America were so opposed to the militarism of the old world from which they had escaped; so keenly alive to the dangers and hardships they had undergone in fleeing from political, religious and military oppression, that they handed down to us "certain rights which must be retained by the people."

They held the spirit of militarism in such abhorrence and hate, they were so apprehensive of the formation of a military machine that would insidiously and secretly advocate the invasion of other lands, that they limited the power of Congress over the militia in providing only for the calling forth of "the militia to execute laws of the Union, suppress insurrections and repel invasions." (See general powers of Congress, Article 1, Section 8, Paragraph 15.)

No power was delegated to send our citizens away to foreign shores to shoot up the people of other lands, no matter what may be their internal or international disputes.

The people of this country did not vote in favor of war. At the last election they voted against war.

To draw this country into the horrors of the present war in Europe, to force the youth of our land into the shambles and bloody trenches of war-crazy nations, would be a crime the magnitude of which defies description. Words could not express the condemnation such cold-blooded ruthlessness deserves.

Will you stand idly by and see the Moloch of Militarism reach forth across the sea and fasten its tentacles upon this continent? Are you willing to submit to the degradation of having the Constitution of the United States treated as a "mere scrap of paper?"

Do you know that patriotism means a love for your country, and not hate for others?

Will you be led astray by a propaganda of jingoism masquerading under the guise of patriotism?

No specious or plausible pleas about a "war for democracy" can becloud the issue. Democracy cannot be shot into a nation. It must come spontaneously and purely from within.

Democracy must come through liberal education. Upholders of military ideas are unfit teachers.

To advocate the persecution of other peoples though the prosecution of war is an insult to every good and wholesome American tradition.

"These are the times that try men's souls."

"Eternal vigilance is the price of liberty."

You are responsible. You must do your share to maintain, support and uphold the rights of the people of this country.

In this world crisis where do you stand? Are you with the forces of liberty and light or war and darkness?

LONG LIVE THE CONSTITUTION OF THE UNITED STATES. Wake up, America! Your Liberties Are in Danger!

The 13th Amendment, Section 1, of the Constitution of the United States says: "Neither slavery nor involuntary servitude, except as a punishment for crime whereof the party shall have been duly convicted, shall exist within the United States, or any place subject to their jurisdiction.

The Constitution of the United States is one of the greatest bulwarks of political liberty. It was born after a long, stubborn battle between king-rule and democracy. (We see little or no difference between arbitrary power under the name of a king and under a few misnamed "representatives.") In this battle the people of the United States established that freedom of the individual and personal liberty are the most sacred things in life. Without them we become slaves.

For this principle the fathers fought and died. The establishment of this principle they sealed with their own blood. Do you want to see this principle abolished? Do you want to see despotism substituted in its stead? Shall we prove degenerate sons of illustrious sires?

The Thirteenth Amendment to the Constitution of the United States, quoted above, embodies this sacred idea. The Socialist Party says that this idea is violated by the Conscription Act. When you conscript a man and compel him to go abroad to fight against his will, you violate the most sacred right of personal liberty, and substitute for it what Daniel Webster called "despotism in its worst form."

A conscript is little better than a convict. He is deprived of his liberty and of his right to think and act as a free man. A conscripted citizen is forced to surrender his right as a citizen and become a subject. He is forced into involuntary servitude. He is deprived of all freedom of conscience in being forced to kill against his will.

Are you one who is opposed to war, and were you misled by the venal capitalist newspapers, or intimidated or deceived by gang politicians and registrars into believing that you would not be allowed to register your objection to conscription? Do you know that many citizens of Philadelphia insisted on their right to answer the famous question twelve, and went on record with their honest opinion of opposition to war, notwithstanding the deceitful efforts of our rulers and the newspaper press to prevent them from doing so? Shall it be said that the citizens of Philadelphia, the cradle of American liberty, are so lost to a sense of right and justice that they will let such monstrous wrongs against humanity go unchallenged?

In a democratic country each man must have the right to say whether he is willing to join the army. Only in countries where uncontrolled power rule can a despot force his subjects to fight. Such a man or men have no place in a democratic republic. This is tyrannical power in its worst form. It gives control over the life and death of the individual to a few men. There is no man good enough to be given such power.

Conscription laws belong to a bygone age. Even the people of Germany long suffering under the yoke of militarism, are beginning to demand the abolition of conscription. Do you think it has a place in the United States? Do you want to see unlimited power handed over to Wall Street's chosen few in America? If you do not, join the Socialist Party in its campaign for the repeal of the Conscription Act. Write to your congressman and tell him you want the law repealed. Do not submit to intimidation. You have the right to demand the repeal of any law. Exercise you rights of free speech, peaceful assemblage and petitioning the government for a redress of grievances. Come to the headquarters of the Socialist Party, 1326 Arch Street, and sign a petition to congress for the repeal of the Conscription Act. Help us wipe out this stain upon the Constitution!

Help us re-establish democracy in America.

Remember, eternal vigilance is the price of liberty.

Down with autocracy!

Long live the Constitution of the United States! Long live the Republic!

Justice Holmes delivered the opinion of the Court:

The most stringent protection of free speech would not protect a man in falsely shouting fire in a theatre and causing a panic. It does not even protect a man from an injunction against uttering words that may have all the effect of force. The question in every case is whether the words used are used in such circumstances and are of such a nature as to create a clear and present danger that they will bring about the substantive evils that Congress has a right to prevent. It is a question of proximity and degree. When a nation is at war many things that might be said in time of peace are such a hindrance to its effort that their utterance will not be endured so long as men fight, and that no court could regard them as protected by any constitutional right. [Footnotes omitted.]

ABRAMS V. UNITED STATES (1919)

This case was heard before the Supreme Court in the same year as the Schenck case, but after the Schenck decision was issued. In this case, five Russian citizens living in the United States were convicted under the 1918 Amendment to the Espionage Act (the Sedition Act) of distributing two antiwar leaflets containing "seditious" messages. Justices Holmes and Brandeis again advocated for a clear and present danger test, but this time they voted against the majority decision to uphold Abrams's lower court conviction. This case marked the beginning of several persuasive Holmes-Brandeis dissenting opinions in support of the "clear and present danger" test. This also is the case where Holmes and Brandeis alluded to Mill's "marketplace of ideas." The text of Abrams's circular appears first and is followed by Holmes and Brandeis's dissenting opinion.

English-Language Circular
THE HYPOCRISY OF THE UNITED STATES AND HER AL-LIES

"Our" President Wilson, with his beautiful phraseology, has hypnotized the people of America to such an extent that they do not see his hypocrisy.

Know, you people of America, that a frank enemy is always preferable to a concealed friend. When we say the people of America, we do not mean the few Kaisers of America, we mean the "People of America." You people of America were deceived by the wonderful speeches of the masked President Wilson. His shameful, cowardly silence about the intervention in Russia reveals the hypocrisy of the plutocratic gang in Washington and vicinity.

The President was afraid to announce to the American people the intervention in Russia. He is too much of a coward to come out openly and say: "We capitalistic nations cannot afford to have a proletarian republic in Russia." Instead, he uttered beautiful phrases about Russia, which, as you see, he did not mean, and secretly, cowardly, sent troops to crush the Russian Revolution. Do you see how German militarism combined with allied capitalism to crush the Russian Revolution?

This is not new. The tyrants of the world fight each other until they see a common enemy—WORKING CLASS—ENLIGHTENMENT as soon as they find a common enemy, they combine to crush it.

In 1815 monarchic nations, combined under the name of the "Holy Alliance" to crush the French Revolution. Now militarism and capitalism combined, though not openly, to crush the Russian Revolution.

What have you to say about it?

Will you allow the Russian Revolution to be crushed? You: Yes, we mean YOU the people of America !

THE RUSSIAN REVOLUTION CALLS TO THE WORKERS OF THE WORLD FOR HELP.

The Russian Revolution cries: "WORKERS, OF THE WORLD! AWAKE! RISE! PUT DOWN YOUR ENEMY AND MINE!

Yes friends, there is only one enemy of the workers of the world and that is CAPITALISM.

It is a crime, that workers of America, workers of Germany, workers of Japan, etc., to fight THE WORKERS' REPUBLIC OF RUSSIA.

AWAKE! AWAKE, YOU

WORKERS OF THE WORLD!

REVOLUTIONISTS

P. S. It is absurd to call us pro-German. We hate and despise German militarism more than do your hypocritical tyrants. We have more reasons for denouncing German militarism than has the coward of the White House.

Yiddish-Language Circular
WORKERS—WAKE UP.

The preparatory work for Russian emancipation is brought to an end by his Majesty, Mr. Wilson, and the rest of the gang; dogs, of all colors!

America, together with the Allies, will march to Russia, not, "God Forbid," to interfere with the Russian affairs, but to help the Czecko-Slovaks in their struggle against the Bolsheviki.

Oh, ugly hypocrites; this time they shall not succeed in fooling the Russian emigrants and the friends of Russia in America. Too visible is their audacious move.

Workers, Russian emigrants, you who had the least belief in the honesty of our government, must now throw away all confidence, must spit in the face of the false, hypocritic, military propaganda, which has fooled you so relentlessly, calling forth your sympathy, your help, to the prosecution of the war. With the money which you have loaned, or are going to loan them, they will make bullets not only for the Germans but also for the Workers Soviets of Russia. Workers in the ammunition factories, you are producing bullets, bayonets, cannon, to murder not only the Germans, but also your dearest, best, who are in Russia and are fighting for freedom.

You who emigrated from Russia, you who are friends of Russia, will you carry on your conscience in cold blood the shame spot as a helper to choke the Workers Soviets? Will you give your consent to the inquisitionary expedition to Russia? Will you be calm spectators to the fleecing blood from the hearts of the best sons of Russia?

America and her Allies have betrayed (the workers). Their robberish aims are clear to all men. The destruction of the Russian Revolution, that is the politics of the march to Russia.

Workers, our reply to the barbaric intervention has to be a general strike! An open challenge only will let the government know that not only the Russian Worker fights for freedom, but also here in America lives the spirit of revolution.

Do not let the government scare you with their wild punishment in prisons, hanging and shooting. We must not and will not betray the splendid fighters of Russia. Workers, up to fight.

Three hundred years had the Romanoff dynasty taught us how to fight. Let all rulers remember this, from the smallest to the biggest despot, that the hand of the revolution will not shiver in a fight.

Woe unto those who will be in the way of progress. Let solidarity live! —THE REBELS.

Justice Holmes, dissenting (with Justice Brandeis):
But as against dangers peculiar to war, as against others, the principle of the right to free speech is always the same. It is only the present danger of immediate evil or an intent to bring it about that warrants Congress in setting a limit to the expression of opinion where private rights are not concerned. Congress certainly cannot forbid all effort to change the mind of the country. Now nobody can suppose that the surreptitious publishing of a silly leaflet by an unknown man, without more, would present any immediate danger that its opinions would hinder the success of the government arms or have any appreciable tendency to do so. . . . But when men have realized that time has upset many fighting faiths, they may come to believe even more than they believe the very foundations of their own conduct that the ultimate good desired is better reached by free trade in ideas—that the best test of truth is the power of the thought to get itself accepted in the competition of the market, and that truth is the only ground upon which their wishes safely can be carried out.

GITLOW V. NEW YORK (1925)

Benjamin Gitlow was convicted in a lower court for violating New York's criminal anarchy statute by publishing and distributing

16,000 copies of the "Left Wing Manifesto." The contents of the Manifesto are too long to present here, but the document called for violent overthrow of the government through mass political strikes, disrupting industrial work, and so on. The Supreme Court upheld Gitlow's lower court conviction. The Court ruled that his "Manifesto" was dangerous enough to warrant limiting Gitlow's protection under the First Amendment. But therein lies the real significance of the case. Gitlow was originally prosecuted under a state law. Before upholding his conviction, the Court ruled that the Fourteenth Amendment required that state laws could not violate the protections guaranteed under the Constitution. Thus Gitlow was able to effectively argue that the First Amendment was a defense against his state prosecution. The Court accepted the rationale of his argument, but still decided that his publication included speech not protected by the First Amendment. Once again, Justices Holmes and Brandeis entered a dissent, arguing that Gitlow's speech did not rise to a "clear and present danger." Below is an excerpt from Justice Edward T. Sanford's majority opinion affirming that the First Amendment is binding on the states. Justice Sanford explains the Court's position that a government has the right to sustain itself by prosecuting those who advocate its demise through nondemocratic means. Then Justices Holmes and Brandeis's dissent, which follows, argues that the clear and present danger test requires that the advocacy of illegal action be immediate and not for some future time.

Excerpt from Justice Sanford's majority opinion:

For present purposes we may and do assume that freedom of speech and of the press—which are protected by the First Amendment from abridgment by Congress—are among the fundamental personal rights and "liberties" protected by the due process clause of the 14th Amendment from impairment by the states. . . .

It is a fundamental principle, long established, that the freedom of speech and of the press which is secured by the Constitution, does not confer an absolute right to speak or publish, without responsibility, whatever one may choose, or an unrestricted and unbridled license that gives immunity for every possible use of language and prevents the punishment of those who abuse this freedom. . . .

That a State in the exercise of its police power may punish those who abuse this freedom by utterances inimical to the public welfare, tending to corrupt public morals, incite to crime, or disturb the public peace, is not open to question. Thus it was held in the *Fox Case,* that a State may punish publication advocating and encouraging a breach of its criminal laws; and, in the *Gilbert Case,* that a State may punish utterances teaching or advocating that its citizens should not assist the United States in prosecuting or carrying on war with its public enemies.

And, for yet more imperative reasons, a State may punish utterances endangering the foundations of organized government and threatening its overthrow by unlawful means. These imperil its own existence as a constitutional state. Freedom of speech and press . . . does not protect disturbances to the public peace or the attempt to subvert the government. It does not protect publications or teaching which tend to subvert or imperil the government or to impede or hinder it in the performance of its governmental duties. It does not protect publications promoting the overthrow of government by force; the punishment of those who publish articles which tend to destroy organized society being essential to the security of freedom and the stability of the State. And a State may penalize utterances which openly advocate the overthrow of the representative and constitutional form of government of the United States and the several States, by violence or other unlawful means. In short this freedom does not deprive a State of the primary and essential right of self preservation; which, so long as human governments endure, they cannot be denied. [Footnotes omitted.]

Justice Holmes, dissenting (with Justice Brandeis):
If what I think the correct [interpretation of the clear and present danger] test is applied, it is manifest that there was no present danger of an attempt to overthrow the government by force on the part of the admittedly small minority who shared the defendant's views. It is said that this Manifesto was more than a theory, that is was an incitement. Every idea is an incitement. It offers itself for belief, and, if believed, it is acted on unless some other belief outweighs it, or some failure of energy stifles the movement at its birth. The only difference between the expres-

sion of an opinion and an incitement in the narrower sense is the speaker's enthusiasm for the result. Eloquence may set fire to reason. But whatever may be thought of the redundant discourse before us, it had no chance of starting a present conflagration. If in the long run the beliefs expressed in proletarian dictatorship are destined to be accepted by the dominant forces of the community, the only meaning of free speech is that they should be given their chance and have their way.

If the publication of this document had been laid as an attempt to induce an uprising against government at once and not at some indefinite time in the future it would have presented a different question.

WHITNEY V. CALIFORNIA (1927)

At 60 years old, Anita Whitney was convicted of violating the California Criminal Syndicalism Act for her membership in the Communist Labor Party (CLP), an organization of radical socialists that advocated for violent overthrow of the government. With legal questions similar to those of the Gitlow *case,* Whitney's *appeal went before the Supreme Court. However, Whitney's attorneys never argued a First Amendment defense, and her conviction was upheld unanimously. Although they did not dissent from the majority of the Court, Justices Brandeis and Holmes took the time to explain in greater detail how the protection of speech should be extended to expression unless the danger it poses is serious and imminent.*

Justice Brandeis's concurring opinion:

Those who won our independence . . . believed that public discussion is a political duty; and that this should be a fundamental principle of the American government. They recognized the risks to which all human institutions are subject. But they knew that order cannot be secured merely through fear of punishment for its infraction; that fear breeds repression; that repression breeds hate; that hate menaces stable government; that the path of safety lies in the opportunity to discuss freely supposed grievances and proposed remedies; and that the fitting remedy for evil counsels is good ones. Believing in the power of reason as applied through public discussion, they eschewed silence coerced by law—the argument of force in its worst form. Recognizing the occasional tyrannies of governing majorities, they amended the Constitution so that free speech and assembly should be guaranteed. . . .

Fear of serious injury cannot long justify suppression of free speech and assembly. Men feared witches and burned women. It is the function of speech to free men from the bondage of irrational fears. To justify suppression of free speech there must be reasonable ground to fear that serious evil will result if free speech is practiced. There must be reasonable ground to believe that that danger apprehended is imminent. There must be reasonable ground to believe that the evil to be prevented is a serious one. Every denunciation of existing law tends in some measure to increase the probability that there will be violation of it.

Condonation of a breach enhances the probability. Expressions of approval add to the probability. Propagation of the criminal state of mind by teaching syndicalism increases it. Advocacy of law-breaking heightens it still further. But even advocacy of violation, however reprehensible morally, is not a justification for denying the free speech where the advocacy falls short of incitement and there is nothing to indicate that the advocacy would be immediately acted on. The wide difference between advocacy and incitement, between preparation and attempt, between assembling and conspiracy, must be borne in mind. In order to support a finding of clear and present danger it must be shown either that immediate serious violence was to be expected or was advocated, or that the past conduct furnished reason to believe that such advocacy was then contemplated.

Those who won our independence by revolution were not cowards. They did not fear political change. They did not exalt order at the cost of liberty. To courageous, self-reliant men, with confidence in the power of free and fearless reasoning applied through the processes of popular government, no danger flowing from speech can be deemed clear and present, unless the incidence of the evil apprehended is so imminent that it may befall before there is opportunity for full discussion. If there be time to expose through discussion the falsehood and fallacies, to avert the evil by the processes of education, the remedy to be applied is more speech, not enforced silence. Only an emergency can justify repression.

NEAR V. MINNESOTA (1931)

In 1927, J.M. Near, a publisher of the Saturday Press, *printed anti-Semitic articles claiming that Jewish gangsters were in control of gambling, bootlegging, and racketeering in Minneapolis. In response to these articles, Minnesota's officials shut down the* Saturday Press *using the state's law allowing state officials to shut down any malicious, scandalous, and defamatory newspaper that is found to be a public nuisance. When the case was brought to the Supreme Court, the Court reversed the prior restraint on Near's publication, concluding that the Minnesota law was in violation of the U.S. Constitution. At the time of this case, prior restraint laws had largely been rejected in England and the United States in favor of subsequent punishment of the press. What follows is an excerpt from the majority opinion, in which Chief Justice Charles E. Hughes speaks to this tradition of protecting the press from prior restraints and ends with a notation of the circumstances under which a prior restraint might be constitutional.*
Chief Justice Hughes delivered the opinion of the Court:

The fact that for approximately one hundred and fifty years there has been almost an entire absence of attempts to impose previous restraints upon publications relating to the malfeasance of public officers is significant of the deep-seated conviction that such restraints would violate constitutional right. Public officers, whose character and conduct remain open to debate and free discussion in the press, find their remedies for false accusations in actions under libel laws providing for redress and punishment, and not in proceedings to restrain the publication of newspapers and periodicals. The general principle that the constitutional guaranty of the liberty of the press gives immunity from previous restraints has been approved in many decisions under the provisions of state constitutions.

The importance of this immunity has not lessened. While reckless assaults upon public men, and efforts to bring obloquy upon those who are endeavoring faithfully to discharge official duties, exert a baleful influence and deserve the severest condemnation in public opinion, it cannot be said that this abuse is greater, and it is believed to be less, than that which characterized the period in which our institutions took shape. Meanwhile, the administration of government has become more complex, the opportunities for malfeasance and corruption have multiplied, crime has grown to most serious proportions, and the danger of its protection by unfaithful officials and of the impairment of the fundamental security of life and property by criminal alliances and official neglect, emphasizes the primary need of a vigilant and courageous press, especially in great cities. The fact that the liberty of the press may be abused by miscreant purveyors of scandal does not make any the less necessary the immunity of the press from previous restraint in dealing with official misconduct. Subsequent punishment for such abuses as may exist is the appropriate remedy, consistent with constitutional privilege. [Footnotes omitted.]

Chief Justice Hughes also explained that certain circumstances would permit prior restraint:
No one would question but that a government might prevent actual obstruction of its recruiting service or the publication of the sailing dates of transports or the number and location of troops. On similar ground, the primary requirements of decency may be enforced against obscene publications. The security of the community of life may be protected against incitements to acts of violence and the overthrow by force of orderly government.

COMMUNICATIONS ACT OF 1934, SECTION 315

When the radio and television broadcasting industry began to grow rapidly in the early twentieth century, Congress passed a series of laws that would help control the delegation of frequencies to radio broadcasters and facilitate the growth of the private commercial broadcasting industry. Later versions of these laws incorporated a public interest requirement of broadcasters in exchange for their licenses to operate. The Communications Act of 1934 and its subsequent amendments established the Federal Communications Commission (FCC) and outlined the most far-reaching regulatory framework for broadcasting. Central to the public interest standard for broadcasters were the requirements associated with Section 315, which details the rules governing access of a broadcasting station to political candidates. What follows is an excerpt from Section 315 of the Communications Act of 1934.

Sec. 315 Candidates for Public Office

(a) Equal opportunities requirement; censorship prohibition; allowance of station use; news appearances exception; public interest; public issues discussion opportunities. If any licensee shall permit any person who is a legally qualified candidate for any public office to use a broadcasting station, he shall afford equal opportunities to all other such candidates for that office in the use of such broadcasting station: Provided, That such licensee shall have no power of censorship over the material broadcast under the provisions of this section. No obligation is imposed under this subsection upon any licensee to allow the use of its station by any such candidate. Appearance by a legally qualified candidate on any

- bona fide newscast,
- bona fide news interview,
- bona fide news documentary (if the appearance of the candidate is incidental to the presentation of the subject or subjects covered by the news documentary), or
- on-the-spot coverage of bona fide news events (including but not limited to political conventions and activities incidental thereto), shall not be deemed to be use of a broadcasting station within the meaning of this subsection. Nothing in the foregoing sentence shall be construed as relieving broadcasters, in connection with the presentation of newscasts, news interviews, news documentaries, and on-the-spot coverage of news events, from the obligation imposed upon them under this chapter to operate in the public interest and to afford reasonable opportunity for the discussion of conflicting views on issues of public importance.
- (b) The charges made for the use of any broadcasting station by any person who is a legally qualified candidate for any public office in connection with his campaign for nomination for election, or election, to such office shall not exceed. . . .

- during the forty-five days preceding the date of a primary or primary runoff election and during the sixty days preceding the date of a general or special election in which such a person is a candidate, the lowest unit charge of the station for the same class and amount of time for the same period; and
- at any other time, the charges made for comparable use of such station by other users thereof.

NEW YORK TIMES V. SULLIVAN (1964)

In this landmark case, Sullivan, an elected official from Montgomery, Alabama, sued the New York Times *after publication of an advertisement making false claims about law enforcement (under his supervision) during a civil rights demonstration. The Supreme Court, for the first time, extended the protection of the First Amendment to the press when covering public officials, by defining a new level of protection for the press against libel suits. In order to win a libel suit against the press, public officials must show "actual malice," meaning that the press knew that the published defamatory material was false or demonstrated a reckless disregard for the truth. Later decisions extended this protection to public figures. Below are some excerpts from the Court's decision.*

Justice William J. Brennan Jr. delivered the opinion of the Court:

Like insurrection, contempt, advocacy of unlawful acts, breach of the peace, obscenity, solicitation of legal business, and the various other formulae for the repression of expression that have been challenged in this Court, libel can claim no talismanic immunity from constitutional limitations. It must be measured by standards that satisfy the First Amendment. . . .

Thus we consider this case against the background of a profound national commitment to the principle that debate on public issues should be uninhibited, robust, and wide-open, and that it may well include vehement, caustic, and sometimes unpleasantly sharp attacks on government and public officials. The present advertisement, as an expression of grievance and protest on one of the major public issues of our time, would seem clearly to qualify for the constitutional protection. The question is whether it forfeits that protection by the falsity of some of its factual statements and by its alleged defamation of respondent.

Authoritative interpretations of the First Amendment guarantees have consistently refused to recognize an exception for any test of truth—whether administered by judges, juries, or administrative officials—and especially one that puts the burden of proving truth on the speaker. The constitutional protection does not turn upon "the truth, popularity, or social utility of the ideas and beliefs which are offered." As Madison said, "Some degree of abuse is inseparable from the proper use of every thing; and in no instance is this more true than in that of the press." ...

That erroneous statement is inevitable in free debate, and that it must be protected if the freedoms of expression are to have the "breathing space" that they "need ... to survive." ...

If neither factual error nor defamatory content suffices to remove the constitutional shield from criticism of official conduct, the combination of the two elements is no less inadequate. This is the lesson to be drawn from the great controversy over the Sedition Act of 1798, ... which first crystallized a national awareness of the central meaning of the First Amendment. ...

Although the Sedition Act was never tested in this Court, the attack upon its validity has carried the day in the court of history. Fines levied in its prosecution were repaid by Act of Congress on the grounds that it was unconstitutional. Calhoun, reporting to the Senate on February 4, 1836, assumed that its invalidity was a matter "which no one now doubts." Jefferson, as President, pardoned those who had been convicted and sentenced under the Act and remitted their fines. ... The invalidity of the Act has also been assumed by Justices of this Court. These views reflect a broad consensus that the Act, because of the restraint it imposed upon criticism of the government and public officials, was inconsistent with the First Amendment. ...

A rule compelling the critic of official conduct to guarantee the truth of all his factual assertions—and to do so on pain of libel judgments virtually unlimited in amount—leads to a comparable "self-censorship." ... Under such a rule, would-be critics of official conduct may be deterred from voicing their criticism, even though it is believed to be true and even though it is in fact true, because of doubt whether it can be proved in court or fear of the expense of having to do so. They tend to make only statements which "steer far wider of the unlawful zone." . . . The rule thus dampens the vigor and limits the variety of public debate. It is inconsistent with the First and Fourteenth Amendments.

The constitutional guarantees require, we think, a federal rule that prohibits a public official from recovering damages for a defamatory falsehood relating to his official conduct unless he proves that the statement was made with "actual malice"—that is, with knowledge that it was false or with reckless disregard of whether it was false or not.

BRANDENBURG V. OHIO (1969)

Brandenburg, a Ku Klux Klan leader, spoke at an Ohio rally at which a cross was burned and some of whose participants were carrying firearms. He invited a news crew to film the activities, and during his speech he made derogatory statements about African Americans and Jews and threatened the president, Congress, and the Supreme Court with the statement, "We're not a revengent organization, but if our president, our Congress, our Supreme Court, continues to suppress the white, Caucasian race, it's possible that there might have to be some revengeance taken." With the news film as clear evidence, Brandenburg was convicted under the Ohio criminal syndicalism statutes for advocating illegal activity. The Supreme Court overturned his conviction, and for the first time ruled that the government had to prove that the "danger" found when applying the clear and present danger test to speech had to be real, imminent, and likely to occur. Thus the Court extended the First Amendment to speech not previously protected and created what is now known as the incitement standard. What follows is an excerpt of the Court's unanimous opinion.
    Per Curiam Opinion

[The] constitutional guarantees of free press do not permit a State to forbid or proscribe advocacy of the use of force or of law violation except where such advocacy is directed to inciting or producing imminent lawless action and is likely to incite or produce such action. As we said in *Noto v. United States,* 367 U.S. 290, 297–298 (1961), "the mere abstract teaching . . . of the moral propriety or even moral necessity for a resort to force and violence, is not the same as preparing a group for violent action and steeling it to such action." A statute which fails to draw this distinction impermissibly intrudes upon the freedoms guaranteed by the First and Fourteenth Amendments. It sweeps within its condemnation speech which our Constitution has immunized from governmental control.

Measured by this test, Ohio's Criminal Syndicalism Act cannot be sustained. The act punishes persons who "advocate or teach the duty, necessity, or propriety" of violence "as a means of accomplishing industrial or political reform"; or who publish or circulate or display any book or paper containing such advocacy; or who "justify" the commission of violent acts "with intent to exemplify, spread or advocate the propriety of the doctrines of criminal syndicalism"; or who "voluntarily assemble" with a group formed "to teach or advocate the doctrines of criminal syndicalism." Neither the indictment nor the trial judge's instruction to the jury in any way refined the statute's bald definition of the crime in terms of mere advocacy not distinguished to imminent lawless action. [Footnotes omitted.]

RED LION BROADCASTING CO. V. FCC (1969)

Red Lion Broadcasting carried, as part of a "Christian Crusade" series, a fifteen-minute segment in which someone's honor and character were attacked. That person demanded free airtime to reply, and the station refused. The lower courts supported the FCC's declaratory order that the station had failed to meet its obligation under the 1949 Fairness Doctrine, which required that broadcasters give balanced airtime coverage to controversial public issues, including a "right of reply" for those subjected to a personal attack. In this landmark case, in which Red Lion challenged the FCC to control radio content, the Supreme Court unanimously upheld the constitutionality of the Fairness Doctrine, ruling that the doctrine

promoted freedom of speech and helped to "preserve an uninhibited marketplace of ideas."
Justice Byron R. White, writing for the Court:

Because of the scarcity of radio frequencies, the Government is permitted to put restraints on licensees in favor of others whose views should be expressed on this unique medium. But the people as a whole retain their interest in free speech by radio and their collective right to have the medium function consistently with the ends and purposes of the First Amendment. It is the right of the viewers and listeners, not the right of the broadcasters, which is paramount. It is the purpose of the First Amendment to preserve an uninhibited marketplace of ideas in which truth will ultimately prevail, rather than to countenance monopolization of that market, whether it be by the Government itself or a private licensee. . . .

In terms of constitutional principle, and as enforced sharing of a scarce resource, the personal attack and political editorial rules are indistinguishable from the equal-time provision of § 315, a specific enactment of Congress requiring stations to set aside reply time under specified circumstances and to which the fairness doctrine and these constituent regulations are important complements. That provision, which has been part of the law since 1927, Radio Act of 1927, § 18, 44 Stat. 1170, has been held valid by this Court as an obligation of the licensee relieving him of any power in any way to prevent or censor the broadcast, and thus insulating him from liability for defamation. The constitutionality of the statute under the First Amendment was unquestioned.

Nor can we say that it is inconsistent with the First Amendment goal of producing an informed public capable of conducting its own affairs to require a broadcaster to permit answers to personal attacks occurring in the course of discussing controversial issues, or to require that the political opponents of those endorsed by the station be given a chance to communicate with the public. Otherwise, station owners and a few networks would have unfettered power to make time available only to the highest bidders, to communicate only their own views on public issues, people and candidates, and to permit on the air only those with whom they agreed. There is no sanctuary in the First Amendment for unlimited private censorship operating in a medium not open to all. . . .

Licenses to broadcast do not confer ownership of designated frequencies, but only the temporary privilege of using them.

FCC v. PACIFICA FOUNDATION (1978)

When a New York radio station owned by the Pacifica Foundation broadcast a program containing George Carlin's monologue "Filthy Words"—containing seven indecent words—the FCC issued a declaratory order that served as a warning to the station. The Pacifica Foundation appealed the order in the lower courts. The Supreme Court upheld the constitutionality of the FCC's decision to punish the station for permitting language on the air that is considered "obscene, indecent, or profane." The Court rationalized the decision to empower the FCC to establish indecency standards on the premise that broadcasting is uniquely pervasive as well as the fact that spectrum scarcity permits the FCC to control content in the interests of the public. The Court did not, however, go so far as to allow the FCC to revoke licenses over indecency violations.

Justice John Paul Stevens, delivering the opinion of the Court:

We have long recognized that each medium of expression presents special First Amendment problems. And of all forms of communication, it is broadcasting that has received the most limited First Amendment protection. Thus, although other speakers cannot be licensed except under laws that carefully define and narrow official discretion, a broadcaster may be deprived of his license and his forum if the Commission decides that such an action would serve "the public interest, convenience, and necessity." Similarly, although the First Amendment protects newspaper publishers from being required to print the replies of those whom they criticize, it affords no such protection to broadcasters; on the contrary, they must give free time to the victims of their criticism.

The reasons for these distinctions are complex, but two have relevance to the present case. First, the broadcast media have established a uniquely pervasive presence in the lives of all Americans. Patently offensive, indecent material presented over the airwaves confronts the citizen, not only in public, but also in the privacy of the home, where the individual's right to be left alone plainly outweighs the First Amendment rights of an intruder. Because the broadcast audience is constantly tuning in and out, prior warnings cannot completely protect the listener or viewer from unexpected program content. To say that one may avoid further offense by turning off the radio when he hears indecent language is like saying that the remedy for an assault is to run away after the first blow. One may hang up on an indecent phone call, but that option does not give the caller a constitutional immunity or avoid a harm that has already taken place.

Second, broadcasting is uniquely accessible to children, even those too young to read. Although Cohen's written message might have been incomprehensible to a first grader, Pacifica's broadcast could have enlarged a child's vocabulary in an instant. Other forms of offensive expression may be withheld from the young without restricting the expression at its source. Bookstores and motion picture theaters, for example, may be prohibited from making indecent material available to children. We held in *Ginsberg v. New York,* 390 U.S. 629, that the government's interest in the "well-being of its youth" and in supporting "parents' claim to authority in their own household" justified the regulation of otherwise protected expression. The ease with which children may obtain access to broadcast material, coupled with the concerns recognized in *Ginsberg,* amply justify special treatment of indecent broadcasting. [Footnotes omitted.]

MILLER V. CALIFORNIA (1973)

Marvin Miller was convicted in a lower court of violating California's obscenity law for distributing advertising brochures containing sexual illustrations. Miller appealed to the U.S. Supreme Court. The Court used this case to weaken the 1957 Roth test so that states would be able to prosecute obscenity cases more successfully. In doing so, Justice Warren E. Burger, delivering the opinion of the Court, amended the Roth test in such a way that state and local standards of obscenity—"contemporary community standards"—do not have to match the national standard. The Court also required that state laws articulate the specific sexual conduct covered by obscenity legislation. Finally, the Court shifted away from the requirement that the work taken as a whole be utterly without redeeming social

*value, requiring instead only that the work taken as a whole lack se-
rious literary artistic, political, or scientific value (known as the
SLAPS test). The following excerpt outlines the new test for obscene
material. If the material in question meets the standard set by the
test, it is not protected expression and is subject to state prosecution.
Excerpt of Justice Burger's majority opinion:*

The basic guidelines for the trier of fact must be: (a) whether "the average person, applying contemporary community standards" would find
that the work, taken as a whole, appeals to the prurient interest, (b)
whether the work depicts or describes, in a patently offensive way, sexual
conduct specifically defined by the applicable state law, and (c) whether
the work, taken as a whole, lacks serious literary, artistic, political, or scientific value. . . . If a state law that regulates obscene material is thus limited, as written or construed, the First Amendment values applicable to
the States through the Fourteenth Amendment are adequately protected.

*Justice Douglas, joined by Justice Brennen, presented a lengthy dis-
sent from the majority opinion. He suggested that it is impossible to
provide a clear definition of obscenity and therefore that it is difficult to know a priori whether one's material might be obscene.*

Obscenity—which even we cannot define with precision—is a hodge-
podge. To send men to jail for violating standards they cannot understand, construe, and apply is a monstrous thing to do in a Nation dedicated to fair trials and due process. . . .

The idea that the First Amendment permits government to ban publications that are "offensive" to some people puts an ominous gloss on
freedom of the press. That test would make it possible to ban any paper
or any journal or magazine in some benighted place. The First Amendment was designed "to invite dispute," to induce "a condition of un-
rest," to "create dissatisfaction with conditions as they are," and even to
stir "people to anger." The idea that the First Amendment permits punishment for ideas that are "offensive" to the particular judge or jury sitting in judgment is astounding. No greater leveler of speech or literature
has ever been designed. To give the power to the censor, as we do today,
is to make a sharp and radical break with the traditions of a free society.
The First Amendment was not fashioned as a vehicle for dispensing

tranquilizers to the people. Its prime function was to keep debate open to "offensive" as well as to "staid" people. The tendency throughout history has been to subdue the individual and to exalt the power of government. The use of the standard "offensive" gives authority to government that cuts the very vitals out of the First Amendment. As is intimated by the Court's opinion, the materials before us may be garbage. But so is much of what is said in political campaigns, in the daily press, on TV, or over the radio. By reason of the First Amendment—and solely because of it—speakers and publishers have not been threatened or subdued because their thoughts and ideas may be "offensive" to some. [Footnotes omitted.]

MIAMI HERALD PUBLISHING CO. V. TORNILLO (1974)

When Pat Tornillo, a candidate for election to the Florida House of Representatives, was denied the right to reply (under a Florida statute) to a highly critical editorial published in the Miami Herald, he sued the newspaper in the Florida court system. When the case reached the Supreme Court, the Court unanimously ruled against mandatory access to the press. Specifically, the Court expressed concern that compelling a publisher to print is as much a violation of the publisher's First Amendment rights as censoring the publisher. An excerpt from the relatively short decision follows.

Chief Justice Burger, delivering the opinion of the Court:

The appellee and supporting advocates of an enforceable right of access to the press vigorously argue that government has an obligation to ensure that a wide variety of views reach the public. The contentions of access proponents will be set out in some detail. It is urged that at the time the First Amendment to the Constitution was ratified in 1791 as part of our Bill of Rights the press was broadly representative of the people it was serving. While many of the newspapers were intensely partisan and narrow in their views, the press collectively presented a broad range of opinions to readers. Entry into publishing was inexpensive; pamphlets and books provided meaningful alternatives to the organized press for the expression of unpopular ideas and often treated events and expressed views not covered by conventional newspapers. A true marketplace of ideas existed in which there was relatively easy access to the channels of communication.

Access advocates submit that although newspapers of the present are superficially similar to those of 1791 the press of today is in reality very different from that known in the early years of our national existence. In the past half century a communications revolution has seen the introduction of radio and television into our lives, the promise of a global community through the use of communications satellites, and the specter of a "wired" nation by means of an expanding cable television network with two-way capabilities. The printed press, it is said, has not escaped the effects of this revolution. Newspapers have become big business and there are far fewer of them to serve a larger literate population. Chains of newspapers, national newspapers, national wire and news services, and one-newspaper towns, are the dominant features of a press that has become noncompetitive and enormously powerful and influential in its capacity to manipulate popular opinion and change the course of events. Major metropolitan newspapers have collaborated to establish news services national in scope. Such national news organizations provide syndicated "interpretive reporting" as well as syndicated features and commentary, all of which can serve as part of the new school of "advocacy journalism."

The elimination of competing newspapers in most of our large cities, and the concentration of control of media that results from the only newspaper's being owned by the same interests which own a television station and a radio station, are important components of this trend toward concentration of control of outlets to inform the public.

The result of these vast changes has been to place in a few hands the power to inform the American people and shape public opinion. Much of the editorial opinion and commentary that is printed is that of syndicated columnists distributed nationwide and, as a result, we are told, on national and world issues there tends to be a homogeneity of editorial opinion, commentary, and interpretive analysis. The abuses of bias and manipulative reportage are, likewise, said to be the result of the vast accumulations of unreviewable power in the modern media empires. In effect, it is claimed, the public has lost any ability to respond or to contribute in a meaningful way to the debate on issues. The monopoly of the means of communication allows for little or no critical analysis of the media except in professional journals of very limited readership. . . .

The obvious solution, which was available to dissidents at an earlier time when entry into publishing was relatively inexpensive, today would be to have additional newspapers. But the same economic factors which have caused the disappearance of vast numbers of metropolitan newspapers, have made entry into the marketplace of ideas served by the print media almost impossible. It is urged that the claim of newspapers to be "surrogates for the public" carries with it a concomitant fiduciary obligation to account for that stewardship. From this premise it is reasoned that the only effective way to insure fairness and accuracy and to provide for some accountability is for government to take affirmative action. The First Amendment interest of the public in being informed is said to be in peril because the "marketplace of ideas" is today a monopoly controlled by the owners of the market. . . .

However much validity may be found in these arguments, at each point the implementation of a remedy such as an enforceable right of access necessarily calls for some mechanism, either governmental or consensual. If it is governmental coercion, this at once brings about a confrontation with the express provisions of the First Amendment and the judicial gloss on that Amendment developed over the years. . . .

Even if a newspaper would face no additional costs to comply with a compulsory access law and would not be forced to forgo publication of news or opinion by the inclusion of a reply, the Florida statute fails to clear the barriers of the First Amendment because of its intrusion into the function of editors. A newspaper is more than a passive receptacle or conduit for news, comment, and advertising. The choice of material to go into a newspaper, and the decisions made as to limitations on the size and content of the paper, and treatment of public issues and public officials—whether fair or unfair—constitute the exercise of editorial control and judgment. It has yet to be demonstrated how governmental regulation of this crucial process can be exercised consistent with First Amendment guarantees of a free press as they have evolved to this time.

GERTZ V. ROBERT WELCH (1974)

In this landmark libel law case, the Supreme Court further defined the law of defamation. With public officials and public figures required to demonstrate actual malice in order to be awarded damages, this court overturned an earlier precedent that established that any parties, public or private, initiating libel suits over news of public interest, had to show actual malice. Attempting to balance the interests of private citizens from libel and protecting the media from excessive monetary awards, the Court stepped back and ruled that private persons do not have to meet the stringent actual-malice standard as set forth in New York Times v. Sullivan, *even if the subject matter was of public interest. Furthermore, the Court established the category of the limited public figure—one who voluntarily thrusts himself into a public controversy in order to affect its outcome. For the purposes of that controversy, the person would have to demonstrate actual malice to win a lawsuit against the press. However, on other, unrelated issues, the same person might be classified as a private figure.*

Excerpt of Justice Lewis Powell's majority opinion:

We begin with the common ground. Under the First Amendment there is no such thing as a false idea. However pernicious an opinion may seem, we depend for its correction not on the conscience of judges and juries but on the competition of other ideas. But there is no constitutional value in false statements of fact. Neither the intentional lie nor the careless error materially advances society's interest in "uninhibited, robust, and wide-open" debate on public issues. They belong to that category of utterances which "are no essential part of any exposition of ideas, and are of such slight social value as a step to truth that any benefit that may be derived from them is clearly outweighed by the social interest in order and morality." . . .

The first remedy of any victim of defamation is self-help—using available opportunities to contradict the lie or correct the error and thereby to minimize its adverse impact on reputation. Public officials and public figures usually enjoy significantly greater access to the channels of effective communication and hence have a more realistic opportunity to counteract false statements than private individuals normally enjoy. Private individuals are therefore more vulnerable to injury, and the state interest in protecting them is correspondingly greater.

More important than the likelihood that private individuals will lack effective opportunities for rebuttal, there is a compelling normative consideration underlying the distinction between public and private defamation plaintiffs. An individual who decides to seek governmental office must accept certain necessary consequences of that involvement in public affairs. He runs the risk of closer public scrutiny than might otherwise be the case. And society's interest in the officers of government is not strictly limited to the formal discharge of official duties. As the Court pointed out in *Garrison v. Louisiana*, 379 U.S., at 77, the public's interest extends to "anything which might touch on an official's fitness for office. . . . Few personal attributes are more germane to fitness for office than dishonesty, malfeasance, or improper motivation, even though these characteristics may also affect the official's private character."

Those classed as public figures stand in a similar position. Hypothetically, it may be possible for someone to become a public figure through no purposeful action of his own, but the instances of truly involuntary public figures must be exceedingly rare. For the most part those who attain this status have assumed roles of especial prominence in the affairs of society. Some occupy positions of such persuasive power and influence that they are deemed public figures for all purposes. More commonly, those classed as public figures have thrust themselves to the forefront of particular public controversies in order to influence the resolution of the issues involved. In either event, they invite attention and comment.

Even if the foregoing generalities do not obtain in every instance, the communications media are entitled to act on the assumption that public officials and public figures have voluntarily exposed themselves to increased risk of injury from defamatory falsehood concerning them. No such assumption is justified with respect to a private individual. He has not accepted public office or assumed an "influential role in ordering society." He has relinquished no part of his interest in the protection of his own good name, and consequently he has a more compelling call on the courts for redress of injury inflicted by defamatory falsehood. Thus, private individuals are not only more vulnerable to injury than public officials and public figures; they are also more deserving of recovery. [Footnotes omitted.]

UNITED STATES V. PROGRESSIVE (1979)

The Progressive, *a small political journal, planned to print an article entitled "The H-Bomb Secret: To Know How Is to Ask Why," writ-*

ten by a freelance journalist who researched the article using public libraries, publicly available documents, and interviews with scientists. Prior to publication the article was circulated among some scientists to verify the factual basis of the article. The U.S. government learned of the article and sought and obtained a federal court order that blocked its publication. A full hearing was scheduled for months later. During this waiting period, a number of other journals and newspapers began printing articles similar to the one the Progressive *intended to publish. Eventually, the government dropped the case.*

Justice Warren delivering the opinion of the court:

Although the defendants state that the information contained in the article is relatively easy to obtain, only five countries now have a hydrogen bomb. Yet the United States first successfully exploded the hydrogen bomb some twenty-six years ago.

The point has also been made that it is only a question of time before other countries will have the hydrogen bomb. That may be true. However, there are times in the course of human history when time itself may have been very important. This time factor becomes critical when considering mass annihilation weaponry; witness the failure of Hitler to get his V-1 and V-2 bombs operational quickly enough to materially affect the outcome of World War II.

Defendants have stated that publication of the article will alert the people of this country to the false illusion of security created by the government's futile efforts at secrecy. They believe publication will provide the people with needed information to make informed decisions on an urgent issue of public concern.

However, this Court can find no plausible reason why the public needs to know the technical details about hydrogen bomb construction to carry on an informed debate on this issue. Furthermore, the Court believes that the defendants' position in favor of nuclear non-proliferation would be harmed, not aided, by the publication of this article.

The defendants have also relied on the decision in the *New York Times* case. In that case, the Supreme Court refused to enjoin the *New York Times* and the *Washington Post* from publishing the contents of a classified historical study of United States decision-making in Viet Nam, the so-called "Pentagon Papers."

This case is different in several important respects. In the first place, the study involved in the *New York Times* case contained historical data relating to events that occurred some three to twenty years previously. Secondly, the Supreme Court agreed with the lower court that no cogent reasons were advanced by the government as to why the article affected national security except that publication might cause some embarrassment to the United States.

A final and most vital difference between these two cases is the fact that a specific statute is involved here. Section 2274 of The Atomic Energy Act prohibits anyone from communicating, transmitting or disclosing any restricted data to any person "with reason to believe such data would be utilized to injure the United States or to secure an advantage to any foreign nation."

Section 2014 of the Act defines restricted data. "'Restricted Data' means all data concerning 1) design, manufacture, or utilization of atomic weapons; 2) the production of special nuclear material; or 3) the use of special nuclear material in the production of energy, but shall not include data declassified or removed from the Restricted Data category pursuant to section 2162 of this title."

As applied to this case, the Court finds that the statute in question is not vague or overbroad. The Court is convinced that the terms used in the statute "communicates, transmits or discloses" include publishing in a magazine. The Court is of the opinion that the government has shown that the defendants had reason to believe that the data in the article, if published, would injure the United States or give an advantage to a foreign nation. Extensive reading and studying of the documents on file lead to the conclusion that not all the data is available in the public realm in the same fashion, if it is available at all.

What is involved here is information dealing with the most destructive weapon in the history of mankind, information of sufficient destructive potential to nullify the right to free speech and to endanger the right to life itself. . . .

A mistake in ruling against *The Progressive* would seriously infringe cherished First Amendment rights. If a preliminary injunction is issued, it will constitute the first instance of a prior restraint against a publication in this fashion in the history of this country, to this Court's knowledge. Such notoriety is not to be sought. It will curtail defendant's First

Amendment rights in a drastic and substantial fashion. It will infringe upon our right to know and to be informed as well.

A mistake in ruling against the United States could pave the way for thermonuclear annihilation for us all. In that event, our right to life is extinguished and the right to publish becomes moot.

In the *Near* case, the Supreme Court recognized that publication of troop movements in time of war would threaten national security and could therefore be restrained. Times have changed significantly since 1931 when *Near* was decided. Now war by foot soldiers has been replaced in large part by war by machines and bombs. No longer need there be any advance warning or any preparation time before a nuclear war could be commenced.

In light of these factors, this Court concludes that the publication of the technical information on the hydrogen bomb contained in the article is analogous to publication of troop movements or locations in time of war and falls within the extremely narrow exception to the rule against prior restraint. [Footnotes omitted.]

PHILADELPHIA NEWSPAPERS, INC. V. HEPPS (1986)

In this landmark case, the Supreme Court shifted the burden of proof from the defendant to the plaintiff in a libel case. Essentially, the Court concluded that when suing the media on matters of public concern, the plaintiff must now prove that the "libelous" allegations are false. This removes the burden of proof from the press so that it does not have a "chilling effect."

Justice Sandra Day O'Connor delivered the opinion of the Court:

There will always be instances when the factfinding process will be unable to resolve conclusively whether the speech is true or false; it is in those cases that the burden of proof is dispositive. Under a rule forcing the plaintiff to bear the burden of showing falsity, there will be some cases in which plaintiffs cannot meet their burden despite the fact that the speech is in fact false. The plaintiff's suit will fail despite the fact that, in some abstract sense, the suit is meritorious. Similarly, under an alternative rule placing the burden of showing truth on defendants, there would be some cases in which defendants could not bear their burden despite the fact that the speech is in fact true. Those suits would succeed despite the fact that, in some abstract sense, those suits are unmeritorious. Under either rule, then, the outcome of the suit will sometimes be at variance with the outcome that we would desire if all speech were either demonstrably true or demonstrably false. . . .

In a case presenting a configuration of speech and plaintiff like the one we face here, and where the scales are in such an uncertain balance, we believe that the Constitution requires us to tip them in favor of protecting true speech. To ensure that true speech on matters of public concern is not deterred, we hold that the common-law presumption that defamatory speech is false cannot stand when a plaintiff seeks damages against a media defendant for speech of public concern. . . .

It is not immediately apparent from the text of the First Amendment, which by its terms applies only to governmental action, that a similar result should obtain here: a suit by a private party is obviously quite different from the government's direct enforcement of its own laws. Nonetheless, the need to encourage debate on public issues that concerned the Court in the governmental-restriction cases is of concern in a similar manner in this case involving a private suit for damages: placement by state law of the burden of proving truth upon media defendants who publish speech of public concern deters such speech because of the fear that liability will unjustifiably result. . . . Because such a "chilling" effect would be antithetical to the First Amendment's protection of true speech on matters of public concern, we believe that a private-figure plaintiff must bear the burden of showing that the speech at issue is false before recovering damages for defamation from a media defendant. To do otherwise could "only result in a deterrence of speech which the Constitution makes free."

We recognize that requiring the plaintiff to show falsity will insulate from liability some speech that is false, but unprovably so. Nonetheless, the Court's previous decisions on the restrictions that the First Amendment places upon the common law of defamation firmly support our conclusion here with respect to the allocation of the burden of proof. In attempting to resolve related issues on the defamation context, the Court has affirmed that "[the] First Amendment requires that we protect some falsehood in order to protect speech that matters." . . . To provide "'breathing space,'" . . . for true speech on matters of public concern, the Court has been willing to insulate even demonstrably false speech from liability, and has imposed additional requirements of fault upon the plaintiff in a suit for defamation. [Footnotes omitted.]

OPERATION DESERT SHIELD GROUND RULES AND SUPPLEMENTARY GUIDELINES (JANUARY 7, 1991)

Any U.S. journalist chosen to travel with the military pool during Operation Desert Shield was provided with the following ground rules. These rules regulated what information was permissible for a journalist to report and what information was prohibited from release. In addition to these content regulations, a number of ground rules dictated the level of involvement of journalists with military troops and the equipment journalists were allowed to use in the field during certain types of operations.

The following information should not be reported because its publication or broadcast could jeopardize operations and endanger lives:

- For U.S. or coalition units, specific numerical information on troop strength, aircraft, weapons systems, on-hand equipment, or supplies (e.g., artillery, tanks, radars, missiles, trucks, water), including amounts of ammunition or fuel moved by support units or on hand in combat units. Unit size may be described in general terms such as "company-size," "multi-battalion," "multi-division," "naval task force," and "carrier battle group." Number and amount of equipment and supplies may be described in general terms such as "large," "small," or "many."
- Any information that reveals details of future plans, operations, or strikes, including postponed or cancelled operations.
- Information or photography, including aerial and satellite pictures, that would reveal the specific location of military

forces or show the level of security at military installations or encampments. Locations may be described as follows: all Navy embark stories can identify the ship upon which embarked as a dateline and will state that the report is coming "from the Persian Gulf," "Red Sea," or "North Arabian Sea." Stories written in Saudi Arabia may be datelined, "Eastern Saudi Arabia," "Near the Kuwaiti border," etc. For specific countries outside Saudi Arabia, stories will state that the report is coming from the Persian Gulf region unless DoD has publicly acknowledged participation by that country.

- Rules of engagement details.
- Information on intelligence collection activities, including targets, methods, and results.
- During an operation, specific information on friendly force troop movements, tactical deployments, and dispositions that would jeopardize operational security and lives. This would include unit designations, names of operations, and size of friendly forces involved, until released by CENT-COM.
- Identification of mission aircraft points of origin, other than as land or carrier based.
- Information on the effectiveness or ineffectiveness of enemy camouflage, cover, deception, targeting, direct and indirect fire, intelligence collection, or security measures.
- Specific identifying information on missing or downed aircraft or ships while search and rescue operations are planned or underway.
- Special operations forces' methods, unique equipment or tactics.
- Specific operating methods and tactics, (e.g., air ops angles of attack or speeds, or naval tactics and evasive maneuvers). General terms such as "low" or "fast" may be used.
- Information on operational or support vulnerabilities that could be used against U.S. forces, such as details of major battle damage or major personnel losses of specific U.S. or coalition units, until that information no longer provides tactical advantage to the enemy and is, therefore, released by

CENTCOM. Damage and casualties may be described as "light," "moderate," or "heavy."

Guidelines for News Media

- News media personnel must carry and support any personal and professional gear they take with them, including protective cases for professional equipment, batteries, cables, converters, etc.
- Night operations—Light discipline restrictions will be followed. The only approved light source is a flashlight with a red lens. No visible light source, including flash or television lights, will be used when operating with forces at night unless specifically approved by the on-scene commander.
- You must remain with your military escort at all times, until released, and follow their instructions regarding your activities. These instructions are not intended to hinder your reporting. They are intended to facilitate movement, ensure safety, and protect operational security.

For news media personnel participating in designated CENTCOM Media Pools:

- Upon registering with the JIB, news media should contact the respective pool coordinator for explanation of pool operations.
- If you are unable to withstand the rigorous conditions required to operate with the forward-deployed forces, you will be medically evacuated out of the area.
- Security at the source will be the policy. In the event of hostilities, pool products will be subject to security review prior to release to determine if they contain information that would jeopardize an operation or the security of U.S. or coalition forces. Material will not be withheld just because it is embarrassing or contains criticism. The public affairs officer on the scene will conduct the security review. However, if a conflict arises, the product will be expeditiously sent to JIB Dhahran for review by the JIB Director.

If no agreement can be reached, the product will be expeditiously forwarded to OASD (PA) for review with the appropriate bureau chief.

- Casualty information, because of concern of the notification of the next of kin, is extremely sensitive. By executive directive, next of kin of all military fatalities must be notified in person by a uniformed member of the appropriate service. There have been instances in which the next of kin have first learned of the death or wounding of a loved one through the news media. The problem is particularly difficult for visual media. Casualty photographs showing a recognizable face, name tag, or other identifying feature or item should not be used before the next of kin have been notified. The anguish that sudden recognition at home can cause far outweighs the news value of the photograph, film or videotape. Names of casualties whose next of kin have been notified can be verified through the JIB Dhahran.

Society of Professional Journalists Code of Ethics (1996)

The Society of Professional Journalists Code of Ethics is voluntarily followed by writers, editors, and news professionals. This version, adopted by the 1996 Society of Professional Journalists National Convention, calls for accuracy of information while reporting, balanced coverage of issues, and accountability, among other desirable practices of journalism professionals.

Preamble
Members of the Society of Professional Journalists believe that public enlightenment is the forerunner of justice and the foundation of democracy. The duty of the journalist is to further those ends by seeking truth and providing a fair and comprehensive account of events and issues. Conscientious journalists from all media and specialties strive to serve the public with thoroughness and honesty. Professional integrity is the cornerstone of a journalist's credibility. Members of the Society share a

dedication to ethical behavior and adopt this code to declare the Society's principles and standards of practice.

Seek Truth and Report It
Journalists should be honest, fair and courageous in gathering, reporting and interpreting information.
Journalists should:

- Test the accuracy of information from all sources and exercise care to avoid inadvertent error. Deliberate distortion is never permissible.
- Diligently seek out subjects of news stories to give them the opportunity to respond to allegations of wrongdoing.
- Identify sources whenever feasible. The public is entitled to as much information as possible on sources' reliability.
- Always question sources' motives before promising anonymity. Clarify conditions attached to any promise made in exchange for information. Keep promises.
- Make certain that headlines, news teases and promotional material, photos, video, audio, graphics, sound bites and quotations do not misrepresent. They should not oversimplify or highlight incidents out of context.
- Never distort the content of news photos or video. Image enhancement for technical clarity is always permissible. Label montages and photo illustrations.
- Avoid misleading re-enactments or staged news events. If re-enactment is necessary to tell a story, label it.
- Avoid undercover or other surreptitious methods of gathering information except when traditional open methods will not yield information vital to the public. Use of such methods should be explained as part of the story.
- Never plagiarize.
- Tell the story of the diversity and magnitude of the human experience boldly, even when it is unpopular to do so.
- Examine their own cultural values and avoid imposing those values on others.
- Avoid stereotyping by race, gender, age, religion, ethnicity, geography, sexual orientation, disability, physical appearance or social status.

- Support the open exchange of views, even views they find repugnant.
- Give voice to the voiceless; official and unofficial sources of information can be equally valid.
- Distinguish between advocacy and news reporting. Analysis and commentary should be labeled and not misrepresent fact or context.
- Distinguish news from advertising and shun hybrids that blur the lines between the two.
- Recognize a special obligation to ensure that the public's business is conducted in the open and that government records are open to inspection.

Minimize Harm
Ethical journalists treat sources, subjects and colleagues as human beings deserving of respect.
Journalists should:

- Show compassion for those who may be affected adversely by news coverage. Use special sensitivity when dealing with children and inexperienced sources or subjects.
- Be sensitive when seeking or using interviews or photographs of those affected by tragedy or grief.
- Recognize that gathering and reporting information may cause harm or discomfort. Pursuit of the news is not a license for arrogance.
- Recognize that private people have a greater right to control information about themselves than do public officials and others who seek power, influence or attention. Only an overriding public need can justify intrusion into anyone's privacy.
- Show good taste. Avoid pandering to lurid curiosity.
- Be cautious about identifying juvenile suspects or victims of sex crimes.
- Be judicious about naming criminal suspects before the formal filing of charges.

- Balance a criminal suspect's fair trial rights with the public's right to be informed.

Act Independently
Journalists should be free of obligation to any interest other than the public's right to know.
Journalists should:

- Avoid conflicts of interest, real or perceived.
- Remain free of associations and activities that may compromise integrity or damage credibility.
- Refuse gifts, favors, fees, free travel and special treatment, and shun secondary employment, political involvement, public office and service in community organizations if they compromise journalistic integrity.
- Disclose unavoidable conflicts.
- Be vigilant and courageous about holding those with power accountable.
- Deny favored treatment to advertisers and special interests and resist their pressure to influence news coverage.
- Be wary of sources offering information for favors or money; avoid bidding for news.

Be Accountable
Journalists are accountable to their readers, listeners, viewers and each other.
Journalists should:

- Clarify and explain news coverage and invite dialogue with the public over journalistic conduct.
- Encourage the public to voice grievances against the news media.
- Admit mistakes and correct them promptly.
- Expose unethical practices of journalists and the news media.
- Abide by the same high standards to which they hold others.

U.S. Department of Defense Directive 5122.5: Nine Principles of Combat Coverage (September 27, 2000)

This directive lists the military's rules for dealing with journalists in areas where there is combat. It explains what journalists should expect from the military during wartime, such as access to military personnel for interviews, what information can be released to the public in reports, and what information is subject to censorship because of its sensitive nature. It outlines similar guidelines for combat coverage that were addressed in the Desert Shield Ground Rules but reflects the new "embedded journalist" approach to war coverage. This directive served as regulation for press coverage during the invasion of Afghanistan in 2001 and of Iraq in 2003.

E3.1.1. Open and independent reporting shall be the principal means of coverage of U.S. military operations.

E3.1.2. Media pools (limited number of news media who represent a larger number of news media organizations for news gatherings and sharing of material during a specified activity), are not to serve as the standard means of covering U.S. military operations. However, they sometimes may provide the only means of early access to a military operation. In this case, media pools should be as large as possible and disbanded at the earliest opportunity (in 24 to 36 hours, when possible). The arrival of early-access media pools shall not cancel the principle of independent coverage for journalists already in the area.

E3.1.3. Even under conditions of open coverage, pools may be applicable for specific events, such as those at extremely remote locations or where space is limited.

E3.1.4. Journalists in a combat zone shall be credentialed by the U.S. military and shall be required to abide by a clear set of military security ground rules that protect U.S. Armed Forces and their operations. Violation of the ground rules may result in suspension of credentials and expulsion from the combat zone of the journalist involved. News organizations shall make their best efforts to assign experienced journalists to combat operations and to make them familiar with U.S. military operations.

E3.1.5. Journalists shall be provided access to all major military units. Special operations restrictions may limit access in some cases.

E3.1.6. Military PA officers should act as liaisons, but should not interfere with the reporting process.

E3.1.7. Under conditions of open coverage, field commanders should be instructed to permit journalists to ride on military vehicles and aircraft when possible. The military shall be responsible for the transportation of pools.

E3.1.8. Consistent with its capabilities, the military shall supply PA officers with facilities to enable timely, secure, compatible transmission of pool material and shall make those facilities available, when possible, for filing independent coverage. If Government facilities are unavailable, journalists, as always, shall file by any other means available. The military shall not ban communications systems operated by news organizations, but electromagnetic operational security in battlefield situations may require limited restrictions on the use of such systems.

E3.1.9. Those principles in paragraph E3.1.8., above, shall apply as well to the operations of the standing DoD National Media Pool system.

U.S. Department of Defense Ground Rules for Embedded Reporters in Iraq (February 10, 2003)

This document, issued by the Department of Defense Office of Public Affairs, outlines the policies and procedures for embedding reporters with the military during operations in Iraq. The concept of embedding reporters within specific military units was first fully implemented during this conflict. Similar to the ground rules given to journalists during Operation Desert Shield in the 1990s, this document covers what information can be released to the public, what information is subject to censorship by the military because of its sensitive nature, and other operations guide-

lines embedded reporters are expected to follow. Below are excerpts of the document.

2. Policy.

2.a. The Department of Defense (DOD) policy on media coverage of future military operations is that the media will have long-term minimally restrictive access to U.S. air, ground and naval forces through embedding. Media coverage of any future operation will, to a large extent, shape public perception of the national security environment now and in the years ahead. This holds true for the U.S. public, the public in allied countries whose opinion can affect the durability of our coalition, and publics in countries where we conduct operations, whose perceptions of us can affect the cost and duration of our involvement. Our ultimate strategic success in bringing peace and security to this region will come in our long-term commitment to supporting our democratic ideals. We need to tell the factual story—good or bad—before others seed the media with disinformation and distortions, as they most certainly will continue to do. Our people in the field need to tell our story—only commanders can ensure the media get to the story alongside the troops. We must organize for and facilitate access of national and international media to our forces, including those forces engaged in ground operations, with the goal of doing so right from the start. To accomplish this, we will embed media with our units. These embedded media will live, work and travel as part of the units with which they are embedded to facilitate maximum, in-depth coverage of U.S. forces in combat and related operations. Commander and public affairs officers must work together to balance the need for media access with the need for operational security.

2.b. Media will be embedded with unit personnel at air and ground forces bases and afloat to ensure a full understanding of all operations. Media will be given access to operational combat missions, including mission preparation and debriefing, whenever possible.

2.c. A media embed is defined as a media representative remaining with a unit on an extended basis—perhaps a period of weeks or even months. Commanders will provide billeting, rations and medical attention, if needed, to the embedded media commensurate with that provided to members of the unit, as well as access to military transportation and assistance with communications filing/transmitting media products, if required.

2.c.1. Embedded media are not authorized use of their own vehicles while traveling in an embedded status.

2.c.2. To the extent possible, space on military transportation will be made available for media equipment necessary to cover a particular operation. The media is responsible for loading and carrying their own equipment at all times. Use of priority inter-theater airlift for embedded media to cover stories, as well as to file stories, is highly encouraged. Seats aboard vehicles, aircraft and naval ships will be made available to allow maximum coverage of U.S. troops in the field.

2.c.3. Units should plan lift and logistical support to assist in moving media products to and from the battlefield so as to tell our story in a timely manner. In the event of commercial communications difficulties, media are authorized to file stories via expeditious military signal/communications capabilities.

2.c.4. No communications equipment for use by media in the conduct of their duties will be specifically prohibited. However, unit commanders may impose temporary restrictions on electronic transmissions for operational security reasons. Media will seek approval to use electronic devices in a combat/hostile environment, unless otherwise directed by the unit commander or his/her designated representative. The use of communications equipment will be discussed in full when the media arrive at their assigned unit.

3. Procedures

3.a. The Office of the Assistant Secretary of Defense for Public Affairs (OASD[PA]) is the central agency for managing and vetting media embeds to include allocating embed slots to media organizations. Embed authority may be delegated to subordinate elements after the commencement of hostilities and at the discretion of the OASD(PA). Embed opportunities will be assigned to media organization, not to individual reporters. [. . .]

3.d. Freelance media will be authorized to embed if they are selected by a news organization as their embed representative. [. . .]

3.f. Embedded media operate as part of their assigned unit. An escort may be assigned at the discretion of the unit commander. The absence of a PA escort is not a reason to preclude media access to operations.

3.g. Commanders will ensure the media are provided with every opportunity to observe actual combat operations. The personal safety of correspondents is not a reason to exclude them from combat areas.

3.h. If, in the opinion of the unit commander, a media representative is unable to withstand the rigorous conditions required to operate with the forward deployed forces, the commander or his/her representative may limit the representative's participation with operational forces to ensure unit safety and inform OASD(PA) through PA channels as soon as possible. Gender will not be an excluding factor under any circumstance.

4. Ground Rules. For the safety and security of the U.S. forces and embedded media, media will adhere to established ground rules. Ground rules will be agreed to in advance and signed by media prior to embedding. Violation of the ground rules may result in the immediate termination of the embed and removal from the area of responsibility (AOR). These ground rules recognize the right of the media to cover military operations and are in no way intended to prevent release of derogatory, embarrassing, negative or uncomplimentary information. Any modification to the standard ground rules will be forwarded through the PA channels to CENTCOM/PA for approval.

Standard ground rules are:

4.a. All interviews with service members will be on the record. Security at the source is the policy. Interviews with pilots and aircrew members are authorized upon completion of missions; however, release of information must conform to these media ground rules.

4.b. Print or broadcast stories will be datelined according to local ground rules. Local ground rules will be coordinated through command channels with CENTCOM.

4.c. Media embedded with U.S. forces are not permitted to carry personal firearms.

4.d. Light discipline restrictions will be followed. Visible light sources, including flash or television lights, flash cameras will not be used when operating with forces at night unless specifically approved in advance by the on-scene commander.

4.e. Embargoes may be imposed to protect operational security. Embargoes will only be used for operational security and will be lifted as soon as the operational security issue has passed.

4.f. The following categories of information are releasable.

4.f.1. Approximate friendly force strength figures.

4.f.2. Approximate friendly casualty figures by service. Embedded media may, within OPSEC limits, confirm unit casualties they have witnessed.

4.f.3. Confirmed figures of enemy personnel detained or captured.

4.f.4. Size of friendly force participating in an action or operation can be disclosed using approximate terms. Specific force or unit identification may be released when it no longer warrants security protection.

4.f.5. Information and location of military targets and objective previously under attack.

4.f.6. Generic description of origin of air operations, such as "land-based."

4.f.7. Date, time or location of previous conventional military missions and actions, as well as mission results are releasable only if described in general terms.

4.f.8. Types of ordnance expended in general terms.

4.f.9. Number of aerial combat or reconnaissance missions or sorties flown in CENTCOM's area of operation.

4.f.10. Type of forced involved (e.g., air defense, infantry, armor, Marines).

4.f.11. Allied participation by type of operation (ships, aircraft, ground units, etc.) after approval of the allied unit commander.

4.f.12. Operation code names.

4.f.13. Names and hometowns of U.S. Military units.

4.f.14. Service members' names and hometowns with the individuals' consent.

4.g. The following categories of information are not releasable since their publication or broadcast could jeopardize operations and endanger lives.

4.g.1. Specific number of troops in units below CORPS/MEF level.

4.g.2. Specific number of aircraft in units at or below the Air Expeditionary Wing level.

4.g.3. Specific numbers regarding other equipment or critical supplies (e.g., artillery, tanks, landing craft, radars, trucks, water, etc.).

4.g.4. Specific numbers of ships in units below the carrier battle group level.

4.g.5. Names of military installations or specific geographic locations of military units in the CENTCOM area of responsibility, unless specifically released by the Department of Defense or authorized by the CENTCOM commander. News and imagery products that identify or include identifiable features of these locations are not authorized for release.

4.g.6. Information regarding future operations.

4.g.7. Information regarding force protection measures at military installations or encampment (except those which are visible or readily apparent).

4.g.8. Photography showing level of security at military installations or encampments.

4.f.9. Rules of engagement.

4.g.10. Information on intelligence collection activities compromising tactics, techniques or procedures.

4.g.11. Extra precautions in reporting will be required at the commencement of hostilities to maximize operational surprise. Live broadcasts from airfields, on the ground or afloat, by embedded media are prohibited until the safe return of the initial strike package or until authorized by the unit commander.

4.g.12. During an operation, specific information on friendly force troop movements, tactical deployments, and dispositions that would jeopardize operational security or lives. Information on on-going engagements will not be released unless authorized for release by on-scene commander.

4.g.13. Information on special operations units, unique operations methodology or tactics, for example, air operations, angles of attack, and speeds; naval tactical or evasive maneuvers, etc. General terms such as "low" or "fast" may be used.

4.g.14. Information on effectiveness of enemy electronic warfare.

4.g.15. Information identifying postponed or cancelled operations.

4.g.16. Information on missing or downed aircraft or missing vessels while search and rescue and recovery operations are being planned or underway.

4.g.17. Information on effectiveness of enemy camouflage, cover, deception, targeting, direct and indirect fire, intelligence collection, or security measures.

4.g.18. No photographs or other visual media showing an enemy prisoner of war or detainee's recognizable face, nametag or other identifying feature or item may be taken.

4.g.19. Still or video imagery of custody operations or interviews with persons under custody.

[. . .]

6. Security

6.a. Media products will not be subject to security review or censorship except as indicated in Para. 6.a.1. Security at the source will be the rule. U.S. military personnel shall protect classified information from unauthorized or inadvertent disclosure. Media provided access to sensitive information, information which is not classified but which may be of operational value to an adversary or when combined with other unclassified information may reveal classified information, will be informed in advance by the unit commander or his/her designated representative of the restrictions on the use or disclosure of such information. When in doubt, media will consult with the unit commander or his/her designated representative.

6.a.1. The nature of the embedding process may involve observation of sensitive information, including troop movements, battle preparations, materiel capabilities and vulnerabilities and other information as listed in Para. 4.g. When a commander or his/her designated representative has reason to believe that a media member will have access to this type of sensitive information, prior to allowing such access, he/she will take prudent precautions to ensure the security of that information. The primary safeguard will be to brief media in advance about what information is sensitive and what the parameters are for covering this type of information. If media are inadvertently exposed to sensitive information they should be briefed after exposure on what information they should avoid covering. In instances where a unit commander or the designated representative determines that coverage of a story will involve exposure to sensitive information beyond the scope of what may be protected by prebriefing or debriefing, but coverage of which is in the best interests of the DOD, the commander may offer access if the reporter agrees to a security review of their coverage. Agreement to security review in exchange for this type of access must be strictly voluntary and if the reporter does not agree, then access may not be granted. If a security review is agreed to, it will not involve any editorial changes; it will be conducted solely to ensure that no sensitive or classified information is included in the product. If such information is found, the media will be asked to remove that information from the product and/or embargo the product until such information is no longer classified or sensitive. Reviews are to be done as soon as practical so as not to interrupt combat operations nor delay reporting. If there are disputes resulting from the security review process they may be appealed through the chain of command, or through PA channels to OASD/PA. This paragraph does not authorize commanders to allow media access to classified information.

6.a.2. Media products will not be confiscated or otherwise impounded. If it is believed that classified information has been compromised and the media representative refuses to remove that information, notify the CPIC and/or OASD/PA as soon as possible so the issue may be addressed with the media organization's management.

CHRONOLOGY

1275	*De Scandalis Magnatum* criminalizes slander in England.
1450	Gutenberg invents the printing press.
1456	Bible is printed on Gutenberg press.
1476	William Caxton sets up the first printing shop in England.
1487	English Court of Star Chamber is established as a separate judicial body from the King's Council.
1538	Proclamation of 1538 establishes first royal licensing system.
1576	Peter Wentworth argues for protection of speech for Parliament in *On the Liberties of the Commons.*
1606	*De Libellis Famosis* case heard before the Star Chamber establishing seditious libel as a crime.
1621	First English newspaper is printed.
1641	Star Chamber is abolished.
1643	England establishes the Ordinance for the Regulation of Printing.
1644	John Milton publishes *Areopagitica.*
1690	First colonial newspaper, *Publick Occurences Both Foreign and Domestick*, is published in America.
1694	Upon expiration of the Printing Act, press becomes free of regulatory prior restraint.

1702	First English Daily newspaper, *Daily Courant,* is published.
1720–1723	English authors Thomas Gordon and John Trenchard publish *Cato's Letters.*
1735	John Zenger goes on trial for seditious libel.
1765–1769	William Blackstone publishes *Commentaries on the Laws of England.*
1781	American Articles of Confederation are ratified.
1787	U.S. Constitution is ratified.
1791	U.S. Bill of Rights is ratified.
1798	Alien and Sedition Act is passed by Congress.
1801	Alien and Sedition Act expires.
1830s	Abolitionist press becomes active.
1859	John Stuart Mill publishes *On Liberty.*
1861–1865	During the Civil War, Lincoln's administration censors the press.
1868	*Regina v. Hicklin* establishes the *Hicklin* rule for obscenity, allowing for easy prosecution of sexually explicit material.
1873	Comstock Act passes.
1890	"The Right to Privacy," is published in the Harvard Law Review.
1917–1918	Espionage and Sedition Acts pass.
1919	U.S. Supreme Court decides *Schenck v. United States* and *Abrams v. United States,* establishing the "clear-and-present-danger" test.
1925	In *Gitlow v. United States,* the Supreme Court determines that the Fourteenth Amendment requires state laws not violate the First Amendment.
1931	*Near v. Minnesota* Supreme Court decision protects the press from most prior restraints on publication.
1934	Communications Act passes Congress, establishing the public interest standard, the Federal Communi-

cations Commission, and an overall regulatory framework for the broadcast industry.

1936   In *Grosjean v. American Press Co.*, the Supreme Court rules that selective, targeted taxes against newspapers are unconstitutional.

1940   Smith Act passes.

1949   Fairness Doctrine is established, setting public interest guidelines for broadcasters.

1950–1953   The Korean War brings a low point for press freedoms during military conflicts.

1956–1973   Vietnam War and the military conflict where the press faced minimal censorship by the U.S. military.

1957   *Roth v. United States* establishes a new standard for measuring obscenity and a strong layer of protection against prosecution for sexually explicit expression.

1964   In *New York Times v. Sullivan*, the Supreme Court concludes that public officials must show actual malice in libel cases, thus providing greater protection for press coverage of public officials.

1966   In *Sheppard v. Maxwell*, the Supreme Court overturns Sheppard's conviction because the pretrial publicity undermined his right to a fair trial.

     Federal Freedom of Information Act passes.

1967   In *Curtis v. Butts*, the Supreme Court extends the "actual malice" standard for libel to public figures.

1969   In *Red Lion v. FCC*, the Supreme Court upholds the constitutionality of the Fairness Doctrine.

     In *Tinker v. Des Moines School District*, the Supreme Court rules that public school students have First Amendment rights provided the exercise of those rights do not interfere with the educational process.

     In *Brandenburg v. Ohio*, the Supreme Court establishes the "incitement" standard protecting speech unless it advocates imminent lawless actions likely to occur as a result.

1971   *New York Times v. United States* decision represents the judicial "high point" of First Amendment protection against government censorship of the press for national security reasons.

1972   In *Branzburg v. Hayes,* the Supreme Court rules that journalists do not enjoy constitutional privilege when subpoenaed to a grand jury.

1973   In *Miller v. California,* the Supreme Court establishes a new test for obscenity, making it easier for states to successfully prosecute sexually explicit material.

1974   In *Gertz v. Welch,* the Supreme Court establishes the concept of limited libel against public figures.

1976   The Government in Sunshine Act opens official meetings of most federal agencies and commissions to the press.

In *Nebraska Press Association v. Stuart,* the Supreme Court rules that the court is limited in its ability to gag the press.

Copyright Act passes Congress, establishing federal guidelines for the protection of creative activity.

1977   *United States v. Progressive* decision suggests a possible shift in judicial commitment to the high standard of press protection against government censorship due to national security concerns.

Zacchini v. Scripps Howard is the only Supreme Court decision ruling that even a news broadcast of a short excerpt of a performance constitutes illegal appropriation if it constitutes the "essence" of the performance.

1978   *FCC v. Pacifica* decision clarifies that the FCC cannot censor indecent material in broadcasting, but can fine offending stations and disc jockeys. Stations are given the option of channeling indecent material into late-night broadcasts.

1980   In *Richmond Newspapers v. Virginia,* the Supreme Court limits trial courts' ability to close the court-room to the press.

Snepp v. United States decision clarifies that employment secrecy contracts trump First Amendment rights to publish details about one's job.

1982   The first use of press pool structure occurs during the British invasion of the Falkland Islands.

1983   During the U.S. invasion of Grenada, the press is banned from covering military maneuvers on the is-land.

1984   The FCC eliminates the Fairness Doctrine.

1988   In *Hazelwood v. Kuhlmeier,* the Supreme Court rules that public secondary school newspapers operating as part of the school curriculum may be censored by the school.

1989   In *Florida Star v. B.J.F.,* the Supreme Court rules that the publication of a rape victim's name does not constitute invasion of privacy.

The first U.S. use of new press pool structure occurs during U.S. invasion of Panama. The press held back until military actions were completed, rendering the strategy ineffective.

1990   In *Milkovich v. Lorain Journal,* the Supreme Court rules that "opinion" is protected from libel lawsuits unless it can be proven factually false.

Children's Television Act passes Congress, requiring minimum hours of educational children's programming per week and limiting commercial minutes during children's programming.

1991   U.S. invasion of Kuwait unveils the first effective use of press pool.

1996   Telecommunications Act passes Congress, setting the stage for deregulation of ownership restrictions.

Communications Decency Act passes Congress, censoring sexually explicit material on the World-Wide Web.

Child Pornography Protection Act passes Congress, criminalizing Internet images of minors (or adults dressed to appear as minors) engaged in sexual acts.

1997   In *Reno v. ACLU,* the Supreme Court strikes down the Communications Decency Act because it censors constitutionally protected expression.

In *Zeran v. America Online,* the Supreme Court rules that Internet service providers are not liable for content posted by a third party.

1998   Digital Millennium Copyright Act passes Congress, extending copyright protection to digital information.

Sonny Bono Copyright Extension Act passes Congress, extending the length of copyright protection for an additional twenty years.

Children's Online Protection Act passes Congress, allowing "community standards" to determine what is harmful to minors on the Internet.

Children's Online Privacy Protection Act passes Congress, requiring that website operators seek parental consent before collecting personal information about children using the Internet.

2001   Children's Internet Protection Act passes Congress, requiring that all libraries receiving federal funds install filters on their Internet computers.

First "embedded" reporters are allowed to participate in the U.S. invasion of Afghanistan.

In October, USA PATRIOT Act passes Congress, enhancing the government's powers to limit access to information about the "war on terror" by the press.

2002   In *Ashcroft v. ACLU,* the Supreme Court strikes down the Children's Online Protection Act because it censors constitutionally protected expression.

In *Ashcroft v. Free Speech Coalition,* the Supreme Court strikes down the Child Pornography Protection Act because it censors constitutionally protected expression.

2003   Many newspapers begin journalists' web logs or "blogs" (an ongoing, indepth and often reflective series of Internet-based "journal" entries) to cover 2004 presidential election.

In *United States v. American Library Association,* the Supreme Court rules that the Children's Internet Protection Act is constitutional.

2004   In *Flynt v. Rumsfeld,* an appellate court rules that reporters do not have a constitutional right to be embedded with military troops.

In *Ashcroft v. ACLU* the Court again strikes down the Children's Online Protection Act because the government did not demonstrate that it represented the least restrictive means (on the First Amendment) to protect children from Internet pornography.

TABLE OF CASES

Rosenbloom v. Metromedia, 403 U.S. 29 (1971)
Roth v. United States, 354 U.S. 479 (1957)
Schenck v. United States, 249 U.S. 47 (1919)
Seattle Times Co. v. Rhinehart, 467 U.S. 20 (1984)
Shields v. Gross, 58 N.Y.2d 388 (1983)
Shoen v. Shoen, 48 F.3d 412 (9th Cir. 1995)
Silkwood v. Kerr-McGee, 563 F.2d 433 (10th Cir. 1977)
Sipple v. Chronicle Publishing, 154 Cal. App. 3d 1040 (1984)
Smith v. Daily Mail, 443 U.S. 97 (1979)
Snepp v. United States, 444 U.S. 507 (1980)
Stanley v. Georgia, 394 U.S. 557 (1969)
Stanley v. McGrath, 719 F.2d 279 (8th Cir. 1983)
Texas Beef Group v. Winfrey, 11 F. Supp.2d 858 (N.D. Texas 1998)
Tinker v. Des Moines School District, 393 U.S. 503 (1969)
Triangle Publications v. Knight-Ridder, 626 F.2d 1171 (5th Cir. 1980)
United States v. ALA, 539 U.S. 194 (2003)
United States v. Caldwell, 434 F.2d 1081 (9th Cir. 1970)
United States v. Hudson & Godwin, 7 Cranch 32 (1812)
United States v. Marchetti, 466 F.2d 1309 (4th Cir. 1972)
United States v. McVeigh, 119 F.3d 806 (10th Cir. 1997)
United States v. Motion Picture Film "The Spirit of '76," 252 F. 946 (S.D. Cal. 1917)
Waits v. Frito-Lay, 978 F.2d 1093 (9th Cir. 1992)
White v. Samsung Electronics of America, 971 F.2d 1395 (9th Cir. 1992)
White v. Samsung Electronics of America, 989 F.2d 1512 (9th Cir. 1992)
Whitney v. California, 274 U.S. 357 (1927)
Yates v. United States, 354 U.S. 298 (1957)
Zacchini v. Scripps-Howard Broadcasting, 433 U.S. 562 (1977)
Zeran v. America Online, 129 F.3d 327 (4th Cir. 1997)
Zurcher v. Stanford Daily, 436 U.S. 547 (1978)

ANNOTATED BIBLIOGRAPHY

Altschull, J. Herbert. 1990. *From Milton to McLuhan: The Ideas Behind American Journalism.* New York: Longman Press. A thorough analysis of the evolution of modern journalism, including the intellectual influences of English libertarianism, French romanticism, and contemporary American political thought.

American Journalism Review. http://www.ajr.org. The *American Journalism Review (AJR)* is a national magazine reporting on print, television, radio, and online media, including how the media report specific stories and broader news coverage trends. The *AJR*'s Web site contains a variety of resources for students as well as journalists, including links to several media organizations devoted to First Amendment protection.

Anderson, Daniel A. 1983. "The Origins of the Press Clause." *UCLA Law Review* 30:455–541. Anderson challenges the assertion that the framers of the Constitution meant "freedom of the press" as merely a prohibition against prior restraint. Anderson draws several conclusions from his study of legislative history, including that the press clause had its own separate and distinct origins from the other rights protected by the First Amendment.

Aufderheide, Patricia. 1999. *Communications Policy and the Public Interest: The Telecommunications Act of 1996.* New York: Guilford Press. A close look at the shifts in policy brought about by the implementation of the Telecommunications Act, including a shift in the rationale for policy-making in the communications industry.

Barron, Jerome A. 1973. *Freedom of the Press for Whom?* Bloomington: Indiana University Press. This is Barron's manuscript-length argument for recognizing a right of access to the media in an age when the mass media have become the most important means of expression at the societal level.

Berlin, Isaiah. 1969. *Four Essays on Liberty.* New York: Oxford University Press. Essays and speeches examining natural human liberties, including the exchange and discussion of ideas. The fourth essay, "John Stuart Mill and the Ends of Life," authoritatively examines Mill's life, his philosophy on personal freedoms, and his most famous work, *On Liberty.*

Bettig, Ron. 1996. *Copyright Culture.* Boulder, CO: Westview Press. A powerful political economy critique of intellectual copyright law as an extension of capitalist economic ideology.

Black, Hugo L. 1960. "The Bill of Rights." *New York University Law Review,* 865–881. A reprint of the historical speech Black delivered to the New York University law school, analyzing the Bill of Rights and its influence on and protection of free speech.

Blackstone, Sir William. *Commentaries on the Laws of England* (4 volumes). 1765–1769. An eighteenth-century discourse on England's common law. Blackstone's *Commentaries* is considered the most influential writing on the development of English law.

Bollinger, Lee C. 1991. *Images of a Free Press.* Chicago: University of Chicago Press. Bollinger examines the interplay between industry and professional trends in the media (i.e., media concentration and entertainment quality of news) and the way the courts have viewed and shaped press freedoms over time. Bollinger anticipates some concerns about the growth of new technologies and new court challenges over press freedoms.

Chamberlin, Bill F., and Charlene Brown, eds. 1982. *The First Amendment Reconsidered: New Perspectives on the Meaning of Freedom of Speech and Press.* New York: Longman Press. A collection of scholarly articles on the twentieth-century development of press freedoms.

Costello, George A., and Johnny H. Killian, eds. 1996. *The Constitution of the United States of America: Analysis and Interpretation.* Washington, DC: Government Printing Office. A detailed examination of the development and elements of the Constitution, including a comprehensive review of major Supreme Court decisions, supplemental rulings, and historical references that influenced the establishment and defense of the First Amendment.

Crozier, Emmet. 1956. *Yankee Reporters, 1861–65.* New York: Oxford University Press. An extensive examination of news coverage during the Civil War, including news content, journalists' ethics, and the use of news sources. The book includes a large index with several maps of Civil War battles.

Curtis, Michael Kent. 2000. *Free Speech, 'The People's Darling Privilege.'* Durham, NC: Duke University Press. An extensive review of influences on freedom of speech and press from the colonial era through the beginning of the twentieth century. Also examines tensions between the press and the military during times of war and the influence of the Fourteenth Amendment on speech freedoms.

Cutler, J. Andrew. 1955. *The North Reports the Civil War.* Pittsburgh: University of Pittsburgh Press. A comprehensive overview of how Union newspapers reported events of the Civil War. The book includes an alphabetical list of northern reporters and newspapers.

Dalglish, Lucy A., Gregg P. Leslie, and Phillip Taylor, eds. 2002. *Homefront Confidential: How the War on Terrorism Affects Access to Information and the Public's Right to Know.* White Paper. The Reporters Committee for Freedom of the Press. A white paper analyzing military efforts to control the content of war reports, the ways in which journalists are censored, and the implications those efforts have on First Amendment press freedoms.

Dennis, Everett E., David Stebenne, John Pavlik, et al. 1991. *The Media at War: The Press and the Persian Gulf Conflict.* New York: Gannett Foundation. A comprehensive examination of the press's interactions with the military during the 1991 Gulf War, including reporting practices and issues of censorship. The book includes copies of documents given to pool reporters sent to the Persian Gulf to cover the war.

D'Ewes, Sir Simonds. *Journal of All the Parliaments During the Reign of Queen Elizabeth.* 1682. A collected journal of the Parliaments during the reign of Elizabeth I, compiled by D'Ewes, who served as a member of the Long Parliament before being expelled after his rebellion against Charles I.

Dickerson, Donna. 1990. *The Course of Tolerance: Freedom of Press in Nineteenth-Century America.* Westport, CT: Greenwood Press. A study of the little-examined state-level prosecutions concerning freedom of the press as they operated from the end of the Sedition Acts in 1801 to the end of the century.

DiStefano, Christine. 1991. *Configurations of Masculinity: A Feminist Perspective on Modern Political Theory.* Ithaca, NY: Cornell University Press. DiStefano reinterprets modern political theories from a feminist perspective, relying on psychological and psychoanalytic methods. She also examines the work of John Stuart Mill from a psychoanalytic feminist approach.

Electronic Frontier Foundation. *http://www.eff.org.* The Electronic Frontier Foundation (EFF) is a membership organization devoted to the protection of civil liberties, including press freedoms. The EFF's Web site serves as an extensive resource for information on issues related to technology and the press and provides a comprehensive archive of digital civil liberties information for the press, policymakers, and the general public.

Emerson, Thomas I. 1970. *The System of Freedom of Expression.* New York: Random House. A historical and political examination of the development of First Amendment protection of freedom of expression. Emerson culls the philosophical, intellectual, and judicial history to develop four central justifications for protecting expression.

Emery, Michael, and Edwin Emery. 1992. *The Press and America,* 7th ed. Englewood Cliffs, NJ: Prentice Hall. This work historically analyzes the development of American journalism, tracing how major events in U.S. history were covered by reporters, editors, and broadcasters and how other forms of media continue to influence news coverage. The work also includes an extensive discussion of women in journalism.

Farrand, Max, ed. 1966. *The Records of the Federal Convention of 1787* (3 volumes). New Haven, CT: Yale University Press. A comprehensive collection of historical records documenting the debates and discussions during the Federal Convention of 1787.

Fialka, John J. 1991. *Hotel Warriors: Covering the Gulf War.* Washington, DC: Woodrow Wilson Center Press. Written by a Gulf War reporter, this book is an indictment on the poor press coverage, for which both the press and the military are responsible.

Fiss, Owen. 1996. *Liberalism Divided: Freedom of Speech and the Many Uses of State Power.* Boulder, CO: Westview Press. An examination of contemporary free-speech issues within the context of liberal and recent ideas of equality and freedom in society. The work includes an examination of what role the state continues to play in this debate.

Fowler, Mark, and Daniel Brenner. 1982. "A Marketplace Approach to Broadcast Regulation." *Texas Law Review* 60:207–257. The influential article in which FCC chairman Mark Fowler laid out the rationale for the deregulatory movement nurtured during the Reagan era.

Friendly, Fred W. 1976. *The Good Guys, The Bad Guys, and the First Amendment.* New York: Vintage Books. Friendly, a former CBS News president (who resigned that post in 1966 when CBS News preempted congressional hearings on Vietnam to air reruns of syndicated programs and soap operas), looks at the strengths and weaknesses of the Fairness Doctrine.

Gleason, Timothy W. 1990. *The Watchdog Concept: The Press and the Courts in Nineteenth-Century America.* Ames: Iowa State University

Press. Analyzes the conflict between the ideal of protecting the press—because, as a watchdog, it is a public servant—and the notion of the press endowed with individual, inherent rights to free expression regardless of its public role.

"Guidance on Embedding." *Committee to Protect Journalists http:www//cpj.org/Briefings/2003/gulf03/embed.html.* A reprint with commentary on the embedded journalist's guide, which includes passages on the journalist's commitment to preserve the security of military operations during the Iraq conflict.

Hachten, William A. 1968. *The Supreme Court on Freedom of the Press: Decisions and Dissents.* Ames: Iowa State University Press. A dated but well-organized look at different aspects of Supreme Court rulings on topics related to freedom of the press, such as the right of distribution, antitrust, taxation, libel, contempt of court, and so on.

Hindman, Elizabeth Blanks. 1997. *Rights v. Responsibilities: The Supreme Court and the Media.* Westport, CT: Greenwood Press. Analyzes the tension between media rights and media responsibilities through sixty years of Supreme Court activity.

Hopkins, Wat W., ed. 2000. *Communications and the Law.* Northport, AL: Vision Press. A collection of comprehensive yet easily accessible chapters reviewing the main areas of media law. Contributions are made by experts in their respective fields.

Horowitz, Robert B. 1989. *The Irony of Regulatory Reform: The Deregulation of American Telecommunications.* New York: Oxford University Press. This book examines the late-twentieth-century deregulatory trend through the specific context of U.S. telecommunications deregulation.

Ingber, Stanley. 1984. "The Marketplace of Ideas: A Legitimizing Myth." *Duke Law Journal* 1: 1–91. Ingber argues that the continued commitment by First Amendment scholars to the marketplace of ideas metaphor as an intellectual or regulatory framework masks the reality that the marketplace is controlled by key self-serving interests. He proposes alternative ways of looking at a framework for articulating First Amendment freedoms.

Ingelhart, Louis E. 1997. *Press and Speech Freedoms in America, 1619–1995: A Chronology.* Westport, CT: Greenwood Press. This book provides an in-depth chronology of views and comments about free expression as well as key incidents and shifts in expressive freedoms. The book does not focus on court decision and opinions, since they are thoroughly covered in existing literature.

Jacobson, David L., ed. 1965. *The English Libertarian Heritage.* New York: Bobbs-Merrill. Jacobson presents a collection of articles excerpted from *The Independent Whig* and *Cato's Letters: Essays on Liberty, Civil and Religious* and places them in the context of the events and policies that led to their composition.

Jaggar, Alison M. 1988. *Feminist Politics and Human Nature.* Totowa, NJ: Rowman and Littlefield. This is an extensive review and historical and critical analysis of four predominant feminist political theories: liberal feminism, Marxist feminism, radical feminism, and socialist feminism.

Katsh, M. Ethan. 1989. *The Electronic Media and the Transformation of Law.* New York: Oxford University Press. A look at the impact of new communication media on law as a process and product.

Kellner, Douglas. 1990. *Television and the Crisis of Democracy.* Boulder, CO: Westview Press. Kellner critically examines the complex history of television, including its ability to present polarized views of conflict and serve the economic and political interests of a few powerful players. He offers suggestions for participatory uses of the media.

Kelser, Charles R., ed. 1987. *Saving the Revolution: The Federalist Papers and the American Founding.* New York: Free Press. A compilation of essays on the publication of *The Federalist Papers'* defense of the Constitution.

Kessler, Lauren. 1984. *The Dissident Press: Alternative Journalism in American History.* Newbury Park, CA: Sage Publications. A look at the important contributions of the dissident press since the 1800s.

Klingler, Richard. 1996. *The New Information Industry: Regulatory Challenges and the First Amendment.* Washington, DC: Brookings Institution Press. A consideration of the challenges regulators face from communications technology, whose innovations are outpacing regulatory efforts. The author cautions against unintended consequences of regulatory choices for the American public.

Knightley, Phillip. 1975. *The First Casualty: From the Crimea to Vietnam: The War Correspondent as Hero, Propagandist, and Myth Maker.* New York: Harcourt Brace. Knightley examines the history of war correspondents from the mid–nineteenth century to the 1970s, analyzing their efforts to report what happened on the front lines. Knightley also considers the changing role of media technology and its impact on war coverage.

Knowlton, Steven R., and Patrick R. Parsons, eds. 1994. *The Journalist's Moral Compass: Basic Principles.* Westport, CT: Praeger. This work poses questions about the basic ethical principles guiding American journalists. In an effort to provide insight into how reporters might justify an invasion of privacy, attempt to report stories objectively, and avoid governmental pressure to influence stories, Knowlton and Parsons present a philosophical guide for students, scholars, and journalists to use as a "moral compass" when reporting. Primary sources include writings of key intellectuals, including Plato, Milton, and more contemporary thinkers. The work also includes the text of the Society of Professional Journalists' Code of Ethics.

Leigh, Robert D. 1947. *A Free and Responsible Press.* Chicago: University of Chicago Press. A report by the Commission on Freedom of the Press examining the role of responsibility of the press and the regulatory implications of that responsibility.

Levy, Leonard W. 1985. *Emergence of a Free Press.* New York: Oxford University Press. Originally published in 1960 (under the title *Legacy of Suppression*), this edition amends the author's original claim that the framers of the Constitution intended freedom of the press only to serve as a protection against prior restraint. Levy presents extensive research evidencing a suppression of press freedoms in colonial America and the historical contributions of English Whig philosophers on America's modern conceptions of press freedom and recognizes a more expansive reading of the meaning of the press clause.

Levy, Leonard, ed. 1966. *Freedom of the Press from Zenger to Jefferson.* New York: Bobbs-Merrill. This work provides a detailed history, along with original documentation, of the development of press freedoms, from the famous Zenger seditious libel trial through the 1798 Alien and Sedition Acts and the ultimate election of Thomas Jefferson.

Linder, Douglas. 2001. *The Trial of John Peter Zenger: An Account.* *http://www.law.umkc.edu/faculty/projects/ftrials/zenger/zengeraccount.html.* A summary of the proceedings of Zenger's trial, including the trial's pivotal role in establishing early press freedoms. Includes the impassioned argument of Zenger's attorney (Andrew Hamilton) to allow truth to be a protection against libel charges.

Lipschultz, Jeremy. 2000. *Free Expression in the Age of the Internet.* Boulder, CO: Westview Press. An exploration of how traditional legal constructs—the marketplace of ideas, social responsibility, and public interest—play out on the Internet. He argues that nonlegal forms of social norms and pressures to conform constrain free expression more than laws.

Litman, Jessica. 2001. *Digital Copyright.* Amherst, NY: Prometheus Books. This book covers a wide range of emerging copyright issues involving digital media. It includes accounts of the Digital Millennium Copyright Act and the story of Napster, and it takes a close look at intellectual property rights.

MacArthur, John R. 1992. *Second Front: Censorship and Propaganda in the Gulf War.* Berkeley: University of California Press. An analysis of the government's effort to control the press and the press's capitulation to the pool system during the 1991 Gulf War.

Martin, Robert W.T. 2001. *The Free and Open Press: The Founding of American Democratic Press Liberty, 1640–1800.* A close examination of the intellectual and theoretical origins of the meaning of press freedom before 1800.

McChesney, Robert W. 1993. *Telecommunication, Mass Media, and Democracy.* New York: Oxford University Press. A detailed study of the early reform efforts to ward off the commercialization of the media prior to the passage of the Communications Act of 1934.

McChesney, Robert W. 1997. *Corporate Media and the Threat to Democracy.* New York: Seven Stories Press. A short monograph that argues for the importance of public participation in democracy. McChesney suggests that corporate control of the media is responsible for declining public participation.

McChesney, Robert W. 1999. *Rich Media, Poor Democracy: Communication Politics in Dubious Times.* McChesney argues that the concentration of media ownership and growing commercialization of the Internet indicate that the media have abdicated any role in nurturing democracy.

McDonald, Forrest. 1985. *Novus Ordo Seclorum: The Intellectual Origins of the Constitution.* Lawrence: University Press of Kansas. McDonald attempts to reconstruct the intellectual environment of the framers of the Constitution by closely examining their understanding of law, history, political philosophy, economics, and public affairs. The book includes an analysis of the Constitutional Convention of 1787.

Media Channel. *http://www.mediachannel.org.* Claiming to be the single largest online media-issues database, MediaChannel.org is dedicated to global media issues, including news, reports, and commentaries from an international network of journalism organizations.

Middleton, Kent R., William E. Lee, and Bill F. Chamberlin. 2004. *The Law of Public Communication,* 6th ed. New York: Pearson Allyn & Bacon. An annually updated text on media law as it affects the daily work of writers, broadcasters, advertisers, Internet service providers, public relations specialists, cable operators, and other media practitioners.

Mill, John Stuart. 1859. *On Liberty.* Edited by Alburey Castell. New York: F.S. Crofts and Co. (1947). Mill's most famous essay, in which he discusses civil and social liberties in England during the nineteenth century. First Amendment scholars particularly note his call for the free flow of ideas, a position dear to most practicing and aspiring journalists.

Miller, John Chester. 1951. *Crisis in Freedom: The Alien and Sedition Acts.* Boston: Little, Brown. A succinct narrative of the history of the Federalist party and the institution of a number of early laws infringing on personal liberties and press freedoms, particularly the Alien and Sedition Acts of 1798.

Milton, John. 1644. *Areopagitica.* Edited by S. Ash. Santa Barbara, CA: Bandana Books (1922). In this essay, considered one of the earliest and most influential writings arguing against censorship, Milton targets the Parliament of England for restricting the freedom of press by requiring the licensing of all printers.

Mott, Frank L. 1969. *American Journalism: A History, 1690–1960.* Toronto: Macmillan and Co. A thorough examination of American journalism history, from colonial American journalists to the tensions between the military and the press during World War I, from the development of yellow journalism at the dawn of the twentieth century to the advent of the modern newspaper.

Nelson, Harold L. 1967. *Freedom of the Press from Hamilton to the Warren Court.* New York: Bobbs-Merrill. A comprehensive historical account of the development of modern press freedoms, from 1800 to the mid-1900s.

Newman, Roger K. 1999. "The Populist Hugo Black." *American Lawyer* 21:40–41. A brief article detailing the political life of Justice Hugo Black, from his former associations with the Ku Klux Klan to his practice of law, his appointment as a senator, and his appointment as a Supreme Court justice. Analyzes Justice Black's legal influence on modern civil liberties, including his involvement in dismantling segregation, developing the First Amendment's religious guarantees in the modern court, and delivering significant judicial opinions regarding the freedom of speech.

Newspapers-USA. *http://www.newspapers-usa.com.* An extensive list of all newspapers published in the United States, including dailies, nondailies, and college publications.

Overbeck, Wayne. 2004. *Major Principles of Media Law.* Belmont, CA: Thompson. A comprehensive and concise summary of media law. Updated annually, this work covers major areas of media law and highlights the most recent developments in communication law through the end of the most recent Supreme Court term.

Pember, Don R. 2003. *Mass Media Law.* New York: McGraw-Hill. A comprehensive look at media law topics presented through lens of judicial decisions. Thorough coverage of the earliest implementation of the Constitution to the most recent Supreme Court decisions. Includes an extensive table of cases.

Powe, Lucas A. 1987. *American Broadcasting and the First Amendment.* Berkeley: University of California Press. An examination of the different regulatory frameworks facing broadcasting and print media. Written in the early stages of the deregulatory movement.

Project for Excellence in Journalism. 2004. "State of the News Media 2004." Journalism.org. *http://www.stateofthenewsmedia.org.* The inaugural report on the economic, ownership, professional health, and future trends of the broadcast, print, Internet, and cable news industry. The Project for Excellence in Journalism intends to publish the report annually.

Ray, William. 1990. *FCC: The Ups and Downs of Radio-TV Regulation.* Ames: Iowa State University Press. A history of the FCC replete with tales about licensing, indecency, and the Fairness Doctrine.

Reporters Committee for Freedom of the Press. *http://www.rcfp.org.* The Committee serves as an international resource on free press issues, providing a quarterly legal review, a biweekly newsletter, and various handbooks on media law issues, all accessible through their Web site. The Committee has been extensively involved in major press freedom cases in the United States and dedicates itself to protecting reporters' interests and defending reporters' First Amendment rights.

Rowland, Willard D., Jr. 1982. "The Further Process of Reification: Continuing Trends in Communication Legislation and Policymaking." *Journal of Communication* 34(2): 114–136. Rowland argues that the deregulatory trend in communications regulation is not a result of regulatory failure but an effort to reshape the regulatory environment to benefit corporate interests.

Rowland, Willard D., Jr. 1997. "The Meaning of the Public Interest in Communications Policy—Part I: Its Origins in State and Federal Regulation." *Communication Law and Policy* 2(3): 309–329. A look at the development of communications policy and the concept of the public interest within the context of other regulatory frameworks and policy goals.

Rowland, Willard D., Jr. 1997. "The Meaning of the Public Interest in Communications Policy—Part II: Its Implementation in Early Broadcast Law and Regulation." *Communication Law and Policy* 2(4): 363–396. A further examination of the concept of the public interest and how it was shaped to reflect specific regulatory structures and goals.

Sanford, Bruce W. 1999. *Don't Shoot the Messenger: How Our Growing Hatred of the Media Theatens Free Speech For Us All.* Lanham, MD: Rowman and Littlefield Publishers. An examination of the erosion of trust between the public and the press. Sanford, a First Amendment attorney, explains how the explosive growth of corporate libel lawsuits against the press is creating an atmosphere of journalistic timidity and alientating the American public from the media.

Schmidt, Benno C., Jr. 1976. *Freedom of the Press vs. Public Access.* New York: Praeger. Considers whether a requirement of access to the media conflicts with the notion of a free press, both print and broadcast.

Scofield, Cora L. 1900. *A Study of the Court of Star Chamber: Largely Based on Manuscripts in the British Museum and the Public Record Office.* Chicago: University of Chicago Press. A thorough history of the development and demise of the Star Chamber in England, including the Chamber's extensive restrictions on the press.

Shapiro, Ian, ed. 2003. John Locke's *Two Treatises of Government and a Letter Concerning Toleration.* New Haven, CT: Yale University Press. Reprints of the complete texts of Locke's most famous political writings accompanied by several interpretive essays by Locke scholars. An introduction places Locke's works in a historical and biographical context.

Shapiro, Martin. 1972. *The Pentagon Papers and the Courts.* San Francisco: Chandler Publishing Co. A comprehensive yet concise study of the famous legal battle between the *New York Times* and the federal government over prior restraint of the press.

Sharkey, Jacqueline. 1991. *Under Fire: U.S. Military Restrictions of the Media from Grenada to the Persian Gulf.* Washington, DC: Center for Public Integrity. A comprehensive study of U.S. military restrictions on the press, from the invasion of Grenada to the 1991 Persian Gulf War. Sharkey concludes that the Department of Defense violated its own guidelines.

Siebert, Frederick Seaton. 1965. *Freedom of the Press in England: 1476–1776.* Urbana: University of Illinois Press. This volume carefully traces the rise and decline of the government's control over the English press and provides accounts of the political and social trends that accompanied these changes. Covers the period of the earliest introduction of printing in England all the way to the American Revolution.

Siebert, Frederick S., Theodore Peterson, and Wilbur Schramm. 1965. *Four Theories of the Press.* Urbana: University of Illinois Press. An examination of four major theories explaining the structure and range of freedoms provided to the press around the world. Contains an extensive bibliography organized by theory.

Sloan, W. David, and James Glen Stovall. 1989. *The Media in America: A History.* Worthington, OH: Publishing Horizons. A straightforward history of the media in the United States.

Smith, Hedrick, ed. 1992. *The Media and the Gulf War: The Press and Democracy in Wartime.* Washington, DC: Seven Locks Press. In a series of essays by journalists, military representatives, and government officials, this book explores several themes explaining military/press tensions, including cultural clashes, efforts at government control of information through the pool system, reasons for government control of the press, and analyses of the pool system's effectiveness.

Smith, Jeffrey A. 1988. *Printers and Press Freedom.* New York: Oxford University Press. A study of the meaning of freedom of the press in the eighteenth century, including the influence of English libertarian philosophies. Smith takes into account the actions of legislatures against journalists and discusses at length the role of seditious libel in early American press freedoms.

Smith, Jeffrey A. 1999. *War and Press Freedom: The Problem of Prerogative Power.* New York: Oxford University Press. Considers the way in which the government's prerogative wartime powers have eaten away at the country's commitment to press freedoms.

Society of Professional Journalists. *http://www.spj.org.* The Society of Professional Journalists (SPJ) is dedicated to the defense of freedom of information and First Amendment rights of journalists and other media practitioners. The Society's Web site provides several legal resources for journalists in addition to coverage of media news. The site also provides a copy of the SPJ's Code of Ethics, designed to guide journalists' reporting methods and practices.

Stone, Geoffrey R. 2003. "Judge Learned Hand and the Espionage Act of 1917: A Mystery Unraveled." *University of Chicago Law Review* 70:335–358. A detailed analysis of Judge Hand's position on press freedoms during a politically challenging time. Includes a contextualized look at Hand's opinion in the *Masses* case.

Tedford, Thomas L. 2001. *Freedom of Speech in the United States,* 4th ed. State College, PA: Strata Publishing. An accessible history of free speech in the United States. Highlights and summarizes landmark court decisions and provides coverage of hate speech, free speech issues for students, and more.

Warren, Samuel, and Louis Brandeis. 1890. "The Right to Privacy." *Harvard Law Review* 4:193–220. A landmark article arguing, ultimately successfully, for the establishment of a tort protecting a right to privacy.

INDEX

ABOUT THE AUTHOR

Nancy C. Cornwell is associate professor of mass communication at Linfield College, McMinnville, Oregon, where she teaches courses in media law and the freedom of expression. She has written numerous articles and book chapters on the First Amendment right of free expression, including hate speech, academic free speech, and related civil rights issues. Her collaborative article "Hate Speech/Free Speech: Using Feminist Perspectives to Foster On-Campus Dialogue" received an award from the National Association of Human Rights Workers' *Journal of Intergroup Relations*. Cornwell has worked with the Michigan chapter of the American Civil Liberties Union, served on the board of its Southwest Michigan chapter, and has published work on the ACLU's response to racial profiling in the post–September 11 environment.